Volume 2 in
Research in Multicultural Education and International Perspectives

Multiple Competencies and Self-Regulated Learning: Implications for Multicultural Education

Series Editors: Farideh Salili & Rumjahn Hoosain

ISBN: 1-930608-92-6 (paper); 1-930608-93-4 (cloth)

Printed in the United States of America

Library of Congress Cataloging-in-Publication Data

Multiple competencies and self-regulated learning implications for multicultural education / edited by Chi-yue Chiu, Farideh Salili, Ying-yi Hong.
    p.   cm. — (Research in multicultural education and international
  perspectives ; v. 2)
Includes bibliographical references.
  ISBN: 1-930608-92-6 (pbk.) — ISBN 1-930608-93-4 (hard)
  1. Multicultural education.   2. Multiple intelligences.   3. Educational tests and
measurements.   4. Self-culture.   5. Motivation in education.   I. Chiu, Chi-yue,
1963– . II. Salili, Farideh.   III. Hong, Ying-yi, 1964– . IV. Series.
  LC1099.M88   2001
  370.117—dc21

2001005432

Multiple Competencies and Self-Regulated Learning: Implications for Multicultural Education

Edited by

Chi-yue Chiu
Farideh Salili
Ying-yi Hong

INFORMATION AGE
P U B L I S H I N G

80 Mason Street
Greenwich, Connecticut 06830

CONTENTS

PART II. Self-Regulated Learning

LIST OF CONTRIBUTORS

Eugene V. Aidman

School of Behavioral and Social Sciences and
   Humanities
University of Ballarat
Victoria, Australia

Jennifer Archer

Faculty of Education
University of Newcastle
New South Wales, Australia

Allan B. I. Bernardo

College of Education
De La Salle University
Manila, the Philippines

Fiona Shui-fun Chan

Department of Psychology
University of Hong Kong
Hong Kong

Jimmy Chan

Department of Psychology
University of Hong Kong
Hong Kong

Chi-yue Chiu

Department of Psychology
University of Hong Kong
Hong Kong

Regina Conti

Department of Psychology
Colgate University
Hamilton, NY

Ho-ying Fu	Graduate School of Business Stanford University Stanford, CA
David Yau-fai Ho	Department of Psychology University of Hong Kong Hong Kong
Ying-yi Hong	Division of Social Science Hong Kong University of Science and Technology Hong Kong
Wai-man Ip	Department of Psychology University of Hong Kong Hong Kong
Judith MacCallum	School of Education Murdoch University Australia
Alex R. Matambo	Faculty of Education University of Zimbabwe Zimbabwe
Si-qing Peng	Guanghua School of Business Peking University China
Farideh Salili	Department of Psychology University of Hong Kong Hong Kong
Robert J. Sternberg	Department of Psychology Yale University New Haven, CT
Diana Tabatabai	Department of Psychology McGill University Montreal, Canada
Yuk-yue Tong	Department of Psychology University of Hong Kong Hong Kong

PREFACE

Although cultural diversity in classrooms is hardly a new phenomenon, its influences on teaching and learning are increasingly discussed. Cultural diversity could lead to better learning and democracy outcomes. However, it also poses challenges for educators and schools. For example, research has revealed marked cultural differences in motivation, learning attitudes, thinking styles and school achievement. Attempts have been made to assure teaching and learning quality by designing standardized curricula and giving standardized tests. However, it is questionable whether standardized tests could capture the diverse aptitudes and skills students with different cultural experiences bring to the classroom. It is also questionable whether a standardized curriculum would lead to positive learning outcomes for all.

In 1998, we convened a conference in the University of Hong Kong, and invited experts from different parts of globe to discuss how to apply psychology to enhance learning and teaching quality. Probably because of the cultural diversity of the conference participants, multicultural education emerged as one of the dominant themes in the conference. For example, in the Opening Address, Robert Sternberg argued for the importance of cultural sensitivity in ability testing. In another keynote address, Martin Maehr discussed the implications of motivation research for designing an optimal achievement environment for culturally diverse students. Professor Sternberg's paper is included in this volume, and Professor Maehr's article was published in a previous volume we edited (*Student Motivation: The Culture and Context of Learning*, Plenum, 2001).

The contributors of this volume include psychologists and education researchers from Africa, Asia, Australia and North, and some of them have extensive experiences in multicultural education. Despite their diverse cultural and professional background, the contributors agree that to meet the challenges posed by cultural diversity, educators need to have the sensitivity to multiplicity of student abilities in aptitude and achievement assessment. Teachers could respond to diversity in student aptitude and learning motivation by designing learner-oriented, individualized teaching programs, and by engaging students in self-regulated learning. In this volume, the contributors have provided convincing evidence and specific examples to argue for the important role of multiple competencies and self-regulated learning in multicultural education.

In preparation of this volume we benefited from the help and advice of many colleagues and students at the University of Hong Kong. We are grateful to scholars who contributed to this book. The book could not have been produced without their help and patience. We wish especially to acknowledge our editorial assistant, Patricia Maggenis. Without her assistance the publication of this book would not be possible. We also wish to express our thanks to our families who supported us with their encouragement. Finally, we offer this book as an invitation to more fruitful intellectual dialogue with our colleagues who are interested in creating an optimal learning environment for culturally diverse students.

Farideh Salili
Chi-yue Chiu
Ying-yi Hong

INTRODUCTION

CHAPTER 1

THE ROLE OF MULTIPLE COMPETENCIES AND SELF-REGULATED LEARNING IN MULTICULTURAL EDUCATION

Chi-yue Chiu, Farideh Salili, and Ying-yi Hong

ABSTRACT

Globalization and increased intercultural contacts have increased the cultural heterogeneity of the student body in schools. This has offered many new challenges to educators and teachers. In this chapter, we outline the background leading to some of these new challenges. We believe that the concept of multiple competencies could offer a new perspective for us to appreciate the limitations of conventional models of ability assessment, student performance evaluation, and provision of educational services to students with special needs. We contend that by measuring a broader range of human abilities, and by focusing on the teaching and assessment of higher order cognition, educators and teachers will be better equipped to recognize the intellectual strengths of different cultural groups, and to design teaching activities to make full use of the strengths brought into the classroom by various cultural groups.

INTRODUCTION

The world is turning into a global village. The transformation has been speeded up to a large extent by recent breakthroughs in telecommunication technology, which have enabled cultures to move across geographical territories on a massive scale. Similarly, through migration and tourism, people are moving across cultures (Hermans & Kempen, 1998; Hong, Morris, Chiu, & Benet-Martinez, 2000).

In North America, the rapid development of multicultural societies has changed the cultural landscape of many major universities. At the University of British Columbia, over half of the students are Asians. European-Canadian students have turned into a numerical minority in this university. Similar changes albeit on smaller scales are taking place in other North American campuses (Maehr & Yamaguchi, 2001). Interestingly, the distribution of Asians in the different academic disciplines is not even. Computer sciences have attracted many students of Indian decent, whereas engineering is particularly popular among Chinese and Korean students.

Increasingly, teachers will find students with diverse ethnic backgrounds in the same classroom. In addition, students from the same ethnic group might have very different cultural experiences, depending on the sociopolitical context in which they grew up. For example, Chinese students may react very differently in a typical North American classroom, depending on whether they are American-born Chinese, or international students from Hong Kong or Mainland China (Salili, Chiu, & Lai, 2001; Salili, Fu, Tong, & Tabatabai, this volume).

Teaching in a multicultural classroom often primes teachers to critically reexamine the most preferred assumptions about education in the culture. It sensitizes teachers to the distinctive culturally conditioned strengths and needs of different student populations, and calls for new theoretical models to guide the design and development of effective practices to educate students with diverse cultural backgrounds. In addition, there is evidence that students learn more and appreciate the value of democracy more in a culturally diverse learning environment than in a culturally homogeneous environment (Gurin, 1999).

The contributors of this volume represent scholars from different countries and intellectual traditions. They are academic or professional psychologists from four different continents: Asia (Hong Kong, Mainland China, the Philippines), Australia, North America (Canada, the United States), and Africa (Zimbabwe). Some of them also have extensive experiences in multicultural education. All of them are experts in multiple competencies and self-regulated learning, and the research insights they offered in this volume are based on individual psychological assessment, experimental studies, systematic observations of student and teacher interactions, action research, survey methods, and in depth qualitative interviews. Despite the wide range of cultural and intellectual traditions represented by these authors, their works converge to a set of psychological principles that give rise to effective learning in diverse cultural contexts.

STUDENT CHARACTERISTICS AND THE CONTEXT OF MULTICULTURAL EDUCATION

Students who diverge from a presumed cultural norm often display variations in achievement behaviors along many important dimensions. In the United States, there is still a big achievement gap between African American students and European American students. Compared to African American students and European American students, Latino American students have the lowest motivation to apply to and enroll in college (Hurtado, Inkelas, Briggs, & Rhee, 1997).

Such cultural differences in motivation and achievement can often be attributed to differences in socioeconomic background, and availability of personal, family, and social resources to pursue one's academic goals. Also, research has shown that students often react to the stereotypic expectations associated with their cultural identity. For example, African American students' achievement motivation is often undermined when the negative stereotype that African American students are typically underachievers is activated (Steele & Aronson, 1995). In addition, high-achieving African American students often possess a marginalized cultural identity because they feel compelled to dissociate themselves from their ethnic community. Yet, their ethnic origin has created a barrier for them to pass into the mainstream culture. Often, high-achieving African American students are portrayed as a "raceless" group (Fordham, 1988).

Asian American students offer another example of how culture forms part of the context of learning in schools. A popular stereotype of Asian American students is that these students are hardworking, and they often outperform their classmates in a multicultural classroom (Stevenson & Lee, 1996). Research has traced the causes of the Asian American students' high school performance to the emphasis on academic success in Asian families and cultures (Harman & Askounis, 1989; Stevenson, 1983), and to Asian American students' diligence (Tsang & Wing, 1985) and conscientiousness (Peng, Owings, & Fetter, 1984).

However, it would be premature to conclude that Asian cultures are superior to other cultures in promoting academic success. First, as noted by Salili and her colleges (Salili, Chiu, & Lai, 2001; Salili, Fu, Tong, & Tabatabai, this volume), in explaining Asian students' achievement behavior, it is important to separate the effects of cultures and those of context.

To separate these two kinds of effects, researchers need to compare the achievement behaviors of at least three student groups: European American students, Asian students studying in Asia, and Asian students studying in North America. Differences between European American students and Asian students in Asia reflect the joint effects of culture and context. Differences between the two Asian groups reflect the effects of context only, whereas differences between North American students and Asian students studying in North America reflect the effect of culture only. When this analysis is performed, the results clearly show that Asian cultural values operating in an authoritarian educational context could produce passive, examination-oriented learning that emphasizes book learning, memorization, and diligence (see Ho, Peng, & Chan, Chapters 3 and 13 of this volume). Consistent with this idea, Salili et al. (this volume) found that compared to Chinese Canadian students and European Canadian students, Hong Kong Chinese students have the worst self-regulatory and cognitive skills, have the greatest tendency to rely on memorization as a study strategy, spend the greatest amount of time on studying, are most anxious about their performance, and feel least confident about their abilities. This examination-oriented passive learning style is negatively related to school achievement among Hong Kong Chinese students (Ho & Spinks, 1985).

Asian students studying in North America also encounter many psychological problems, although these problems may not be shown in their achievement behaviors. Probably because Asian American students are strongly driven by their academic performance, many of them experience a feeling of anxiety and psychological distress (Sue & Okaszki, 1990).

In short, the preceding analysis suggests that in multicultural education, the best strategy is not to identify a model ethnic student group and to unilaterally impose the dominant norm of this ethnic group onto other cultural groups. The preceding analysis also suggests that the cultural norm may interact with the learning context to affect learning behavior and achievement outcomes. Thus, it is important to examine how to transform school culture in order to create a learning environment that will make the best use of the latent abilities of the students from diverse cultural groups (Maehr & Yamaguchi, 2001). This takes us to consider the conception of student abilities in a culturally heterogeneous educational context.

ASSESSMENT OF MULTIPLE COMPETENCIES

One issue raised by culturally diverse education is the conceptualization of human abilities. Since the successful construction of the first intelligence test by Binet and Simon in 1905, IQ tests have been used to predict school performance. A conventional view of intelligence tests is that these tests measure some stable human abilities that are determined largely by one's genetic constitution. In addition, these abilities account for a large percentage of variance in intellectual behavior (see Chan, this volume). Some theorists have pointed to the possibility that the same set of correlated cognitive abilities, often referred to as the g-factor, is a major determinant of individual differences in school performance in all cultures.

However, based on his cross-cultural observations, Sternberg (see Sternberg, this volume) rejects this conventional view of intelligence. He argues that intelligence tests do not measure stable, genetic cognitive dispositions of individuals. Instead, they measure the kind of expertise that are valued and emphasized in Western schools. He observed that in cultures that have different school practices and require different kinds of expertise, the role of the g-factor in predicting school performance is much less important than other abilities. For example, Oksgaki and Sternberg (1993) noted that compared to Asian and Anglo parents, Latino parents valued social kinds of expertise more and cognitive kinds of expertise less. As teachers in the United States tend to value cognitive abilities over other kinds of expertise, Anglo and Asian students tend to do better in schools than do Latino students. The implications of these findings for multicultural education, according to Sternberg (this volume) are very clear:

> Until we expand our notions of abilities, and recognize that when we measure them, we are measuring developing forms of expertise, we will be consigning many potentially excellent contributors to our society to bleak futures. We will also be potentially overvaluing students with expertise for success in a certain kind of schooling, but not necessarily for success later in life.

To prepare students for the different kinds of intellectual undertakings, Sternberg proposes assessing a broader range of expertise that includes important life skills, such as analytical, creative, and practical abilities. The idea of assessing and recognizing students' multiple competencies has received increasing recognition worldwide. In Chan's review (this volume) of the changing models of intellectual abilities that guide educational practices in Hong Kong, Chan noted that there is a trend for ability assessment to (a) shift from general abilities to specific competencies, (b) include in the list of measured abilities cognitive, affective, and social, practical competencies, and (c) consider the interaction of latent abilities and environmental factors in the conceptualization of human intelligence.

One important implication of the concept of multiple competencies is its emphasis on the authentic assessment of students' learning and performance (Armstrong, 1994). Multiple competencies assessment focuses on a student's strengths. It seeks to establish a learning environment where students irrespective of their cultural background have the opportunity to succeed. By providing multiple sources of evaluation, teachers provide a culture-fair assessment of students' performance and give every student an equal chance to succeed. In addition, multiple competencies assessment typically focuses on the processes as much as the final products of learning in student assessment, and includes assessment of higher order thinking skills.

Bernardo (this volume) and Aidman (this volume) offer two examples of how to assess higher order thinking skills and knowledge representation in a culture-fair manner. When Bernardo taught his Filipino students probabilistic reasoning, he presented students with four types of basic probability problems and asked them to create their own analogous problem after each study problem. By analyzing how the problem elements and their relations are presented in the students' constructed analogous problems, teachers are able to discern how students represent the information from a problem.

Similarly, teachers can assess students' representation of knowledge using the implicit concept mapping method Aidman introduced in this volume. In this method, students make a series of similarity and dissimilarity judgments between concepts they have learned. Using a variety of proximity matrix decomposition techniques (e.g., clustering analysis, multidimensional scaling), it is then possible to construct for each learner a visual representation of the concepts on a conceptual map. By visually revealing the ways students organize the knowledge they hold, the technique helps students to identify their misconceptions and poor understanding of the subject matter. Students may also compare their knowledge maps with those of experts in the same domain of knowledge. Thus, this assessment technique gives students a "picture" of their unique learning experiences, and engages students in a continual process of self-reflective learning and revision.

MULTICULTURAL EDUCATIONAL INTERVENTION AND SELF-REGULATED LEARNING

As noted, students coming from diverse cultural backgrounds may bring with them learning patterns conditioned by their cultural experiences. Educators often address the issue of student diversity by offering students from disadvantaged cultural groups special intervention programs. As Maehr and Yamaguchi (2001, p. 127) noted, although some of these programs have used almost "everything we know about effective instruction for students at risk to direct all aspects of school and classroom organization toward the goal of preventing academic deficits from appearing in the first place," (see Slavin, Madder, Dolan, & Wasik, 1996), some researchers have reported disappointing results on the effectiveness of such programs in attaining lasting results (Stringfield, Millsap, & Herman, 1997).

In light of the previous discussion on the moderating effects of school context, it is not surprising that some educators have argued for the transformation of the school culture as a means to address issues related to student diversity. Armstrong (1994) noted that conventionally, teachers and educators have the tendency to view learning problems as deficits, and label individual students in terms of specific impairments. Once psychologists have reliably identified these deficits, they would seek to remediate the impairments by separating the "problem" students from the mainstream students for specialized treatment. Indeed, this conventional view of learning difficulties has guided the development of various special treatment programs.

Informed by the concept of multiple competencies, many educators have developed an alternative growth paradigm to help students with special needs. In this paradigm, teachers use authentic assessment to identify individual students' special needs and assist students to learn and grow by developing a varied set of learning activities. What this paradigm calls for is a fundamental change in the school culture. In this connection, Maehr and Yamaguchi (2001, p. 132) have commented that "a school culture that promotes and values competitiveness and comparison is likely to condition how a special reading program will be read by students, parents as well as staff." David Ho's rich personal observations of such a school culture in Hong Kong, Taiwan, and Mainland China attest to the validity of Maehr and Yamaguchi's assertion. In Chapter 13 of this volume, Ho and his colleagues compare the educational systems in Confucian-heritage societies to sorting machines that "sort students into institutions ranked hierarchically on the basis of examination marks and warping human development in the process."

In direct contrast to competitive school cultures are school cultures that "assume that all children can learn, and value effort and progress in the learning process. This kind of school culture is likely to define special attention to differences as a step toward engaging in the learning community, rather than separation into a labeled category" (Maehr & Yamaguchi, 2001, p. 132). As a need and a solution to the issue of managing student diversity in a multicultural classroom, educators need to go beyond introduction of superficial changes to the ethnic composition of a multicultural classroom. Such changes only serve to create the impression that schools value multicultural education. What educators really need to do is to create an optimal learning environment that values student diversity, while at the same time focuses on the fundamental purpose of schooling and learning (Maehr & Yamaguchi, 2001).

Many contributors of this volume believe that current research and conceptualizations on the universal principles of self-regulated learning (see Salili, Chiu, & Hong, 2001) may provide a useful framework to guide transformation of school culture. As noted, the contributors themselves are from diverse cultural backgrounds. Despite the heterogeneity of their cultural experiences, they seem to agree that teachers could apply *universal* principles of self-regulated learning to create an optimal learning environment that values student diversity and focuses on the basic purposes of learning. Salili et al. (this volume) showed that for Hong Kong Chinese students, Chinese Canadian students, and European Canadian students, self-regulation correlated positively with effort invested in learning, a sense of self-efficacy, and the willingness to adopt a learning goal. In addition, a sense of self-efficacy was positively related to academic performance in all three groups. Matambo (Chapter 12) also reported that among high school students in Zimbabwe, the use of self-regulated learning strategies is positively related to academic performance.

Self-regulated learning is goal-directed. Thus, setting appropriate goals is essential to effective learning in all cultures. In this connection, Conti (Chapter 9) found that among American college freshmen, those who reflect on their reasons for going to college, compared to those who do not, have a clearer sense of direction and higher academic achievement in college. On the other hand, students who are motivated primarily by a need to meet rigidly imposed standards tend to have more problems in emotional adjustment.

Not only do effective learners have goals, they have mastery-oriented goals. Archer (Chapter 7) observed that in her sample of Australian college students, those who did well in a course aspired to doing the best they could. This goal seemed to have provided them with a framework to develop effective study strategies, such as looking for major themes, relating new information to prior knowledge, reading widely and making their own notes in addition to copying down notes presented by lecturers during the massed lectures, and exercising self-discipline. By contrast, those who had bad grades possessed an academic alienation goal; they wanted to do the least just to pass the course. These students found the course boring and did not enjoy reading about the subject. They had no sophisticated methods of note taking and did not relate new information to prior knowledge.

MacCallum (Chapter 10) reported similar findings with her Australian junior secondary school students. She found that when students focused on learning, they generally performed well. In addition, they would work hard and seek help when they encountered learning obstacles. Although students who wanted to demonstrate their abilities through doing well in school works tended to have good academic results, they nonetheless were likely to limit their effort and were motivated by extrinsic reasons (the motivation to please teachers and parents). Ip and Chiu (Chapter 11) also found that students who focus on performance tend to infer their level of intelligence from their performance. To avoid negative evaluation, they may avoid challenging learning tasks. In addition, when they encounter achievement setbacks, they are likely to blame their abilities for the setbacks. By contrast, when students focus on learning, they make use of all available learning opportunities to improve their skills. As in the Archer study (Chapter 7), MacCallum (Chapter 10) found that students who possessed an academic alienation goal tended to dislike effort as well as academic support from peers.

In their review of the relevant literature, Ip and Chiu (Chapter 11) have identified a number of elements of effective self-regulated learning. These elements include:

Set reasonably challenging goals.   When students attempt to master a task that requires reasonably advanced skills, they find the task engaging, are motivated to apply their cognitive abilities to master the task, and will develop more advanced skills and strategies.

Develop an intrinsic interest in learning.   Students will have strong intrinsic motivation when the learning environment does not emphasize evaluation, and the students are given the chance to become an autonomous learner. When students take ownership of their learning, they tend to be creative, motivated, and persistent in learning.

Believe in the malleability of abilities.   When students believe that abilities are fixed, they focus on assessing their abilities rather than improving them. When students believe that abilities are malleable qualities that can be improved, they will focus on how to improve themselves (Hong, Chiu, Dweck, Lin, & Wan, 1999).

Believe that effort and strategies will lead to improvement in abilities.   Some students believe that effort implies lack of ability: Only unintelligent students need to work hard. This belief will reduce students' motivation to work hard to improve themselves. When students believe that they can become smarter by working harder, they will be more willing to shape up their skills (Hong, 2001).

Do not blame the unchangeable aspects of the self for one's failures.   Some students attribute their failures to fixed aspects of the self (e.g., intelligence). They become helpless in failure situations. Teachers can motivate students to change such maladaptive attributions.

Take responsibility for one's failure and take remedial actions.   Some students externalize the responsibility of their failures (attribute the failures to external causes) and therefore do not assume the responsibility of taking remedial actions. Teachers can help students to take responsibility for their failures by emphasizing the link between internal, alterable qualities (effort and strategies) and performance.

Learn from one's mistakes.   Failures are unavoidable when students set challenging goals for themselves. Students should learn not to view setbacks too negatively. They can use failures to identify room for improvement and set realistic goals for the future.

CONCLUSION

Globalization and increased intercultural contacts have increased the cultural heterogeneity of the student body in schools. This has offered many new challenges to educators and teachers. In this chapter, we have outlined the background leading to some of these new challenges. We believe that the concept of multiple competencies could offer a new perspective for us to appreciate the limitations of conventional models of ability assessment, student performance evaluation, and provision of educational services to students with special needs. We contend that by measuring a broader range of human abilities, and by focusing on the teaching and assessment of higher order cognition, educators and teachers will be better equipped to recognize the intellectual strengths of different cultural groups, and to design teaching activities to make full use of the strengths brought into the classroom by various cultural groups.

We however are wary of the claim that the goals of multicultural education could be attained simply by increasing the cultural heterogeneity of the student body in schools and by recognizing the strengths of different cultural groups. Research has shown that the qualities students acquired from their culture interact with the school culture. Thus, educators should apply universal principles of self-regulated learning to create an optimal learning environment for all students. In this environment, cultural diversity will be respected and valued. In addition, learning activities will be designed to achieve the fundamental purposes of effective learning in schools.

Now that we have outlined the basic themes of this volume, it is our pleasure to invite readers to discover for themselves the numerous insights that the chapter contributors of this volume have on these themes.

REFERENCES

Armstrong, T. (1994). *Multiple intelligences in the classroom.* Alexandria, VA: Association for Supervision and Curriculum Development.

Fordham, S. (1988). Racelessness as a factor in Black students' success. *Harvard Educational Review, 58,* 54–83.

Gurin, P. (1999). Expert report for Gratz et al. vs. Bollinger et al., No 97-75321 (E. D. Mich.) and Grutter et al. vs. Bollinger et al., No. 97-75928 (E. D. Mich.), http://www.umich.edu.

Harman, J., & Askounis, A. (1989). Asian American students: Are they really a "model minority"? *The School Counselor, 37,* 109–113.

Hermans, H.J.M., & Kampen, H.J.G. (1998). Moving cultures: The perilous problems of cultural dichotomies in a globalizing society. *American Psychologist, 53,* 1111–1120.

Ho, D.Y.F., & Spinks, J.A. (1985). Multivariate prediction of academic performance by Hong Kong university students. *Contemporary Educational Psychology, 10,* 249–259.

Hong, Y. (2001). Chinese students' and teachers' inferences of effort and ability. In F. Salili, C.Y. Chiu, & Y.Y. Hong (Eds.), *Student motivation: The culture and context of learning* (pp. 105–120). New York: Kluwer Academic/Plenum.

Hong, Y., Chiu, C.Y., Dweck, C.S., Lin, D.M., & Wan, W. (1999). Implicit theories, attributions, and coping: A meaning system approach. *Journal of Personality and Social Psychology, 77,* 588–599.

Hong, Y., Morris, M.W., Chiu, C.Y., & Benet-Martinez, V. (2000). Multicultural minds: A dynamic constructivist approach to culture and cognition. *American Psychologist, 55,* 709–720.

Hurtado, S., Inkelas, K.K., Briggs, C., & Rhee, B.S. (1997). Differences in college success and choice among racial/ethnic groups. *Research in Higher Education, 38,* 43–75.

Maehr, M.L., & Yamaguchi, R. (2001). Cultural diversity, student motivation and achievement. In F. Salili, C.Y. Chiu, & Y.Y. Hong (Eds.), *Student motivation: The culture and context of learning* (pp. 123–148). New York: Kluwer Academic/Plenum.

Okagaki, L., & Sternberg, R.J. (1993). Parental beliefs and children's school performance. *Child Development, 64,* 36–56.

Peng, S., Owings, J., & Fetter, W. (1984). *School experiences and performance of Asian American high school students.* Washington, DC: U. S. Department of Education.

Salili, F., Chiu, C.Y., & Hong, Y.Y. (Eds.). (2001), *Student motivation: The culture and context of learning.* New York: Kluwer Academic/Plenum.

Salili, F., Chiu, C.Y., & Lai, S. (2001). The influence of culture and context on students' motivational orientation and performance. In F. Salili, C.Y. Chiu, & Y.Y. Hong (Eds.), *Student motivation: The culture and context of learning* (pp. 221–247). New York: Kluwer Academic/Plenum.

Slavin, R.E., Madder, N.A., Dolan, L.J., & Wasik, B.A. (1996). *Every child, every school: Success for all.* Thousand Oaks, CA: Corwin Press.

Stringfield, S., Millsap, M.A., & Herman, Wasik R. (1997). *Urban and suburban/rural special strategies for educating disadvantaged children: Findings and policy implications of a longitudinal study.* Washington, DC: Department of Education.

Steele, C.M., & Aronson, J. (1995). Stereotype threat and the intellectual test performance of African Americans. *Journal of Personality and Social Psychology, 69,* 797–811.

Stevenson, H.W. (1983). *Making the grade: School achievement in Japan, Taiwan, and the United States.* Stanford, CA: Center for Advanced Study in the Behavioral Sciences.

Stevenson, H.W., & Lee, S.Y. (1996). The academic achievement of Chinese students. In M.H. Bond (Ed.), *The handbook of Chinese psychology* (pp. 124–142). Hong Kong: Oxford University Press.

Sue, S., & Okazaki, S. (1990). Asian American educational achievement: A phenomenon in search of an explanation. *American Psychologist, 45,* 913–920.

Tsang, S.L., & Wing, L.C. (1985). *Beyond Angel Island: The education of Asian Americans.* New York: ERIC/CUE.

PART I

MULTIPLE COMPETENCIES

CHAPTER 2

INTELLIGENCE TESTS AS MEASURES OF DEVELOPING EXPERTISE

Robert J. Sternberg

ABSTRACT

This chapter describes how tests of intelligence measure developing expertise. The general conception of intelligence as developing expertise is described and then research examples are given that, in conjunction, seem odd under traditional interpretations of abilities but that make sense as a whole in the context of the developing-expertise model. It is concluded that this new model offers potential for better understanding intelligence-related phenomena.

INTRODUCTION

This chapter describes how tests of intelligence measure developing expertise. The general conception of intelligence as developing expertise is described and then research examples are given that, in conjunction, seem odd under traditional interpretations of abilities but that make sense as a whole in the context of the developing-expertise model. It is concluded that this new model offers potential for better understanding intelligence-related phenomena.

The conventional view of intelligence tests is that these tests measure some relatively stable attributes of individuals, which develop as an interaction between heredity and environment. Factor analysis and related techniques then can be used to determine the structure of intellectual abilities, as illustrated by the massive analysis of Carroll (1993).

The argument of this article, advancing that of Sternberg (1998), is that this view of what intelligence tests measure is both naive and wrong. In reality, what these tests measure is a form of developing expertise. Good performance on intelligence tests requires a certain kind of expertise, and to the extent this expertise overlaps with the expertise required by schooling or by the work place, there will be a correlation between the tests and performance in school or in the work place. But such correlations represent no intrinsic relationship between intelligence and other kinds of performance, but rather overlaps in the kinds of expertise needed to perform well under different kinds of circumstances. The goal of this article is to carry the argument made by Sternberg (1998) a step further by showing that a conjunction of research results that would seem puzzling and contradictory when taken together make sense as a whole when considered from the standpoint of ability tests as measuring developing expertise.

There is nothing privileged about the intelligence tests. One could as easily use, say, academic achievement to predict intelligence-related scores. For example, it is as simple to use the SAT-II (a measure of achievement) to predict the SAT-I (a measure presently called the Scholastic Assessment Test and formerly called the Scholastic Aptitude Test) as vice versa, and of course, the levels of prediction will be the same. Both tests measure achievement, although the kinds of achievements they measure are different.

According to this view, although ability tests may have temporal priority relative to various criteria in their administration (i.e., ability tests are administered first, and later, criterion indices of performance, such as grades or achievement test scores, are collected), they have no psychological priority. All of the various kinds of assessments are of the same kind psychologically. What distinguishes ability tests from other kinds of assessments is how the ability tests are used (usually predictively) rather than what they measure. There is no qualitative distinction among the various kinds of assessments. All tests measure various kinds of developing expertise.

Conventional tests of intelligence and related abilities measure achievement that individuals should have accomplished several years back. Tests such as vocabulary, reading, comprehension, verbal analogies, arithmetic problem solving, and the like are all, in part, tests of achievement. Even abstract-reasoning tests measure achievement in dealing with geometric symbols, skills taught in Western schools (Laboratory of Comparative Human Cognition, 1982). One might as well use academic performance to predict ability-test scores. The problem regarding the traditional model is not in its statement of a correlation between ability tests and other forms of achievement but in its proposal of a causal relation whereby the tests reflect a construct that is somehow causal of, rather than merely temporally antecedent to, later success.

THE G-FACTOR AND THE STRUCTURE OF ABILITIES

Some intelligence theorists point to the stability of the alleged general factor of human intelligence as evidence for the existence of some kind of stable and overriding structure of human intelligence. But the existence of a g factor reflects nothing more than an interaction between whatever latent abilities individuals may have and the kinds of expertise that are developed in school. With different forms of schooling, g could be made either stronger or weaker. In effect, Western forms and related forms of schooling may, in part, create the g phenomenon.

Suppose, for example, that children were selected from an early age to be schooled for a certain trade. Throughout most of human history, this is in fact the way most children were schooled. Boys, at least, were apprenticed at an early age to a master who would teach them a trade. There was no point in their learning skills that would be irrelevant to their lives.

To bring the example into the present, imagine that we decided, from an early age, that certain students would study English (or some other native language) to develop language expertise; other students would study mathematics to develop their mathematical expertise. Still other students might specialize in developing spatial expertise to be used in flying airplanes or doing shop work or whatever. Instead of specialization beginning at the university level, it would begin from the age of first schooling.

These students then would be given an omnibus test of intelligence or any broad-ranging measure of intelligence. There would be no general factor because people schooled in one form of expertise would not have been schooled in others. One can imagine even a negative correlation between scores on the so-called intelligence test. The reason for the negative correlation would be that developing expertise in one area would preclude developing expertise in another because of the form of schooling.

Lest this tale sound far-fetched, I hasten to add that it is a true tale of what is happening now in some places. In the United States and most of the developed world, of course, schooling takes a fairly standard course. But this standard course, and the value placed upon it, is not uniform across the world.

In a collaborative study, children of near Kisumu, Kenya, conducted with Elena Grigorenko, Kate Nokes, Wenzel Geissler, Ruth Prince, and Frederick Okatcha (see Sternberg & Grigorenko, 1997), we devised a test of practical intelligence that measures informal knowledge for an important aspect of adaptation to the environment near Kisumu, namely, knowledge of the identities and use of natural herbal medicines that could be used to fight infections. By *informal knowledge,* we are referring to kinds of knowledge not taught in schools and not assessed on tests given in the schools.

The idea of our research was that children who knew what these medicines were, what they were used for, and how they should be dosed would be in a position better to adapt to their environments than would children without this informal knowledge. We do not know how many, if any, of these medicines actually work, but from the standpoint of measuring practical intelligence in a given culture, the important thing is that the people in Kenya believe that the medicines work.

We found substantial individual differences in the children's tacit knowledge of these natural herbal medicines. More important, however, was the correlation between scores on this test and scores on an English language vocabulary test (the Mill Hill), a Dholuo equivalent (Dholuo is the community and home language), and the Raven Coloured Progressive matrices. We found significantly negative correlations between our test and these tests. The better children did on the test of indigenous tacit knowledge, the worse they did on the academic ability tests, and vice versa (Sternberg et al., 2001). Why might we have obtained such a finding?

Based on ethnographic observation, we believe the reason is that parents near Kisumu may emphasize either a more indigenous or a more Western education. Some parents (and their children) see little value to school. They do not see how success in school connects with the future of children who will basically spend their whole lives living in a village near Kisumu without the need for the expertise the school teaches. Other parents and children seem to see Western schooling as of value in itself or potentially as a ticket out of the confines of the village. The parents thus tend to emphasize one type of education or the other for their children, with corresponding results. The kinds of developing expertise the families value differ, and so therefore do scores on the tests. From this point of view, the intercorrelational structure of tests tells us nothing intrinsic about the structure of intelligence per se, but rather, something about the way abilities as developing forms of expertise structures themselves in interaction with the demands of the environment.

Nuñes (1994) has reported related findings based on a series of studies she conducted in Brazil (see also Ceci & Roazzi, 1994). Street children's adaptive intelligence is tested to the limit by their ability to form and successfully run street businesses. If a child fails to run such a business successfully, he risks starvation or even death at the hands of death squads, should he resort to stealing. Nuñes and her collaborators have found that the same children who are running successful street businesses may be failing mathematics in school.

From a conventional-abilities standpoint, this result is puzzling. From a developing-expertise standpoint, it is not. Street children grow up in an environment that fosters the development of practical but not academic mathematical skills. We know that even conventional academic kinds of expertise often fail to show transfer (e.g., Gick & Holyoak, 1980). It is scarcely surprising, then, that there would be little transfer here. The street children have developed the kinds of practical expertise they need for survival and even success, but they will get no credit for these skills when they take conventional ability tests.

It also seems likely that if the scales were reversed, and privileged children who do well on conventional ability tests or in school were forced out on the street, many of them would not survive long. Indeed, in the ghettoes of urban America, many children and adults who, for one reason or another, end up on the street, in fact barely survive or do not make it at all.

Jean Lave (1989) has reported similar findings with Berkeley housewives shopping in supermarkets. There just is no correlation between their ability to do the mathematics needed for comparison shopping, and their scores on conventional paper-and-pencil tests of mathematical skills. And Ceci and Liker (1986) similarly found that expert handicappers at race-tracks generally had only average IQs. There was no correlation between the complexity of the mathematical model they used in handicapping and their scores on conventional tests. In each case, important kinds of developing expertise for life were not adequately reflected by the kinds of developing expertise measured by the conventional ability tests.

The problem with the conventional model of abilities does not just apply in what to us are exotic cultures or exotic occupations. In a collaborative study with Michel Ferrari, Pamela Clinkenbeard, and Elena Grigorenko (Sternberg, Ferrari, Clinkenbeard, & Grigorenko, 1996), high school students were tested for their analytical, creative, and practical abilities via multiple-choice and essay items. The multiple-choice items were divided into three content domains: verbal, quantitative, and figural. Students' scores were factor analyzed and then later correlated with their performance in a college-level introductory-psychology course (Sternberg, Grigorenko, Ferrari, & Clinkenbeard, 1999).

We found that when students were tested not only for analytical abilities, but for creative and practical abilities too (as follows from the model of successful intelligence, Sternberg, 1985, 1997), the strong general factor that tends to result from multiple-ability tests disappears. Of course, there is always some general factor when one factor analyzes but does not rotate the factor solution, but the general factor was weak, and of course disappeared with a varimax rotation. We also found that all of analytical, creative, and practical abilities predicted performance in the introductory-psychology course (which itself was taught analytically, creatively, or practically, with assessments to match). Moreover, although the students who were identified as high analytical were from the traditional population-primarily white, middle- to upper middle-class, and well educated, the students who were identified as high creative or high practical were much more diverse in all of these attributes.

Thus, conventional tests may favor a small segment of the population by virtue of the narrow kind of developing expertise they measure. When one measures a broader range of developing expertise, the results look quite different. Moreover, the broader range of expertise includes kinds of skills that will be important in the world of work and in the world of the family.

Analytical, creative, and practical abilities, as measured by our tests or anyone else's, are simply forms of developing expertise. All are useful in various kinds of life tasks. But conventional tests unfairly advantage those students who do well in just a narrow range of kinds of expertise. By expanding the range of developing expertise we measure, we discover that many children not now identified as able have, in fact, developed important kinds of expertise.

Teaching in a way that departs from notions of abilities based on a general factor also pays dividends. In a recent set of studies we have shown that third-grade and eighth-grade students, who are taught social studies (a unit in communities) or science (a unit on psychology) for successful intelligence (analytically, creative, and practically, as well as for memory), outperform students who are taught just for analytical (critical) thinking or just for memory (Sternberg, Torff, & Grigorenko, 1998a, b). The students taught "triarchically" outperform the other students not only on performance assessments that look at analytical, creative, and practical kinds of achievements, but even on tests that measure straight memory (multiple-choice tests already being used in the courses).

Thus, teaching students in a way that takes into account their more highly developed expertise, and that also enables them to develop other kinds of expertise, results in superior learning outcomes, regardless of how these learning outcomes are measured. The children taught in a way that enables them to use kinds of expertise other than memory actually remember better, on average, than do children taught for memory.

We have also done studies in which we have measured informal procedural knowledge in children and adults. We have done such studies with business managers, college professors, elementary-school students, sales people, college students, and general populations. This important aspect of practical intelligence, in study after study, has been found to be uncorrelated with academic intelligence as measured by conventional tests, in a variety of populations, occupations, and at a variety of age levels (Sternberg,

Wagner, Williams, & Horvath, 1995). Moreover, the tests predict job performance as well as or better than do tests of IQ. Most recently, we have developed a test of common sense for the work place that predicts self-ratings of common sense but not self-ratings of various kinds of academic abilities.

Although the kinds of informal procedural expertise we measure in these tests do not correlate with academic expertise, they do correlate across work domains. For example, we found that sub-scores (for managing oneself, managing others, and managing tasks) on measures of informal procedural knowledge are correlated with each other and that scores on the test for academic psychology are moderately correlated with scores on the test for business managers (Sternberg, Wagner, Williams, & Horvath, 1995). So the kinds of developing expertise that matter in the world of work may show certain correlations with each other that are not shown with the kinds of developing expertise that matter in the world of the school.

It is even possible to use these kinds of tests to predict effectiveness in leadership. Studies of military leaders showed that tests of informal knowledge of military leaders predicted the effectiveness of these leaders, whereas conventional tests of intelligence did not. We also found that although the test for managers was significantly correlated with the test for military leaders, only the latter test predicted superiors' ratings of leadership effectiveness (Sternberg et al., 2000).

Both conventional academic tests and our tests of practical intelligence measure forms of developing expertise that matter in school and on the job. The two kinds of tests are not qualitatively distinct. The reason the correlations are essentially null is that the kinds of developing expertise they measure are quite different. The people who have good abstract, academic kinds of expertise are often people who have not emphasized learning practical, everyday kinds of expertise, and vice versa, as we found so strongly in our Kenya study. Indeed, children who grow up in challenging environments such as the inner city must develop practical over academic expertise as a matter of survival. As in Kenya, these practical expertise can be expected better to predict their survival than can academic kinds of expertise. The same applies in business, where tacit knowledge about how to perform on the job is as likely or more likely to lead to job success than is the academic expertise that in school seems so important.

Practical kinds of expertise matter in schools too. In a study at Yale, Wendy Williams and I (cited in Sternberg, Wagner, & Okagaki, 1993) found that a test of tacit knowledge for college predicted grade point average as well as did an academic-ability test. But a test of tacit knowledge for college life better predicted adjustment to the college environment than did the academic test.

TAKING TESTS

Developing expertise applies not only to the constructs measured by conventional intelligence tests, but also to the very act of taking the tests. In a collaborative study in Bagamoyo, Tanzania, with Elena Grigorenko and Professor Mbise, we have been investigating dynamic tests administered to children (Sternberg et al., in press). Although dynamic tests have been developed for a number of purposes (see Grigorenko & Sternberg, 1998; Sternberg & Grigorenko, 2001), one of our particular purposes was to look at how dynamic testing affects score patterns. In particular, we developed more or less conventional measures but administered them in a dynamic format. First students took a pretest. Then they received a short period of instruction (generally no more than 10 to 15 minutes) on how to improve their performance in the expertise measured by these tests. Then the children took a posttest. A control group received the tests but no instruction.

A first finding was that the correlation between pretest scores and posttest scores, although statistically significant, was weak in the experimental (but not control) group (about .3). In other words, even a short period of instruction fairly drastically changed the rank orders of the students on the test. The critical question, of course, is not whether there is a change, but what it means. In particular, which predicts other kinds of cognitive performance better, pretest scores or posttest scores? We found that posttest scores predicted other kinds of cognitive performance about four times as well as did pretest scores.

We again interpret these results in terms of the model of developing expertise. The Tanzanian students had developed very little expertise in the skills required to take American-style intelligence tests. Thus even a short intervention could have a fairly substantial effect on their scores. When the students developed somewhat more of this test-taking expertise through a short intervention, their scores changed and became more reflective of their true capabilities for cognitive work.

Sometimes the expertise children learn that is relevant for in-school tests may actually hurt them on conventional ability tests. In one example, we studied the development of children's analogical reasoning in a country day school that taught in English in the morning and in Hebrew in the afternoon (Sternberg & Rifkin, 1979). We found a number of second-grade students who got no problems right on our test. They would have seemed, on the surface, to be rather stupid. We discovered the reason why, however. We had tested in the afternoon, and in the afternoon, the children always read in Hebrew. So they read our problems from right to left, and got them all wrong. The expertise that served them so well in their normal environment utterly failed them on the test. Our sample was upper-middle-class children who, in a year or two, would know better. But imagine what happens with other children in less supportive environments who develop kinds of expertise that may serve them well in their family or community lives or even school life, but not on the tests. They will appear to be stupid rather than lacking the kind of expertise the tests measure.

Patricia Greenfield (1997) has done a number of studies in a variety of cultures and found that the kinds of test-taking expertise assumed to be universal in the US and other Western countries are by no means universal. She found, for example, that children in Mayan cultures (and probably in other highly collectivist cultures as well) were puzzled when they were not allowed to collaborate with their parents or others on test questions. In the United States, of course, such collaboration would be viewed as cheating. But in a collectivist culture, someone who had not developed this kind of collaborative expertise, and moreover, someone who did not use it, would be perceived as lacking important adaptive skills (see also Laboratory of Comparative Human Cognition, 1982).

CONCLUSION

Intelligence tests measure developing expertise. Tests can be created that favor the kinds of developing expertise developed in any kind of cultural or sub-cultural milieu. Those who have created conventional tests of abilities have tended to value the kinds of skills most valued by Western schools. This system of valuing is understandable, given that Binet and Simon (1905) first developed intelligence tests for the purpose of predicting school performance. But in the modern world, the conception of abilities as fixed or even as predetermined is an anachronism. Moreover, the set of abilities measured by conventional tests encompass only a small portion of the kinds of developing expertise relevant for life success. It is for this reason that conventional tests predict only about 10 percent of individual-difference variation in various measures of success in adult life (Herrnstein & Murray, 1994).

Not all cultures value equally the kinds of expertise measured by these tests. In a study comparing Latino, Asian, and Anglo subcultures in California, for example, we found that Latino parents valued social kinds of expertise as more important to intelligence than did Asian and Anglo parents, who more valued cognitive kinds of expertise. Predictably, teachers also more valued cognitive kinds of expertise, with the result that the Anglo and Asian children would be expected to do better in school, and did (Okagaki & Sternberg, 1993). Until we expand our notions of abilities, and recognize that when we measure them, we are measuring developing forms of expertise, we will be consigning many potentially excellent contributors to our society to bleak futures. We will also be potentially overvaluing students with expertise for success in a certain kind of schooling, but not necessarily for success later in life.

REFERENCES

Binet, A., & Simon, T. (1905). Méthodes nouvelles pour le diagnostic du niveau intellectuel des anormaux. *L'Année psychologique*, 11, 191–336.

Carroll, J.B. (1993). *Human cognitive abilities: A survey of factor-analytic studies*. New York: Cambridge University Press.

Ceci, S.J., & Liker, J. (1986). Academic and nonacademic intelligence: An experimental separation. In R.J. Sternberg & R.K. Wagner (Eds.), *Practical intelligence: Nature and origins of competence in the everyday world* (pp. 119–142). New York: Cambridge University Press.

Ceci, S.J., & Roazzi, A. (1994). The effects of context on cognition: Postcards from Brazil. In R.J. Sternberg & R.K. Wagner (Eds.), *Mind in context: Interactionist perspectives on human intelligence* (pp. 74–101). New York: Cambridge University Press.

Gick, M.L., & Holyoak, K.J. (1980). Analogical problem solving. *Cognitive Psychology*, 12, 306–355.

Grigorenko, E.L., & Sternberg, R.J. (1998). Dynamic testing. *Psychological Bulletin*, 124, 75–111.

Greenfield, P.M. (1997). You can't take it with you: Why assessments of abilities don't cross cultures. *American Psychologist*, 52, 1115–1124.

Herrnstein, R.J., & Murray, C. (1994). *The bell curve*. New York: Free Press.

Laboratory of Comparative Human Cognition. (1982). Culture and intelligence. In R.J. Sternberg (Ed.) *Handbook of human intelligence* (pp. 642–718). New York: Cambridge University Press.

Lave, J. (1989). *Cognition in practice*. New York: Cambridge University Press.

Nuñes, T. (1994). Street intelligence. In R.J. Sternberg (Ed.), *Encyclopedia of human intelligence* (Vol. 2, pp. 1045–1049). New York: Macmillan.

Okagaki, L., & Sternberg, R.J. (1993). Parental beliefs and children's school performance. *Child Development*, 64, 36–56.

Sternberg, R.J. (1985). *Beyond IQ: A triarchic theory of human intelligence*. New York: Cambridge University Press.

Sternberg, R.J. (1997). *Successful intelligence*. New York: Plume.

Sternberg, R.J. (1998). Abilities are forms of developing expertise. *Educational Researcher*, 27, 11–20.

Sternberg, R.J., Ferrari, M., Clinkenbeard, P.R., & Grigorenko, E.L. (1996). Identification, instruction, and assessment of gifted children: A construct validation of a triarchic model. *Gifted Child Quarterly*, 40, 129–137.

Sternberg, R.J., Forsythe, G.B., Hedlund, J., Horvath, J., Snook, S., Williams, W.M., Wagner, R.K., & Grigorenko, E.L. (2000). *Practical intelligence in everyday life*. New York: Cambridge University Press.

Sternberg, R.J., & Grigorenko, E.L. (1997 Fall). The cognitive costs of physical and mental ill health: Applying the psychology of the developed world to the problems of the developing world. *Eye on Psi Chi, 2*(1), 20–27.

Sternberg, R.J., & Grigorenko, E.L. (2001). *Dynamic testing.* New York: Cambridge University Press.

Sternberg, R.J., Grigorenko, E.L., Ferrari, M., & Clinkenbeard, P. (1999). A triarchic analysis of an aptitude-treatment interaction. *European Journal of Psychological Assessment, 15* (1), 1–11.

Sternberg, R.J., Grigorenko, E.L., Ngorosh, D., Tantufuye, E., Mbise, A., Nokes, C., Jukes, M., & Burdy, D.A. (in press). Assessing intellectual potential in rural Tanzanian school children. *Intelligence.*

Sternberg, R.J., Nokes, K., Geissler, P.W., Prince, R., Okatcha, F., Bundy, D.A., & Grigorenko, E.L. (2001). The relationship between academic and practical intelligence. A case study in Kenya. *Intelligence, 29,* 401–418.

Sternberg, R.J., & Rifkin, B. (1979). The development of analogical reasoning processes. *Journal of Experimental Child Psychology, 28,* 469–478.

Sternberg, R.J., Torff, B., & Grigorenko, E.L. (1998a). Teaching for successful intelligence raises school achievement. *Phi Delta Kappa, 79,* 667–669.

Sternberg, R.J., Torff, B., & Grigorenko, E.L. (1998b). Teaching triarchically improves school achievement. *Journal of Educational Psychology, 90,* 374–384.

Sternberg, R.J., Wagner, R.K., & Okagaki, L. (1993). Practical intelligence: The nature and role of tacit knowledge in work and at school. In H. Reese & J. Puckett (Eds.), *Advances in lifespan development* (pp. 205–227). Hillsdale, NJ: Erlbaum.

Sternberg, R.J., Wagner, R.K., Williams, W.M., & Horvath, J. (1995). Testing common sense. *American Psychologist, 50,* 912–927.

CHAPTER 3

AUTHORITY AND LEARNING IN CONFUCIAN-HERITAGE EDUCATION:

A RELATIONAL METHODOLOGICAL ANALYSIS

David Yau-fai Ho, Si-qing Peng, and Shui-fun Fiona Chan

ABSTRACT

The authors confront the paradox of Confucian-heritage education: the apparent contradiction between the alleged superior academic achievement by Asian students, and the many ills of Confucian-heritage education voiced by critics. A review of the evidence leads to three conclusions: (a) Examination superstition continues to subvert the goals of education; (b) students rely heavily on memorization and repeated practice in order to do well in examinations; and (c) there is no evidence of superior academic achievement by Asian students other than merely knowledge acquisition and retention. Two methodological foci are identified. The first focus argues for using the student-in-relations as the unit of analysis, in line with methodological relationalism. The role definition of teachers and students is regarded as potent determinants of learning outcomes. The second focus decries the preoccupation with academic achievement, narrowly conceived, in educational research. It views success in learning as being relative to educational goals. We argue that the key for transforming Confucian-heritage education—and other educational systems—lies in confronting authority relationships in the world of learning, and particularly in redefining the teacher-student relationship.

> *I learned to sharpen my tongue when I went from the East to the West, and to dull it, somewhat, when I returned from the West to the East.*
> *Of what use is a pen to a student, if with his pen he cannot beguile examiners to win high marks?*
> *Dear is Confucius. But dearer still is thought liberation.*

INTRODUCTION

In this chapter, we confront a paradox that has caught the attention of educators in both the East and the West. Following Ho (1994), we call this the paradox of Confucian-heritage education. On the one hand, Confucian-heritage cultures place a high value on educational achievement; children are highly motivated to succeed in school. Superior levels of achievement in mathematics and/or science by Chinese and Japanese children have been consistently reported in cross-national studies (Ho, 1994; IEA, 1988; Stevenson & Lee, 1996). On the other hand, critics of Confucian-heritage educational systems point to their many ills: the authoritarian atmosphere in the classroom in general and of the teacher-student relationship in particular; outmoded instructional methods; overemphasis on examinations; lack of cultivation of creativity and independent, critical thinking; and excessive pressure to succeed, often at the expense of the students' mental health. Thus, the questions must be raised: What are the costs of the lopsided emphasis on academic achievement to psychological development? What are the cultural values underlying the ills of Confucian-heritage education?

A more restricted statement of the paradox has come to be known as the paradox of the Chinese learner (Watkins & Biggs, 1996): How can Chinese learners be so successful academically when the way they are taught and their learning appears to rely so heavily on rote memorization? Framing the paradox in this way begs a fundamental question concerning the definition of academic success and how it can be meaningfully measured. Moreover, from a methodological point of view, it is ill advised to focus on the characteristics of the individual learner, rather than on the learner-in-context. This occasions a closer examination of what analytic framework is suitable in educational research.

These questions provide the foci for the following analysis. Resolving the paradox requires, however, a prior examination of the evidence concerning the alleged reliance on rote memorization and superior academic performance by Asian students. Most important, confronting the paradox of Confucian-heritage education compels us to ask: What are the goals of education? Specifically, do examinations serve to advance, or to subvert, the goals of education?

A REVIEW OF THE EVIDENCE

Rote Memorization or Lack of Metacognitive Abilities

Concerning the paradox of the Chinese learner, Watkins and Biggs (1996) conclude that the alleged reliance on rote memorization is a widely held Western stereotype and misconception, and is largely unfounded. In self-report questionnaires, students from Confucian-heritage cultures report a stronger preference for deep (high-level and meaning-based), and a weaker preference for surface (rote), learning strategies, than that of Western students, both in their own countries and overseas in Australia (Biggs, 1996, p. 49).

The conclusion of Watkins and Biggs may be questioned on empirical and methodological grounds. Empirically, data on schoolchildren from six rather different countries summarized by Watkins (1996, Table 1.6) indicate that Hong Kong schoolchildren were not the only ones who were both lower in surface strategy and higher in deep strategy than their Australian counterparts. Malaysian and Nepalese schoolchildren showed a similar trend—that is, students who did not come from Confucian-heritage cultures also compared favorably with Western students. Chinese learners are not alone in this respect. Are we then to say that non-Confucian Asian cultures have also contributed to the favorable comparisons with Western cultures in students' learning strategies? As cultural psychologists are aware, to invoke culture in the explanation of phenomena is laden with intellectual traps.

Methodologically, problems of measurement have to be addressed. The self-report questionnaires used fall short of the classical psychometric requirements of reliability and validity. Reported reliabilities were rather low and only marginally adequate; mean correlations with academic grades, though in the expected directions, were of the order of .20 or lower (Watkins, 1996, Tables 1.2, 1.4). Also, under relentless attack, rote memorization has gotten a bad name. Thus social desirability, as a response set in self-report measures, is an issue. More fundamentally, to say that one prefers the deep strategy is not to say that one has indeed mastered it. If research were to zero in on assessing the mastery of interrelating ideas and reading extensiveness, essential to successful applications of the deep strategy, how would the Chinese learner fare? An investigative research by Ho, Chan, and Peng (this volume) speaks directly on this question. The conclusion: poorly.

Other researchers have also refuted the alleged Chinese learner's reliance on rote memorization, saying that it is a bias of Western observers. Gow, Bella, Kember, and Hau (1996) state that "memorization could coexist with understanding in Chinese students" (p. 123). This they hail as a "recent discovery"—which would sound strange to cognitive psychologists and, of course, to the Chinese students themselves. As the authors themselves are aware, rote memorization intended for the reproduction of information (e.g., regurgitation to "satisfy" unimaginative examiners) must be distinguished from memorization as a step in the learning process toward understanding. It must also be distinguished from repetitive practice, which is commonly used by Asian students.

Gow et al. (1996) conclude: "The learning approaches of Chinese students cannot be adequately described by a deep/surface dichotomy" (p. 123). We would go further: Learning approaches cannot be adequately described by any dichotomy, such as deep versus surface approaches or rote memorization versus understanding. Such dichotomization is misleading. In real life, learning moves forth and back between the surface and the deep. Some memorization is essential to understanding, and understanding enhances retention. To avoid being misunderstood, we wish to make clear that we have said nothing to defend, much less to endorse, the Chinese learner's strategies. Rather, the point is that, as seekers of meaning, humans would find it rather difficult not to generate, even from rote memorization, some understanding. In sum, the research focus on rote memorization is misplaced, and we must confront the paradox of the Chinese learner afresh.

Educators generally agree that the ultimate goal of learning is not just the acquisition and retention of knowledge, but the capacity to apply and even to generate knowledge. Accordingly, the extent to which metacognitive abilities are mastered—to reflect on one's thinking and learning— ought to be the most meaningful measure of success or failure in learning, and hence a focus of research. The evidence presented by Ho, Chan, and Peng (this volume) points to a weakness in metacognitive abilities among Chinese university students: to think critically, independently, and reflectively; to develop coherent arguments supported by evidence or rational analysis; to apply knowledge to solve novel problems; or to gain insights into relations between academic learning and everyday life experiences. Likewise, results reported by Salili, Chiu, and Lai (2001) indicate that Chinese students in Hong Kong made less use of appropriate metacognitive and learning strategies than European-Canadian students. They were more concerned with their academic performance, spent more time studying, but felt less competent and more anxious. This pattern of results points to wastage: The students consume much of their emotional energy worrying, and the quantity of time they spend on studying is not matched by quality.

Quantity Means Quality?

Diligence is highly valued in Confucian-heritage education, but it is all too commonly equated with monotonous repeated practice. Among Japanese students, there is a popular saying: "Four hours of sleep and pass, five hours of sleep and fail." Attending school is not enough; many Asian students enroll in private cram schools after their regular school hours. Research results indicate that Chinese schoolchildren spend an inordinate amount of time on homework—far more than their counterparts in the United States—leaving precious little time for leisure, reading for pleasure, and other educational activities, but the amount of time spent on homework has no consistent relation with academic achievement (see Ho, 1994, pp. 299–301, for a summary).

We must, therefore, question if the stress on quantity represents a misguided belief that doing more automatically means doing better. The traditional learning style may be described as a compulsive study orientation: stressing (a) book learning; (b) memorization; and (c) compulsion, hardship, and the need for punishment in the learning process. Studious students are referred to as "book worms." They "read books in a dead manner"—not in the manner of "lively learning and lively application." This orientation, however, is negatively correlated with academic performance by university students in Hong Kong (Ho & Spinks, 1985). Not being considered is how effectively the time on studying is spent, as when memorization and repeated practice do not translate into understanding, let alone creativity. Asian countries are beginning to be awakened to these problems. In mainland China, for instance, the Ministry of Education has been calling for lessening the burden of homework for schoolchildren. But its effectiveness appears to be inversely related to the number of documents issued for this purpose (numbering 48 between 1995 and 1999).

Academic Success?

What is academic success? What are the measures that would be more meaningful and useful to personal and national development than GPAs or achievement tests? Most important, is academic success the only, or ultimate, goal of education? Answers to these questions are laden with educational values. They entail a central issue underlying the paradox: the nature of the evidence upon which supporters and critics of Confucian-heritage education make their claims and counterclaims.

In North America, the superior educational and occupational achievements of Asians are well documented (Vernon, 1982). Asian-Americans have higher levels of educational achievement than the national average, as indicated by percentages of high school and college graduates, GPAs, and finalists and winners of prestigious competitions (Sue & Okazaki, 1990; see also Stevenson & Lee, 1996). Furthermore, their achievement levels are higher than what would be predicted from their IQs (Flynn, 1991). These studies, however, provide evidence on the superior performance of Asian students in North American universities, not on the success or failure of Confucian-heritage education.

Studies yielding evidence for the superior academic achievement of students in Confucian-heritage cultures have relied largely on quantitative data, in the form of achievement test results, obtained in large-scale international surveys. Among the best known are studies conducted by the International Association for the Evaluation of Educational Achievement (IEA, 1988). They show consistently that Korea, Japan, and Singapore—all sharing the Confucian heritage—rank among the top countries in mathematics and science achievement. Greater methodological rigor may be found in studies by Stevenson and his associates (for a summary, see Ho, 1994; Stevenson & Lee, 1996). They contribute to establish the superior achievement in mathematics by Chinese and Japanese students on a firm empirical ground.

No wonder educators in the United States are alarmed. The United States has been consistently outperformed by other countries. Stevenson and Stigler (1992) raise a pointed question: Why our schools are failing and what we can learn from Japanese and Chinese education? Many U.S. educators have joined the chorus call to learn from the East. To critics of Confucian-heritage education, this is disconcerting. Underachievement of schools in the United States may be symptomatic of deep-seated problems in its educational system. But might an importation of Confucian-heritage education make things worse? What to learn—and not to learn—from the East requires a more judicious assessment.

Stevenson and Lee (1996) state that "there is compelling evidence of superior academic achievement by Chinese students" (p. 129). This verdict is less compelling when we take note of its unwarranted overgeneralization. For the sake of clarity, we restrict "Chinese students" to refer only to those in Asia. The evidence is derived from cross-national comparisons of achievement by schoolchildren in three areas of study: mathematics, reading, and science; the case for superior achievement in reading, in particular, is not strong. These comparisons are restricted to urban populations— a serious limitation in view of the fact that about 70% of the population in mainland China is rural. Comparisons of achievement at the tertiary level are lacking. But they are important, because they serve to reveal how successfully the schools have prepared students for higher education. Also lacking are comparisons in other areas of study, such as languages and humanities. But they too are important, because achievement in these areas may depend on factors that are very different from those for achievement in mathematics and science. In support of this contention, data on secondary school examination results in Hong Kong (Spinks & Ho, 1984, Table V) show very small correlations (less than .13) between mathematics and languages (Chinese or English).

There is *no* evidence, let alone compelling evidence, of superior academic achievement by Chinese students, if achievement is gauged in terms of metacognitive or knowledge-generation abilities, rather than merely knowledge acquisition and retention. One would think that these abilities become increasingly important as students move from lower to higher levels of education. Yet, in Hong Kong, both pre-university (Salili, Chiu, & Lai, 2001) and university students (Ho, Chan, & Peng, this volume) show a lack of metacognitive abilities.

Examinations to Serve Education, or to Subvert its Goals?

In retrospect, the superior academic achievement of students in Confucian-heritage cultures, measured in terms of achievement tests and examination results, is hardly surprising at all. People usually do better on tasks to which they attach importance and on which they spend a great deal of time. Motivation and effort are key factors. Indeed, one would be hard put to find an explanation if they do not perform better than, say, students in the United States. A more meaningful consideration is that educational values underlie the standards according to which academic success is measured.

In Confucian-heritage education, passing examinations is the dominant standard. So students, like their counterparts elsewhere, do what their culture expects of them. They study hard and perform well in examinations. But examination results are a function of the manner in which examinations are conducted. Kim and Michael (1995) find little, if any, relation between school achievement and creativity measures among Korean high school students. In Hong Kong, university entrance examination results correlate negatively with self-rated creative ability (Zhang & Sternberg, 1998). Perhaps even more revealing is that Chinese history, probably the most "Confucian" among the subjects in the entrance examination, correlates positively with authoritarianism (Ho & Spinks, 1985). Typically, school examinations emphasize accuracy in the reproduction of informational content, a low-level cognitive activity (cf. Watkins & Biggs, 1996).

So to concentrate their efforts on reproducing information accurately, students rely on memorization and repeated practice. Symptomatic of the notorious syllabus-bound mentality, teachers cover and students study only or mainly materials prescribed in the syllabus (Ho, Chan, & Peng, this volume). Frequently students approach their teachers prior to examinations in the hope of getting "tips" on what questions might be set in examinations. The syllabus-bound mentality extends even into tertiary education. Gow et al. (1989) state that tertiary students in Hong Kong concentrate their efforts on materials covered by the syllabus and on which they may be examined; they typically rely on handouts or notes taken in lectures, and use texts or recommended readings only as supplements. Thus students learn to play the examination game, for failure to do so means elimination from the educational system—a personal failure, and a disgrace to the family. They view education in utilitarian terms, as a means to an end.

The harmful effects of pushing too hard and too early are evident. An inspection of the norms provided by Biggs (1992, Tables 7.1–7.4) indicate an increased surface and a decreased deep approach to learning, for both males and females, from Primary 5–6 to junior secondary Forms 1–3 in Hong Kong (contrary to the erroneous statement of Salili, 1996, p. 96). Having gone through the academic mill and survived competitive examinations, students are intellectually exhausted upon entering university. What has not survived is the thirst for knowledge; intellectual curiosity is nearly extinct. They have had enough of what is commonly referred to as the "Peking Duck" (i.e., forced feeding) style of instruction. Yee (1995) uses the term *anti-intellectualism* (p. 53) to characterize university students in Hong Kong. Most telling and depressing is to find a decline, from the first to the final year, in deep motivation, achieving strategy (manifest in good study skills), enthusiasm, interest in study, and competitive drive (Gow et al., 1996, p. 119). Increasingly, they restrict their studies to what is specifically set out in the curriculum—that is, increasingly they succumb to the syllabus-bound mentality.

A common complaint among university teachers is that schools fail to prepare students for higher education; another is that the students feel that they are entitled to a diploma, without having to work hard to earn it (Ho, Chan, & Peng, this volume). This contrasts with the pattern in the United States, where the motivation to learn is much stronger at the tertiary level in comparison with the secondary level. Thus, if academic achievement is gauged developmentally, in terms of how successfully the completion of one educational level prepares the student for the next and eventually for life, then the evidence points again to a failure of Confucian-heritage education.

Mao Tse-tung (1964/1974), a fierce critic of Chinese education, minced no words:

> At present, there is too much study going on, and this is exceedingly harmful … the burden is too heavy, it puts middle-school and university students in a constant state of tension … The students should have time for recreation, swimming, playing ball, and reading freely outside their course work…

Our present method of conducting examinations is a method for dealing with the enemy, not a method for dealing with people. It is a method of surprise attack, asking oblique or strange questions. This is still the same method as the old eight-legged essay.... I am in favour of publishing the questions in advance and letting the students study them and answer them with the aid of books.... [If] some students answer half of them and answer them well, and some of the answers are very good and contain creative ideas, then one can give them 100 per cent.... Whispering in other people's ears and taking examinations in other people's names used to be done secretly. Let it now be done openly....

At present, we are doing things in too lifeless a manner.... The present method of education ruins talent and ruins youth. (pp. 203–205)

Mao's ideas on education continue to echo and reverberate among contemporary educators in mainland China (e.g., Yang, 1996). If some other students answer all ... [the] questions and answer them correctly, without any creative ideas, they should be given 50 or 60%.

In sum, examinations continue serve to subvert, not to advance, the goals of education. Confucian-heritage education is dominated by what could be called *examination superstition*: examination results = academic performance = academic achievement = future academic achievement = occupational success or failure = socioeconomic status = personal and familial achievement = personal worth and glory/disgrace to the family. A popular saying in mainland China states: "Exams, exams, exams, the magic weapon of teachers; marks, marks, marks, the lifeblood of students." The Japanese term it *examination hell*. The core values underlying the system of imperial examinations in traditional China, which served as a ladder for social ascendancy, have remained intact.

Conclusions

The examination of the evidence above leads to the following conclusions.

1. Examination superstition continues to dominate Confucian-heritage education. As they are presently conducted, examinations assess knowledge acquisition and retention, at the expense of knowledge application and generation.
2. Students rely heavily on memorization and repeated practice in order to do well in examinations.
3. Asian students perform poorly, if academic success is gauged in terms of approaches to learning and mastery of metacognitive abili-

ties, and how developmentally the completion of one educational level prepares them for the next and eventually for life.

The evidence, in short, points to a failure of Confucian-heritage education. To trace the source of this failure, a new analytic scheme for research is needed—for focusing on rote memorization or academic success measured in terms of examination results or achievement tests is misplaced.

A RELATIONAL ANALYTIC SCHEME

All education takes place within some defined context, both as a cause and a consequence of learning. Researchers (e.g., Gow et al., 1996; Watkins & Biggs, 1996) have taken pains to explain that approaches to learning are highly dependent on the students' intentions and perceptions of what is expected of them to receive good grades, and the context (e.g., school milieu) in which teaching and learning takes place. Still, they rely primarily on the individual learner as the unit of analysis. The measures of learning approaches they use yield scores on the characteristics of the learner, not of the learner-in-context. Detailed observations reveal, however, that the behavior of Chinese students may be radically different in the presence or absence of authority figures and, more generally, in different interpersonal relationships (Ho, Chan, & Peng, this volume). Hence a sound strategy is to begin with an analysis of learning contexts, after which, and only after which, the world of individual learners may be better understood.

According to methodological relationalism, a general framework for analyzing human thought and action (Ho 1998b), the analysis of learning contexts has priority over that of individual students. Learning contexts may be defined in terms of situations (e.g., inside and outside the classroom), which are transient in nature. In contrast, learning contexts defined in terms of role relationships are enduring. A role relationship is a relational construct that relates two roles, not persons. For instance, the role of students is defined in relation to that of teachers, and vice versa. The teacher-student role relationship imposes constraints on how students and teachers behave toward each other. The attributes of role relationships are irreducible to those of situations or individuals. Moreover, construals of one's role determine largely how one would define situations. The methodological import is that the analysis of role relationships precedes those of individual students and learning situations.

Role relationships are relational, not individual, constructs. Accordingly, methodological relationalism repudiates treating the individual student as the fundamental unit of analysis. Instead, it employs two units: persons-in-relation (focusing on persons, e.g., teachers and students, interacting within a learning context), and student-in-relations (focusing on a student in different learning contexts). Persons-in-relation is useful for analyzing the teacher-student and other interpersonal relationships in-depth. Using this unit takes into account self-perceptions of the teacher and the student, as well as their reciprocal perceptions of each other. The attributes of the teacher-student dyad and their influence on learning are the objects of research. Student-in-relations is useful for analyzing the definition of the student's role. Using this unit enables the investigator to focus on how an individual student functions in different relationships, and is, therefore, particularly suitable for idiographic studies. It helps to locate problems of learning in role relationships, not in the abstract individual student. In sum, analyzing role relationships (using, e.g., the teacher-student dyad) serves as a vantage for a deeper understanding of individual students (using student-in-relations).

Among the most important role relationships are those between students and authority figures (e.g., parents, teachers, and school principals). Culturally defined, authority relationships are invariant across situations. In particular, the teacher-student relationship exerts a pervasive influence on teacher-student interactions and hence on learning. According to Ho's (1998b) scheme of classification, the attributes of the teacher-student relationship are secondary (vs. primary, e.g., familial), inclusive (vs. exclusive, e.g., as in the case of marital partners), and above all unequal (vs. equal). The teacher is held responsible for overseeing, evaluating, and reporting the learning performance of student. In this way, the teacher has the authority to exercise considerable control over the student and perhaps even his or her future career. Authority is thus immanent in the teacher-student relationship. This calls for a deeper analysis of how authority relationships are structured in Confucian-heritage education.

AUTHORITY IN CONFUCIAN-HERITAGE EDUCATION

Traditionally, the study of Confucian educational philosophy falls within an interface between Sinology and educational philosophy. The source of discourse is confined to the classics and subsequent commentaries on Confucian thought regarding the role of education in general, and of the teacher in particular, in human development. Respect for learning, self-cultivation, and building moral character are among the central themes. Many Confucian ideas have a modern ring: teaching through setting a personal example (modeling, in psychological parlance), teaching without words, and education for all without distinctions. However, we must avoid equating Confucian educational philosophy with Confucian-heritage education. We must ask: To what extent has Confucian educational philosophy been faithfully put into practice in Confucian-heritage education? Moreover, there are signs that Confucian educational values are becoming increasingly irrelevant in recent decades—thus raising the question of whether the notion of Confucian-heritage education is still applicable (Ho, Chan, & Peng, this volume). This important question, beyond the scope of this chapter, deserves urgent research attention.

The behavioral science literature, for the most part, has been ignored in the discourse on Confucian educational philosophy. Consequently, the discourse is about cultural prescriptions of what ought to be, not empirical facts of what is. It also leaves out the discussion of continuities and departures from tradition. In the present discourse, we redress the imbalance of over relying on the classics, and base our analysis on the behavioral science literature, particularly that on socialization in Confucian-heritage cultures. A survey of this literature reveals a high degree of consensus among scholars: Status and authority relationships are well defined, rigidly hierarchical, and authoritarian. The Chinese pattern of socialization governed by filial piety predisposes children toward a generalized tendency to distance themselves from those of disparate statuses; to fear, and at the same time to resent, authority figures; to adopt silence, negativism, passive resistance or passive aggression as behavioral styles in dealing with authority demands; to displace or turn inward aggression; and to dissociate affect from role behavior (Ho, 1998a). The evidence converges on the conclusion that the socialization pattern is biased toward the development of authoritarian moralism and cognitive conservatism (Ho, 1994, 1998a). Authoritarian moralism embodies two salient features of Confucian societies: authoritarianism and pervasiveness in applying moral precepts as the primary standard for judging people. Cognitive conservatism refers to a disposition toward resisting cognitive change and preserving existing knowledge structures. Authoritarian moralism and cognitive conservatism operating within the individual mirror the ideological conservatism of Confucianism governing human relationships as well as educational and sociopolitical institutions.

Three Dogmas of Confucian Educational Philosophy

A central influence of Confucianism on learning and education concerns the representation of truth transmitted to, and subsequently experienced and internalized by, the student (Ho, 1994). Confucian thinking on morality and, by extension, knowledge in general assumes that there is a fundamental distinction between right and wrong—one that cannot be disputed because it is an extension of the cosmic principle into the realm of knowledge. The human mind is capable of discerning this distinction, and the function of education is to enforce making it. Therefore, students must be taught the correct knowledge, and not to question it. This knowledge is contained in the teachings of sages in the classics. The written word is sacred and comes to be identified with truth. Having learned the classics, teachers are charged with the responsibility of passing correct knowledge onto their students. Thus, Confucianism sets the stage for learning through inculcating into the student's mind its representation of truth.

Three dogmas are thus implicit in the Confucian educational philosophy. The first dogma asserts that education is the acquisition of correct knowledge, not the discovery or generation of new knowledge. This dogma effectively leaves creativity out of consideration. Moreover, acquiring unorthodox or "incorrect" knowledge is harmful and, therefore, must be prohibited. Seen in this light, the campaign against "spiritual pollution" in mainland China not long ago was a legacy of Confucianism. The second dogma asserts the superiority of the written word over oral discourse. Once written and accepted as orthodox, a text is enshrined with authority not to be challenged. This may provide an insight into why traditionally composition is valued so highly, at the expense of training in oral discourse. Exercising caution in speaking is a virtue; spontaneity is recklessness. The third dogma asserts that the teacher is the repository of knowledge, to be passed onto his students. The older the teacher, the greater the repository of knowledge. Hence the polite form of address for the teacher is *laoshi* (literally, aged teacher).

Together, these three dogmas define the parameters of authority in the Confucian world of learning. As expressions of ideological conservatism, they are responsible for reinforcing the development of cognitive conservatism in teachers and, through them, in students. Though under attack and weakened in modern times, they remain the core values underlying the definition of the teacher-student relationship and the student's role. Challenge to these dogmas lies at the root of the tension between the critics and defenders of Confucian-heritage education.

The Teacher-Student Relationship

In Confucianism, the teacher-student relationship is modeled after the father-son relationship, which is governed by the ethic of filial piety. This modeling is reflected in the Chinese language. The term for *master* is *shifu*, which translates literally into teacher-father. A popular saying states: "One day as teacher amounts to a lifetime as father." Not surprisingly, authoritarianism and attitudes toward filial are positively correlated among teachers in Taiwan (Ho & Lee, 1974).

The definition of the teacher-student relationship is marked by its imperative nature: pervasive, stringent, and intolerant of deviation. It constrains, even inhibits, the student's freedom of action, self-assertion, and development of individuality. It impedes the free exchange between teachers and students that is essential for learning (Ho, Chan, & Peng, this volume). Teachers do not allow their authority to be challenged. Students are afraid of their teachers, and dare not ask "provocative" questions. Ironically, the Chinese terms for learning are *xuewen* (learning-questioning) and *xuexi* (learning-exercise). The inhibition of asking and questioning means that *xuexi* is emphasized, at the expense of *xuewen*.

The dominance of the teacher-student relationship implies *role dominance* for both teachers and students, which overrides personality and situational factors in teaching and learning. The model teacher teaches by setting a personal example; he is principled, caring, but stern. As stated in the *Three-Character Classic*, a primer for beginners produced in the thirteenth century and memorized by countless Chinese children until recent times: "Rearing without education is the fault of the father; teaching without strictness is the fault of the teacher." The teacher, in short, is the embodiment of authority.

The Confucian definition of the teacher's role entails both affective and instrumental (e.g., instructional) functions. It recognizes that emotions could interfere with the attainment of educational goals. For educational efforts to be effective, emotional detachment has to be maintained. More than anyone else, the teacher, as a master-educator of superior self-cultivation, is expected to maintain control over his emotions. Otherwise, the student would think that the teacher has failed to act in accordance with his own teachings. The teacher's affection and caring for his students have to be concealed in his heart. He must be stern, or at least appear stern, in front of his students. He is stingy in giving praise for good efforts, but harsh in making demands and ready to use shaming or to administer physical punishment when his demands are not met. As a popular saying puts it: "Stern teachers produce outstanding pupils."

The model student is diligent, humble, obedient, and deferential. Role prescriptions for the student in relation to the teacher are respect and unquestioned obedience, as are those for the son in relation to the father. This romanticized ideal, however, falls far short of reality. In real life, the Chinese father-son relationship is marked by affective distance, tension, and even antagonism (Ho, 1998a). The behavioral patterns of Chinese students reported by Ho, Chan, and Peng (this volume), therefore, would come as no surprise: fear, docility, silence, negativism, resentment, and outward compliance (but inward defiance) in front of their teachers; disrespect, noncompliance, and passive-aggression behind their backs. More portentous is the observation, especially visible in Hong Kong, that some students openly disobey and disrespect their teachers; in turn, teachers regularly complain that present day students are "hard to teach." So much for the myth of the obedient and respectful Chinese student.

Under ordinary circumstance, psychological mechanisms (e.g., role-affect dissociation, displacement, and turning aggression inwards) are at work to hold resentment and aggression in check. Students would "dare to be angry, but not to voice a protest" and "forbear and swallow one's voice." Under extraordinary circumstances, however, the psychological mechanisms break down and aggression might erupt into the open. During the Great Cultural Revolution, aggression did erupt, this time in the form of unprecedented collective violence. Prompted by Mao Tse-tung, students revolted against institutional authority. They humiliated and in many instances acted with physical violence toward their teachers and professors.

The Role of Students: Action Rules

A role comprises a set of implicit action rules for successful performance. The action rules for a "successful" student in Confucian-heritage education are now made explicit (cf. Ho, 1994; Ho, Chan, & Peng, this volume).

1. The most important thing is to obtain good grades in examinations.
2. Study hard, do lots of homework, and practice repeatedly the materials prescribed in the syllabi. Do not "waste" time on outside reading or learning.
3. If you do not succeed, keep trying until you do.
4. Be respectful and obedient toward teachers. Do not challenge their authority and run the risk of invoking their displeasure or retribution.
5. The safest strategy is to keep silent in the classroom, except when the teacher gives you an opportunity to say something. To avoid exposing oneself to ridicule by the teacher or classmates, do not ask too many questions, make mistakes, or express unpopular, deviant, or "strange" ideas.

These action rules define the role of a student as a passive recipient, not an active seeker or generator of knowledge. Education is viewed in instrumental terms: Scholastic success is necessary for getting good jobs, which are, in turn, necessary for attaining higher socioeconomic status. Learning is viewed as a necessary hardship to be suffered, not as personal enrichment to be enjoyed.

TOWARD A TRANSFORMATION OF EDUCATION

Claims about the superior academic achievement of Asian students have not silenced the critics. Criticisms of Confucian-heritage education have been persistently voiced, not only by Asians but also by Westerners who work within Confucian-heritage educational systems and have an in-depth knowledge of their operations. Perhaps a paradox within the paradox is that it is the Asians themselves who have been the most vocal in raising concerns about education in Asia. These concerns have less to do with academic performance than with creativity, cognitive socialization, and broadly defined educational goals. They reflect an intellectual tradition that places development of the whole person at the heart of education, and discontent with how far reality falls short of the ideals of that tradition.

It is most ironic that, as reported by *Newsweek* ("Now, please think," 1999), "As Americans embrace testing, Asians pursue creativity" (front cover). The Chinese government (Central Committee of the Chinese Communist Party and State Council of the People's Republic of China, 1999) has proclaimed cultivating creativity as one of the central goals of education. Singapore, always conscious of how it fares internationally, especially in comparison with Hong Kong, joins the chorus for educational reforms in Asia. In the 7th International Conference on Thinking held in Singapore, June 1–6, 1997, Prime Minister Goh called for promoting greater creativity and independent thought among the island's examination-obsessed students to prepare the nation for the 21st century. The Education Ministry plans to cut back on learning content knowledge. Instead, information technology will help develop communication skills and independent learning. What is critical, he said, is to ignite a passion for learning, instead of studying for the sake of getting good grades in examinations. Unfortunately, Goh failed to address the irony of attempting to promote creativity and independent thought in the context of an autocratic sociopolitical ethos.

The key for a transformation of education in Confucian-heritage cultures—and others, we would argue—lies in confronting authority in the world of learning. In line with the relational methodological analysis above, role dominance implies that the teaching and learning behaviors may change radically when the roles of teachers and students are redefined; in turn, this necessitates a redefinition of the teacher-student relationship.

Redefining the Teacher-Student Relationship

We define the teacher-student relationship as *the relational context in which the student (and the teacher) discovers, applies, and generates knowledge.*

This relationship forms the foundation upon which teaching and learning proceed. A good teacher forms facilitative relationships with his or her students, in the context of which the optimal conditions for active learning are created. Teaching is not instruction: Quality teaching does not stress the imparting of knowledge, much less of "spoon feeding" students. Rather, it creates an atmosphere in which students are encouraged to be independent, to express themselves, and even to challenge authority. A facilitative relationship has to be created; it is not present at the beginning. Creating this relationship is a joint endeavor. The act of creation transforms its creators. In an important sense, then, learning is self-learning, and education is self-transformation.

Redefining the teacher-student relationship will not succeed without a more fundamental redefinition of authority in the world of learning. This requires liberation from the dogmas of Confucian-heritage education. First, "the sea of learning knows no bounds." What constitutes correct or incorrect knowledge occasions debate and investigation; it cannot be pre-ordained. Second, oral discourse is no less important than writing. Silence is deadly for learning. Third, "the waves of Changjiang, pushed from behind, keep pressing forward." Great teachers, therefore, expect their students to surpass themselves. Learning is static when teachers are regarded as the embodiment of authority, not to be challenged.

Redirecting Future Research

The analysis above serves to identify two key methodological foci for directing future research. The first focus aims to rectify the overreliance on individual variables (e.g., learner and teacher characteristics) in research. Attempts to assess the individual learner without reference to learning contexts (e.g., authority relationships) are at best incomplete. In line with methodological relationalism, the units of analysis are not individual, but relational variables (e.g., student-in-relations). In particular, the role definition of teachers and students should be recognized as potent determinants of learning outcomes.

The second focus decries the preoccupation with academic achievement, narrowly conceived, in educational research. It views success in learning as relative to the goals of education. Accordingly, it insists on a prior examination of our educational values on which the standards for assessing success are based. From this perspective, international research playing the game of ranking achievement across countries represents misdirection and wastage of resources. Research using more meaningful standards for assessing success, such as the development of metacognitive, creative, and knowledge-generation abilities, now demands due attention.

REFERENCES

Biggs, J.B. (1992). *Why and how do Hong Kong students learn? Using the learning and study process questionnaires* (Education Paper 14). Hong Kong: University of Hong Kong, Department of Education.

Biggs, J.B. (1996). Western misperceptions of the Confucian-heritage learning culture. In D.A. Watkins & J.B. Biggs (Eds.), *The Chinese learner: Cultural, psychological and contextual influences* (pp. 45–67). Hong Kong & Victoria, Australia: Comparative Education Research Centre & The Australian Council for Educational Research Ltd.

Central Committee of the Chinese Communist Party, & State Council of the People's Republic of China. (1999, June 13). *Deepening educational reform and implementing quality education.* Beijing: Author. (Also published in *People's Daily,* 1999, June 17.)

Flynn, J.R. (1991). *Asian Americans: Achievement beyond IQ.* Hillsdale, NJ: Erlbaum.

Gow, L., Bella, J., Kember, D., & Hau, K.T. (1996). The learning approaches of Chinese people: A function of socialization processes and the context of learning? In M.H. Bond (Ed.), *The handbook of Chinese psychology* (pp. 109–123). Hong Kong: Oxford University Press.

Gow, L., Bella, J., Kember, D., Stokes, M., Stafford, K., Chow, R., & Hu, S. (1989). Approaches to study of tertiary students in Hong Kong. *Bulletin of the Hong Kong Psychological Society,* Nos. 22/23, 57–77.

Ho, D.Y.F. (1994). Cognitive socialization in Confucian heritage cultures. In P. Greenfield & R. Cocking (Eds.), *The development of the minority child: Culture in and out of context* (pp. 285–313). Hillsdale, NJ: Erlbaum.

Ho, D.Y.F. (1998a). Filial piety and filicide in Chinese family relationships: The legend of Shun and other stories. In U. P. Gielen & A. L. Comunian (Eds.), *The family and family therapy in international perspective* (pp. 134–149). Triest: Edizioni LINT.

Ho, D.Y.F. (1998b). Interpersonal relationships and relationship dominance: An analysis based on methodological individualism. *Asian Journal of Social Psychology, 1,* 1–16.

Ho, D.Y.F., & Lee, L.Y. (1974). Authoritarianism and attitudes toward filial piety in Chinese teachers. *Journal of Social Psychology, 92,* 305–306.

Ho, D.Y.F., & Spinks, J.A. (1985). Multivariate prediction of academic performance by Hong Kong university students. *Contemporary Educational Psychology, 10,* 249–259.

International Association for the Evaluation of Educational Achievement (IEA). (1988). *Science achievement in seventeen countries: A preliminary report.* Oxford: Pergamon Press.

Kim, J., & Michael, W.B. (1995). The relationship of creativity measures to school achievement and preferred learning and thinking style in a sample of Korean high school students. *Educational and Psychological Measurement, 55,* 60–74.

Mao, T.T. (1974). Remarks at the Spring Festival (summary record). In S. Schram (Ed.), *Mao Tse-tung unrehearsed: Talks and letters: 1956–71* (J. Chinnery & Tieyun, Trans., pp. 197–211). Middlesex: Penguin. (Originally given on 1964, February 13).

Now, please think: As Americans embrace testing, Asians pursue creativity. (1999, September 6). *Newsweek*, 36–47.

Salili, F. (1996). Accepting personal responsibility for learning. In D.A. Watkins & J.B. Biggs (Eds.), *The Chinese learner: Cultural, psychological and contextual influences* (pp. 85–105). Hong Kong & Victoria, Australia: Comparative Education Research Centre & The Australian Council for Educational Research Ltd.

Salili, F., Chiu, C.Y., & Lai, S. (2001). The influence of culture and context on students' motivational orientation, learning patterns and performance. In F. Salili, C. Chiu, & Y. Hong (Eds.), *Student motivation: The culture and context of learning*. New York: Plenum.

Spinks, J.A., & Ho, D.Y.F. (1984). Chinese students at an English-language university: Prediction of academic performance. *Higher Education, 13,* 657–674.

Stevenson, H.W., & Lee, S.Y. (1996). The academic achievement of Chinese students. In M.H. Bond (Ed.), *The handbook of Chinese psychology* (pp. 124–142). Hong Kong: Oxford University Press.

Stevenson, H.W., & Stigler, J. (1992). *The learning gap: Why our schools are failing and what we can learn from Japanese and Chinese education.* New York: Summit Books.

Sue, S., & Okazaki, S. (1990). Asian-American educational achievements: A phenomenon in search of an explanation. *American Psychologist, 45,* 913–920.

Vernon, P.E. (1982). *The abilities and achievements of Orientals in North America.* New York: Academic Press.

Watkins, D.A. (1996). Learning theories and approaches to research: A cross-cultural perspective. In D.A. Watkins & J.B. Biggs (Eds.), *The Chinese learner: Cultural, psychological and contextual influences* (pp. 3–24). Hong Kong & Victoria, Australia: Comparative Education Research Centre & The Australian Council for Educational Research Ltd.

Watkins, D.A., & Biggs, J.B. (Eds.). (1996). *The Chinese learner: Cultural, psychological and contextual influences.* Hong Kong & Victoria, Australia: Comparative Education Research Centre & The Australian Council for Educational Research Ltd.

Yang, D.P. (1996, September). Continuing to uphold the spirit of Mao Zedong's criticism of feudalistic traditional education. *Chinese Education,* No. 3, 9–10. (In Chinese)

Yee, A.H. (1995). Higher education in Hong Kong. In A.H. Yee (Ed.), *East Asia higher education: Traditions and transformations* (pp. 36–54). Oxford: Pergamon.

Zhang, L., & Sternberg, R.J. (1998). Thinking styles, abilities, and academic achievement among Hong Kong university students. *Educational Research Journal, 13*(1), 41–62.

CHAPTER 4

IMPLICIT CONCEPT MAPPING:

METHODOLOGY AND APPLICATIONS IN KNOWLEDGE ASSESSMENT

Eugene V. Aidman

ABSTRACT

The learning enhancement capacities of concept mapping are often hindered by the initial learner resistance to the technique. A new computerized method of implicit cognitive mapping (Aidman & Egan, 1996, 1998) addresses this obstacle by helping the learner to visualize their intuitive conceptualizations. The method teaching applications will be discussed along with validation data.

INTRODUCTION

This chapter reports a segment of a large-scale study into concept mapping as a tool for knowledge assessment (cf. Aidman & Egan, 1998; Aidman & Ward, 2001). The term concept mapping will be used in a narrow and specific sense—referring to a group of graphic methods of structural representation of individuals' knowledge in a given domain (Novak, 1990; Trochim, 1989), as one of the family of methods for visual representation of knowledge. These methods have rapidly expanded over the last two decades and can be traced back to Information Mapping (Horn, 1989), Mind Mapping (Svantesson, 1989; Woycoff, 1991) and Entailment Meshes (Pask, 1984). Among these methods, concept mapping is perhaps the only one that has shown considerable potential both as a viable new learning technique and, possibly, a valid assessment tool (Novak, 1993; Sandoval, 1995). The method has gained wide recognition as a viable new learning technique that helps learners to visualize their understanding of what they learn (Novak, 1990). However, concept mapping and other knowledge visualization methods involve more than just converting the linear discourse of a discipline into a pictorial form. More importantly, they play a key role of knowledge integration—thus providing for a "vision of the forest behind the trees" that retains most of the original complexity in a more compact and manageable form. This "nutshell conceptual picture" of the subject has been shown to be useful in learners' navigating through their subject (Novak, 1993; Sandoval, 1995). Our research has shown that it can also be used in evaluating the quality of knowledge it represents (Aidman & Egan, 1998; Aidman & Ward, 2001).

As predicted by Novak (1990), concept mapping is promising to generate a "quantum leap" in quality of education. However, in order to produce it the idea of concept mapping needs to be supported by a sound methodology, which should provide a vehicle for, and environment conducive to, meaningful learning (Novak, 1990). One of the most important elements of such an environment is the ways in which learner knowledge is assessed (Fisher, 1990). Academic assessment tends to drive most students' learning and as Tamir (1993) pointed out, it has typically driven the curriculum. So, when in this assessment driven curriculum the students are faced with predominantly multiple-choice and other declarative knowledge-based assessment tasks, they are not encouraged to develop their expertise in the subject by building their own, deep understanding of it. Instead, they often opt for rote learning, coaching themselves on "what is going to be on the exam." Even performance-based assessment tasks in science subjects (i.e., computational solutions or practical problems) involve substantial inferential leaps beyond the immediate performance that have very little empirical substantiation (Ruiz-Primo & Shavelson, 1996). It appears that a multitude of assessment tools are required if academic curriculum is to meet the challenge of supporting the development of learners' expertise in their subjects. These tools need to look beyond declarative knowledge, in order to be able to tap into procedural and implicit elements of it (Blais, 1993). Concept mapping is one obvious candidate for such a tool: incorporating concept mapping into the assessment process has been found a viable addition to traditional assessment tasks (Moreira, 1985; Raferty & Fleshner, 1993; Trigewell & Sleet, 1990) and is likely to encourage its use as a learning technique, as well as the use of other deep learning strategies (Aidman & Egan, 1998; Roth, 1994).

Since pioneering efforts of Novak and his colleagues (cf. Novak, 1977, 1981, 1990) who defined concept mapping as a "schematic device for representing a set of concept meanings embedded in a framework of propositions" (Novak & Gowin, 1984, p.15), concept mapping has established its utility in both exploratory and evaluative representations of knowledge. This method is now widely used in science teaching (Sandoval, 1995), as well as in a range of contexts such as teacher education (Winitzky, Kauchack & Kelly, 1994), program evaluation and planning (Trochim, 1989; Trochim, Cook, & Setze, 1994), instructional design (Barenholtz & Tamir, 1992; Edmondson, 1994, 1995; Starr & Krajcik, 1990) and evaluation of conceptual change (Beyerbach & Smith, 1990; Songer & Mintzes, 1994; Trowbridge & Wandersee, 1994; Wallace & Mintzes, 1990). Studying individual differences in conceptual structures offers promise as a means of evaluating and assessing knowledge. The relationship between concept mapping and academic assessment has, however, received relatively little attention (Beyerlein, Beyerlein, & Markley, 1991; Wilson, 1994).

By visually revealing the ways a person organizes the knowledge that they hold, concept mapping helps the learner to identify misconceptions and a poor understanding, and encourages new interpretations of old ideas, as well as other forms of creative thinking (Roth, 1994). It has been suggested that concept maps have the potential to monitor students evolving understanding of a given area (Trowbridge & Wandersee, 1994).

Concept mapping measures developed so far have shown only low to moderate correlations with achievement measures such as course grades and scholastic aptitude tests (see Novak, Gowin, & Johansen, 1983). However, concept maps have been able to discriminate between divergent groups of learners (Markham, Mintzes, & Jones, 1994; Wilson, 1994). It is possible that inconsistencies between concept mapping scores and conventional knowledge assessment as found in some studies are due to limitations of measures derived from concept mapping. This chapter will outline the rationale for a more effective concept mapping measurement system than is generally employed, followed by two examples of its application and a discussion of how it might be used in a range of concept mapping applications.

Two distinct approaches have been used to quantify concept maps. The predominant system stems from the original work of Novak (1981) and entails scoring the number of concepts the person links, levels of hierarchy, valid relationships, branching, cross-links and examples (Novak & Gowin, 1984). The several weighting schemes that have been used to quantify these elements (Markham, Mintzes, & Jones, 1994; Stuart, 1985) all involve manual scoring by domain experts and in some cases control for inter-rater reliability. Measures established by this method yield reasonable differentiation between expert and novice learners (Beyerlein, Beyerlein, & Markley, 1991; Gobbo & Chi, 1986) and change as understanding of the subject increases (Trowbridge & Wandersee, 1994; Wallace & Mintzes, 1990). The measures also provided some reflection of learner achievement in physics (Pankratius, 1990), chemistry (Wilson, 1994), human movement (Blais, 1993), and biology (Songer & Mintzes, 1994). The accuracy of this methodology, however, has not gone much beyond crude classifications such as between "high" and "low" achievers in secondary school chemistry (Wilson, 1994) or between non-major freshmen and advanced graduates in biology (Markham, Mintez, & Jones, 1994). Often individual maps are collapsed into group matrices (Wilson, 1994), which leads to further loss of discriminating power.

Trochim (1989) and his colleagues have used a different approach, which involves direct learner rating of inter-concept similarities and subsequent multivariate decomposition of the concept proximity matrix resulting in a reconstruction of underlying cognitive maps. The map is then interpreted, usually by the learners themselves (cf. Trochim, Cook, & Setze, 1994). The concept proximity matrix is usually decomposed by multidimensional scaling and cluster analysis (Keith, 1989; Trochim, 1989). The methodology has recently "tended to include other methods of multivariate decomposition such as *pathfinder* analysis (Schvaneldt, 1991) which led to successful hybrid approaches (Wilson, 1994) combining both Trochim's and Novak's ideas of map quantification.

Trochim's model of conceptualization is essentially based on Kelly's (1955) long established *personal construct* framework and its repertory grid methodology (Fransella & Bannister, 1977; Neimeyer, 1989). There are clear parallels between Trochim's *generation, structuring* and *representation* phases (Trochim & Linton, 1986) and Kelly's stages of construct *elicitation* and *evaluation*. Unlike Kelly's, however, Trochim's approach has primarily concentrated on generating collective cognitive representations, and mainly for exploratory purposes (Caracelli, 1989; Trochim, 1989). At the same time the use of this methodology in reconstruction and assessment of individual concept maps has remained largely unexplored.

Even more important is a need for a tool that could assist the learner in eliciting and visualizing their existing, often intuitive conceptualizations. One such tool is based on *implicit concept mapping*—a method of inferring cognitive representations through various sets of learner judgments, usually similarity—contrast judgments (i.e., concept proximity judgments). Our group has developed "implicit" mapping assessment tasks for undergraduate statistics (Pierce & Roberts, 1995), sport psychology (Scott, 1993) and introductory psychology (Aidman & Egan, 1998; Aidman & Ward, 2001). The following description of the two latter studies exemplifies the general methodology we employed to examine the utility of implicit concept mapping in assessing students' knowledge and evolving expertise in their respective domains/ fields of study.

GENERAL METHODOLOGY

Both Aidman and Egan (1998) and Aidman and Ward (2001) studies utilized a modified repertory grid format to generate learner-derived concept proximity data, resulting in an individual concept proximity matrix for each student. The mapping task, which was administered via a knowledge mapping software package *DCS-4* (Burmistrov & Shmeliov, 1991, 1992), required participants to make a series of similarity and contrast judgments between concepts. Each concept takes its turn at the top of the list *(header concept)* and the task is to select from the remaining list one concept that is most similar to the header, but also two concepts most in contrast to it (an example can be seen in Figure 1). The process is repeated with subsequent header concepts selected from the list until the list is exhausted. The resulting proximity data form an [n*n] nonsymmetrical square matrix $A_n = a_{ij}$, where n = number of concepts mapped. Each matrix cell is filled with one of only three values: $a_{ij} = 1$ if jth concept was judged as similar to ith concept, $a_{ij} = -1$ if jth concept was judged as contrasting ith concept, and $a_{ij} = 0$ if neither similarity nor contrast among ith and jth concepts was recorded. In other words, a "+1" flags similarity, a "−1" flags contrast and a zero is reserved for all middle-range/ non-judged comparisons.

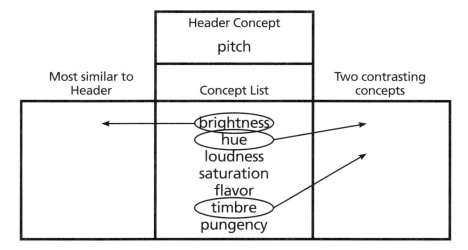

Figure 1.   A computer screen dump showing the process of concept comparison: Moving concepts left if similar to Header and right if contrasting.

Details of the subsequent data analysis are presented elsewhere (Aidman & Egan, 1998). In principle, though, a simple modification to the resulting proximity matrix (i.e., the normalized matrix S_n of scalar products of its rows) can be factor- and cluster-analyzed to generate spatial-dimensional and hierarchical cluster tree representations of the individual's map (Aidman & Egan, 1998). The same proximity matrix can be analyzed to compute global structural characteristics of the map, such as cognitive complexity, internal consistency and taxonomic organization. The visualization, achieved through factorial (cf. Figures 3 and 5) and cluster-tree (cf. Figures 2 and 4) decomposition of individual concept proximity matrices, can be interpreted—by experts or the learners themselves—as a reconstruction of their *implicit* concept maps. This allows one to generate a range of concept mapping indices that can be validated against conventional academic assessment. The studies that follow provide two concrete examples of how this general methodology can be applied.

"EXPERT" AND "NOVICE" IMPLICIT MAPS: ARE THE DIFFERENCES RELATED TO ACHIEVEMENT?

Aidman and Egan (1998) had 100 psychology undergraduates perform a computerized mapping task, described above, that required the students to judge similarity between a group of concepts from the introductory psychology course. The concepts (see Figure 1) were selected to represent a compact segment from the prescribed study content in human perception (Weiten, 1992). It also afforded clear expectations of the maps produced by different learners: modality-based classifications were expected from "novices" and poor learners while successful learners were expected to base their maps on more advanced distinctions between *primary qualities, intensity* and *complexity* of sensory stimulation.

The study was conducted in two stages. The first stage involved one expert in the particular knowledge domain (human perception) examining the implicit concept maps of a second expert, and inferring the criteria used by a second expert to correctly differentiate between a number of concepts within that domain.

The second stage involved the reconstruction and analysis of implicit concept maps of 100 psychology undergraduate students. These maps were reconstructed using the computer-based procedure described above. Student maps were analyzed for complexity, internal consistency and global similarity to expert and novice "model" maps.

The results of stage one showed that the criteria used by the first expert to differentiate concepts at each stage of the cluster analysis (Figure 2) were accurately inferred by the second expert. The factorial reconstruction

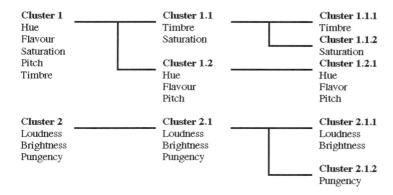

Figure 2.   Cluster tree representation of the expert's (lecturer's) model map.

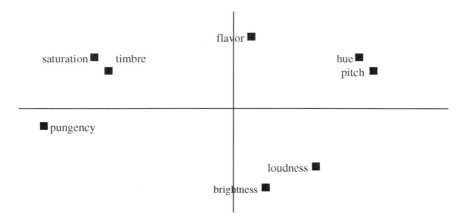

Figure 3.   A spatial-factorial representation of the expert's (lecturer's) map.

(Figure 3) was also accurately interpreted. In both cases, the second expert rated the first's map as an accurate and expert representation of the knowledge domain. The implication of this is that concept maps, which are essentially structural representations of semantic distances between concepts, can reflect substantive characteristics of knowledge that are *accurate, meaningful* and can be *shared.*

Second stage results showed that the students' reconstructed implicit concept maps essentially fell into three distinct categories. Two qualified examiners, who had no knowledge of the students' academic results, independently evaluated student maps by analyzing their factorial and cluster representations. With high inter-rater consistency (.89), the two raters classified those maps that followed the more advanced distinctions between

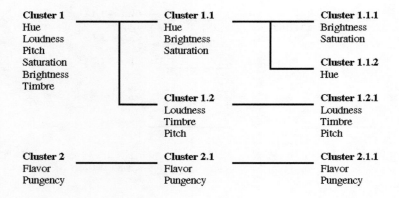

Figure 4.   Cluster tree representation of the novice model map.

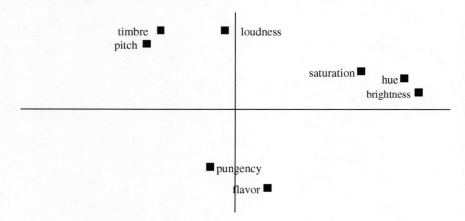

Figure 5.   A spatial-factorial representation of the novice model map.

primary qualities, intensity, and *complexity* of sensory stimulation into the expert category. These were remarkably similar to the lecturer's map reconstructed in stage one. Nearly two-thirds of the students distinguished the concepts by sensory modality and were classified into the "novice" category, and about one-fifth used a combination of both novice and expert structures—their maps were classed as "*mixed.*"

All student maps were compared to expert (Figures 2 and 3) and novice (see Figures 4 and 5) model maps. As expected, there was a strong positive correlation between the degree of similarity to the expert model and the students' score on the relevant questions on their formal academic test. Perhaps more important, the degree of similarity to the expert model predicted the students' performance on the overall test, which covered a range of other topics (see Table 1).

Table 1. Formal Assessment Test Performance by Different Mapping Groups.

Mapping Groups	Total Test Mark[a]		Subject Score[b]	
	Mean	SD	Mean	SD
Expert	13.25	1.66	1.44	0.42
Mixed	12.25	1.68	1.43	0.39
Novice	11.41	1.49	1.23	0.45
Other	11.30	1.67	0.96	0.69

Note. [a] The 40 item test yielded a maximum overall text mark of 18;
[b] The 4 question subtest yielded a maximum subtext score of 1.8.

With those students whose concept maps evidenced expert knowledge, the strength of correlation between students' similarity to expert model score and actual test mark increased as the consistency of student maps increased (see Table 2). This relationship between the properties of students' implicit maps and their academic achievement was further examined in the next study.

Table 2. Intercorrelations Between Similarity to Expert Model Score (STEM) and Test Mark at Different Levels of Consistency in the Combined Expert/Mixed Group

Map Consistency	Correlation of Test Mark and STEM	p=	N=
> .85	.45	.004	34
> .88	.47	.003	32
> .92	.63	.000	25
> .95	.67	.001	17
= 1.00	.94	.002	6

IMPLICIT CONCEPT MAPS: STRUCTURE VERSUS CONTENTS

Aidman and Ward (2001) extended the methodology described above to include both measures of structural properties of the individual implicit maps and their content-based expert evaluation. A different group of 65 introductory psychology students were asked to work with a set of basic "personality" concepts in a mapping procedure identical to the one presented in Figure 1. The resulting concept proximity matrices were not only scored for complexity (differentiation) and internal consistency, but also individually factor- and cluster-analyzed. Hierarchical cluster tree and unrotated factorial representations were generated for each individual map (examples can be seen in Figures 6 and 7). Students were asked to interpret their own cluster trees and factor plots by naming the clusters and factor axes (a brief statement accompanying the name was allowed). Three independent experts (lecturers in the subject) rated the clarity and accuracy of these interpretations, as well as the soundness of cluster trees and the factorial representations themselves. These data were compared with the overall grade the students had obtained in the Introductory Psychology course prior to participating in the study.

The results showed that, while the internal consistency of students' implicit maps of personality concepts was associated with the grades, it could only differentiate top students (A grade) from the rest of the field (see Figure 8). The expert ratings of both cluster tree and factorial representations of the students' implicit maps—and, particularly, expert ratings of their

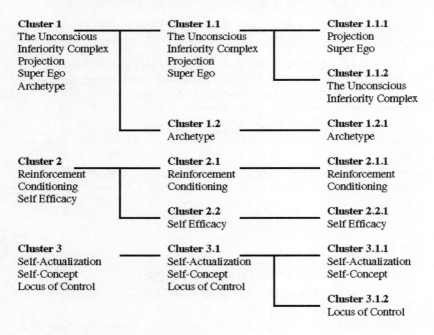

Figure 6.   Cluster tree representation of a student implicit map of personality concepts.

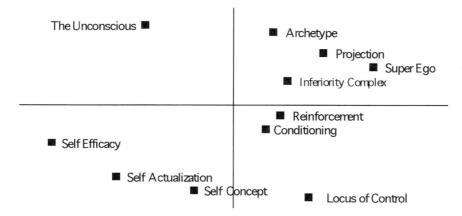

Figure 7. A spatial-factorial representation of a student implicit map of personality concepts.

interpretations by map owner—showed a more refined association with the overall grade (see Figure 9). Leaving aside the controversial issue of how representative the grades are of the students' knowledge of the subject, this study confirmed that structural assessment of implicit maps needs to be complemented by content-based evaluation in order to achieve a more accurate estimate of the learner's level of expertise in the subject. Implicit mapping may be used as a reliable source of material for such content-based evaluation particularly, the cluster and factorial representations of the maps.

IMPLICIT CONCEPT MAPS: DOMAIN SPECIFIC VERSUS GENERIC ASSESSMENT DEVICE

Aidman and Egan's (1998) results showed that implicit mapping is sensitive to individual differences in both domain specific and more generic characteristics of learners' knowledge. This was evidenced in concept mapping indices correlating with both the students' overall marks on a formal academic test covering the mapped content among other topics and the sub-test scores reflecting exclusively the mapped content. Interestingly enough, the latter association is weaker than the former, indicating that concept mapping may reflect generic learner characteristics just as effectively—if not better—than their domain specific knowledge.

In a broader context, the utility of concept mapping measures in the assessment of individuals' knowledge beyond the content from which those measures are derived is not only entirely consistent with conventional academic assessment practices, but is necessary for any assessment

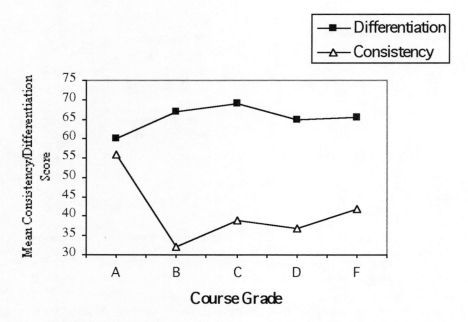

Figure 8.   Structural assessment of implicit maps of personality concepts: Map complexity (differentiation) and internal consistent scores for students with differ- ent levels of achievement (grades) in the course.

method if it is to find widespread use. In this sense the results demon- strated an acceptable level of concurrent validity of concept mapping against conventional academic assessment. At the same time, however, as was expected, the association found between concept mapping and tradi- tional assessment is incomplete (evidenced by low to moderate correla- tions of various concept mapping indices and standard multiple-choice test scores). This incomplete association indicates that apart from the shared variance in learners' knowledge reflected in both concept mapping and multiple-choice test scores, there is a unique variance in learners' perfor- mance that can be explained only by concept mapping. Concept mapping thus appears to tap either abilities that are not well measured by common assessment techniques or abilities that are not assessed at all. Although insufficient to reach a firm conclusion, the results indicate that concept mapping reflects generic learner characteristics better than their domain specific knowledge, which is consistent with a widely held view that concept mapping is a more sensitive form of knowledge assessment (Markham, Mintzes, & Jones, 1994), and one that tends to discriminate more effec- tively between rote and meaningfully learned knowledge.

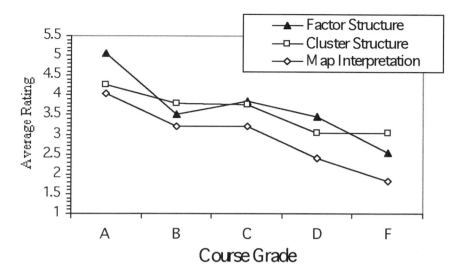

Figure 9.   Expert ratings of cluster structure, factor structure, and own map interpretation (personality concepts) for students with different levels of achievement (grades) in the course.

Although earlier reports (Novak, Gowin, & Johansen, 1983) indicated that concept mapping scores did not correlate with common assessment techniques, such as multiple choice questions, associations were evident with tests requiring higher levels of understanding. Markham, Mintzes, and Jones (1994) submit that these findings illustrate the inadequacies of traditional assessment techniques in differentiating between a deeper level, meaningful understanding of a given domain, and a superficial, rote-learned one. Our results support this contention, though partially and indirectly, in showing stronger concept mapping correlations with more generic learner appraisal (which is more likely to be influenced by overall quality of learning practices than by a narrow domain achievement). The findings thus provide further support to Novak's (1990) claim that concept mapping should lead to more meaningful (and less rote) learning. This support, however, comes from a distinctly different perspective: the ability of concept mapping assessment to capture the quality of the learner's broader knowledge base, beyond the memorized material in a narrow domain, provides a powerful encouragement to adopt sound learning strategies, whether or not concept mapping is among them. Thus, concept mapping assessment becomes instrumental in overall enhancement of learner practices whether or not they include concept mapping as a learning strategy.

FUTURE RESEARCH AND APPLICATIONS

The studies discussed in this chapter exemplify a meaningful and efficient application of concept mapping in academic assessment. Implicit mapping tasks have been developed in a number of knowledge domains including undergraduate statistics (Roberts, 1995), sport psychology (Scott, 1993) and personality assessment (Aidman, 2001). The approach is not, however, without its downside. Validation studies conducted so far (Aidman & Egan, 1998; Aidman & Ward, 2001; Roberts, 1995) have uncovered a number of methodological restrictions that merit separate consideration and will be only briefly outlined here.

First, as implicit mapping employs predetermined sets of concepts, the quality of these sets becomes critical. For example, although the computerized mapping task can accept any set of terms or labels, it has become evident from a number of our pilot studies that some sets produce better discrimination of learners than others. The characteristics of the better concept sets are of prime interest for future research. The data available to date suggest that the development of such sets should be based on a reasonable hypothesis about experts and novices using different classification criteria or differently judging particular concepts (the current study, for instance, predicted classification by sensory modality from novices while expecting "experts" to use more advanced criteria of primary quality, intensity and complexity of sensory stimulation). After the initial hypothesis is confirmed in a pilot study, mapping of the trialed concept set is likely to produce effective differentiation of learner knowledge, derived from both structural measures (such as complexity and internal consistency of the map) and content measures (such as similarity to "expert" maps).

Second, the efficiency of a mapping task dramatically improves when its concept set is hierarchically leveled. That is, all the concepts that are being mapped belong to the same generic category (being a specimen of a higher order concept). For instance, Aidman and Egan's (1998) study employed a taxonomy of "sensory input parameters," while Aidman and Ward's (2001) used a more complicated class of personality concepts, where classification had to be created by the learner (that is why directly comparing student maps with "expert" model(s) was inappropriate—these are yet to be established). In general, different taxonomies seem particularly suitable for mapping tasks: one could map biological species or anatomical organs, classes of visual illusions or emotions, personality traits or defense mechanisms, chemical elements or types of engineering devices, and so on.

Continuing validation of implicit mapping procedures is an important direction for future research, particularly an analysis of the convergent validity of this method and Novak's concept mapping scoring system. If the two methods converge, then implicit mapping would be worth a serious consideration as an economical alternative to the Novak system.

In summary, the two studies, discussed in this chapter, demonstrate that empirical reconstruction of individual *implicit concept maps* from direct ratings of concept proximity can produce a viable concept mapping assessment methodology. Provided certain requirements are met in the development of concept lists for mapping assessment, structural properties of the learner maps such as map complexity, internal consistency and content-oriented measures of similarity to "expert" map(s) can predict the student's proficiency in the domain subject and corresponding academic achievement.

The learners' evaluations of the new method indicate that, if utilized judiciously, it may become a welcome addition to the academic assessment arsenal. Aidman and Ward's (2001) participants were asked to compare the implicit mapping assessment task with conventional multiple choice tests on their perceived levels of difficulty and the afforded opportunity to demonstrate their knowledge of the subject. The participants' ratings showed that the mapping task was seen as much more difficult ($p < .001$), less boring (more challenging, $p < .002$), and more encouraging ($p < .04$). However, in terms of affording opportunities to demonstrate students' knowledge of the subject, implicit mapping was rated lower than conventional tests ($p < .04$)—a result that may be indicative of the existing assessment culture, including preconceptions of what expertise actually is, and the resulting expectations communicated to students.

Many informal comments from participants in Aidman and Egan's (1998) study confirmed the challenging and stimulating properties of implicit mapping, and further indicated that it involved a more stimulating *process* of assessment—one that encouraged learning modes and processes they had not employed before, such as analyzing inter-concept similarity and contrast that requires working with concepts beyond their definitions. This capacity of concept mapping assessment to promote deeper learning strategies makes it worthy of serious consideration as a method of knowledge assessment with tertiary students, as it appears to be a valid step toward encouraging *meaningful* learning in those domains where *procedural* knowledge (as opposed to *declarative* knowledge) is of prime importance.

REFERENCES

Aidman, E.V., & Egan G. (1998). Academic assessment through concept mapping: Validating a method of implicit map reconstruction. *International Journal of Instructional Media, 25*(3), 277–294.

Aidman E., & Ward, J. (2001, July 9–12). *Implicit concept mapping in academic assessment: Predicting individual course achievement in undergraduate psychology from struc-*

tural properties and content evaluation of computer-reconstructed post-instruction concept maps. Paper presented at *"Tertiary Teaching and Learning: Dealing with Diversity"* Conference, Darwin, NT, Australia.

Aidman E.V. (2001) Integrating implicit representations of self and significant others: Construing or stereotyping? In R. Roth & S.E.S. Neil (Eds.), *A matter of life: Psychological theory, research, and practice* (pp. 77–83). Berlin: Pabst Science.

Barenholtz, H., & Tamir, P. (1992). A comprehensive use of concept mapping in design instruction and assessment. *Research in Science and Technological Education, 10* (1), 37–52.

Beyerbach, B.A., & Smith, J.M. (1990). Using a computerized concept mapping program to assess pre-service teachers' thinking about effective teaching. *Journal of Research in Science Teaching,* 27(10), 961–971.

Beyerlein S.T., Beyerlein M.M., & Markley, ? (1991). Measurement of cognitive structure in the domain of art and history. *Empirical Studies of the Arts, 9*(1), 35–50.

Blais, C. (1993). Concept mapping of movement-related knowledge. *Perceptual & Motor Skills, 76,* 767–774.

Burmistrov, I.V., & Shmeliov, A.G. (1991). *DCS: Diagnostics of Conceptual Systems* [Computer software]. Moscow: Human Technologies.

Burmistrov, I.V., & Shmeliov, A.G. (1992). Exsort and DCS: Prototype program shells using a psychosemantic approach to concept acquisition, representation and assessment. In P. Brusilovsky & V. Stefanuk (Eds.), *Proceedings of the East-West Conference on Emerging Computer Technologies in Education* (pp. 46 -51). Moscow: International Center for Science and Information Technology.

Caracelli, V.J. (1989). Structured conceptualization: A framework for interpreting evaluation results. Special Issue: Concept mapping for evaluation and planning. *Evaluation and Program Planning,* 12(1), 45–52.

Caputi, P., Breiger, R., & Pattison, P. (1990). Analysing implications grids using hierarchical models. *International Journal of Personal Construct Psychology, 3,* 77–90.

Cropper, S., Eden, C., & Ackermann, F. (1990). Keeping sense of accounts using computer based cognitive maps. *Social Science Computer Review, 8*(3), 345–365.

Dumont, 1. (1989). Validity of multidimensional scaling in the context of structured conceptualization. *Evaluation and Program Planning, 12,* 81–86.

Edmondson, K.M. (1994). Concept maps and the development of cases for problem-based learning. *Academic Medicine, 69*(2), 108–110.

Edmondson, K.M. (1995). Concept mapping for the development of medical curricula. *Journal of Research in Science Teaching, 32*(7), 777–793.

Fisher, K.M. (1990). Semantic networking: The new kid on the block. *Journal of Research in Science Teaching,* 27(10), 1001–1018.

Fransella, F., & Bannister, D. (1977). *A manual for repertory grid technique.* London: Academic Press.

Gobbo, C., & Chi, M. (1986). How knowledge is structured and used by expert and novice children. *Cognitive Development, 1,* 221–237.

Goldsmith, T.E., & Johnson, P.J. (1990) A structural assessment in classroom learning. In R.W.Schvaneldt (Ed.), *Pathfinder associative networks: Studies in knowledge organization.* Norwood, NJ: Ablex.

Jonassen, D.H. (1992). What are cognitive tools? In P.A.M. Kommers, D.H. Jonassen, & J.T. Mayes, (Eds.), *Cognitive tools for learning* (pp. 1–6). Berlin: Springer-Verlag.

Keith, D. (1989). Refining concept maps: Methodological issues and an example. Special Issue: Concept mapping for evaluation and planning. *Evaluation and Program Planning, 12*(1), 75–80.

Kelly, G.A. (1955). *The psychology of personal constructs.* New York: Norton.

Linton R. (1989). Conceptualizing feminism: Clarifying social science concepts. *Evaluation and Program Planning, 12,* 25–29.

Markham, K.M., Mintzes, J.J., & Jones, M.G. (1994). The concept map as a research and evaluation tool: Further evidence of validity. *Journal of Research in Science Teaching, 31*(1), 91–101.

Martin, J., Slemon, A.G., Hiebert, B., Hallberg, E.T., & Cummings, A.L. (1989). Conceptualizations of novice and experienced counselors. *Journal of Counselling Psychology, 4,* 395–400.

Neimeyer G.J. (1989). Applications of repertory grid technique to vocational assessment. *Journal of Counselling and Development, 67,* 585–589.

Novak, J.D. (1977). *A theory of education.* Ithaca, NY: Cornell University Press.

Novak, J.D. (1981). Applying learning psychology and philosophy of science to biology teaching. *The American Biology Teacher, 41*(8), 466–474.

Novak, J.D. (1990). Concept mapping: A useful tool for science education. *Journal of Research in Science Teaching, 27*(10), 937–949.

Novak, J.D. (1993). Human constructivism: A unification of psychological and epistemological phenomena in meaning making. *International Journal of Personal Construct Psychology, 6*(2), 167–193.

Novak, J.D., & Gowin, D.B. (1984). *Learning how to learn.* London: Cambridge University Press.

Novak, J., Gowin, D.B., & Johansen G.T. (1983). The use of concept mapping and knowledge vee mapping with junior high school science students. *Science Education, 67*(5), 625–645.

Pankratius, W.J. (1990). Building an organized knowledge base: Concept mapping and achievement in secondary school physics. *Journal of Research in Science Teaching, 27*(10), 315–333.

Roberts, L. (1995, November). *Applications of concept mapping in teaching undergraduate statistics.* Seminar presentation. Ballarat, Australia.

Roth, W.M. (1994) Student views of collaborative concept mapping: An emancipatory research project. *Science Education, 78*(1), 1–34.

Ruiz-Primo, M.A., & Shavelson, R.J. (1996) Problems and issues in the use of concept maps in science assessment. *Journal of Research in Science Teaching, 33*(6), 569–600.

Sandoval, J. (1995) Teaching in subject matter areas: Science. *Annual Review of Psychology, 46,* 355–374.

Schvaneldt, R.W. (Ed.). (1990). *Pathfinder associative networks: Studies in knowledge organization.* Norwood, NJ: Ablex.

Scott, B. (1993). *Personality and cognitive differences: Individual and team sport selection behaviour.* Unpublished Graduate Thesis.

Starr, M.L., & Krajcik, J.S. (1990). Concept maps as a heuristic for science curriculum development: Toward improvement in process and product. Special Issue: Perspectives on concept mapping. *Journal of Research in Science Teaching, 27*(10), 987–1000.

Stuart, H.A. (1985). Should concept maps be scored numerically? *European Journal of Science Education, 7,* 3–8.

Tamir, P. (1993) Focus on student assessment. *Journal of Research in Science Teaching, 30*(6), 535–536.

Trapp, A., Reader, W., & Hammond, N. (1992). Tools for knowledge mapping. A framework for understanding. In P. Brusilovsky & V. Stefanuk (Eds.), *Proceeding of the East-West Conference on Emerging Computer Technologies in Education* (pp. 306–312). Moscow: International Center for Science and Information Technology.

Trochim W.M.K. (1989) An introduction to concept mapping for planning and evaluation. *Evaluation and Program Planning, 12,* 1–16.

Trochim, W.M.K., Cook, J.A., & Setze, R.J. (1994). Using concept mapping to develop a conceptual framework of staff's views of a supported employment program for individuals with severe mental illness. *Journal of Consulting & Clinical Psychology, 62,* 766–775.

Trowbridge, 1.E., & Wandersee, J.H. (1994). Identifying critical junctures in learning in a college course on evolution. Special Issue: The teaching and learning of biological evolution. *Journal of Research in Science Teaching, 31*(5) 459–473.

Wallace, J.D., & Mintzes, J.J. (1990). The concept map as a research tool: Exploring conceptual change in biology. Special Issue: Perspectives on concept mapping. *Journal of Research in Science Teaching, 27*(10), 1033–1052.

Weiten, W. (1992). *Psychology: Themes and variations.* Pacific Grove: Brooks/ Cole.

Wilson, J. M. (1994). Network representations of knowledge about chemical equilibrium: variations and achievement. *Journal of Research in Science Teaching, 31*(10), 1133–1147.

Winitzky, N., Kauchak, D., & Kelly, M. (1994). Measuring teachers' structural knowledge. *Teaching and Teacher Education, 10*(2), 125–139.

CHAPTER 5

ANALOGICAL PROBLEM CONSTRUCTION AS AN INDICATOR OF UNDERSTANDING IN MATHEMATICS PROBLEM SOLVING

Allan B.I. Bernardo

ABSTRACT

The paper describes the use of analogical problem construction to assess students understanding of math problems. High school students studied examples and solutions for four problems, and then wrote analogous problems for each. The constructed problems were analyzed in terms of the types of errors, and how errors related to problem understanding and to subsequent analogous transfer.

INTRODUCTION

Developing understanding of mathematics concepts and procedures is one of the most fundamental concerns of mathematics education. Related to this concern is a more basic problem of knowing how a student actually understands concepts and procedures at different points in the learning process. This paper describes an attempt to use analogous problems constructed by students as an indicator of their understanding of the structure and elements of specific types of word problems.

Many people, including educators and psychologists, have come to think of "understanding" as having different meanings. In this paper, a cognitive science perspective is used to define understanding as *how a person represents the information from a problem or situation for use in a cognitive process like problem solving or reasoning.* By defining understanding in this way, the task of assessing how students understand concepts and procedures becomes much more difficult. This is because we can no longer simply stop at determining whether the student can or cannot define or use a concept. Instead, we require a finer description of how a student comes to represent the different pieces of information in a situation and how these relate to each other. To compound this problem, we must also be able to describe how these representations or understandings change and evolve during the learning process.

Much work has been done in cognitive science that tries to describe models of understanding for specific types of problems, concepts, and situations in the various areas of mathematics. These models adopt a range of methods for verifying the representations that underlie the students' understanding of specific problems and domains. Some methods use the analysis of written problem-solving solutions and explanations (e.g., Nuñez & Bryant, 1995; Reeve & Pattison, 1996; Singer & Resnick, 1992), think-aloud procedures (e.g., Schoenfeld, 1985; Wenger, 1987), computer-based assessments and computer simulations (e.g., Kintsch & Greene, 1985; Lesh, 1990; Lipson, Faletti & Martinez, 1990), among others.

In this study, the analogical problem construction procedure was used as a possible means of determining how students understand the problem structure of word problems in basic probability. The analogical problem construction procedure is a learning task that has been shown to be effective in facilitating analogical transfer in mathematics word problems (Bernardo, 2001a, 2001b). The procedure involves asking the students to write their own problems after they are presented and made to study the solution for a particular problem type. The students are told to make their own problem, one that can be solved using the same solution as for the one they just studied.

In the present study, the focus was on the problems that the students wrote. The study sought to determine whether the problems that the students wrote could reveal characteristics of how the students understood the problems they were presented. The assumption was that the students would reflect their knowledge of the problem structure in the way they form their own problems. If they were able to grasp the problem structure correctly, they could design their problem to mirror this problem structure. On the other hand, if the students failed to understand the problem structure, this would also reflect in their inability to construct an analogous problem. The study also sought to establish some relationship between the students' understanding (as indicated by the nature of problems constructed) and the analogical problem solving performance.

METHOD

Participants

Twenty-five male and female, junior and senior students from St. Mary's High School and La Salle Greenhills High School participated in the study as part of a class requirement. None of the subjects have had formal lessons on basic probability, but all of them have had two years of formal lessons in algebra.

Materials

Four types of basic probability problems were used: conjunction problems with independent events, conjunction problems with dependent events, disjunction problems with exclusive events, and disjunction problems with intersecting events. The first three problem types either involved the adding or multiplying the probabilities of two events. The last problem type involved adding and subtracting probabilities corresponding to the likelihood of two events. (See the appendix for examples of the problem types.)

For each problem type, four analogous problems were created, making a total of 16 problems. Each analog involved a superficially different set of objects, relations, and stories. For each problem, a study sheet was made. The study sheet included the text of the problem on the topmost part, a summary of the principles of probability involved, a description of the solution equation and procedures, and the computation of the final solution using the given solution equation. The study sheet was attached to another sheet, which was used for the problem-construction task. In this attached sheet the subject was told to make their own problems similar to the one they just studied. They were also given suggestions regarding objects and events they can use in the problem they would create.

From the 16 problems, four clusters of problems were created, with each cluster comprising one problem from each problem type. The study sheets for each problem in a cluster were arranged so that the two conjunction problems were paired in sequence, and the two disjunction problems were also paired in sequence. The sequence of problems within a pair and the sequence of pairs was counterbalanced across all subjects.

For the analogical problem-solving phase, test sheets were prepared for each of the 16 problems. In the test sheets, the problem was typed on top of the page, and the rest of the page was left blank for the solutions. The test sheets were combined in the same four clusters as the study sheets, but the four sheets were arranged in a random order. A subject information sheet was also made; this sheet asked the subject for basic demographic information and details about their math and language background.

All the materials for one subject were combined in one booklet, which contained: (a) the general instructions for the task and specific instructions for the study phase; (b) the four study sheets attached to the problem-construction sheets for one cluster; (c) the instructions for the test phase; (d) the four test sheets from another cluster; and (e) the subject information sheet. It should be emphasized that the subjects constructed their own problems based on different sets of study problems.

Procedure

The participants, divided into two groups, were asked to sign an informed consent form, after they signed they were given a test booklet. They were asked to carefully read the instructions, and the experimenter answered all questions about the task. After all the questions were answered, the participants proceeded to the study phase. They were given 2 minutes to study each problem and they were informed when they had 30 seconds left. The participants were then instructed to create their own analogous problem after each study problem. They were given 4 minutes to complete this task, and they were also told when they had 30 seconds left. After the participants completed the study phase, they were asked to read the instructions for the test phase. The experimenter answered all questions about this part of the study, and the participants proceeded to the test problems. They were given 3 minutes to answer each test problem without directly referring to the study problems; they were also told when they had 30 seconds left. Before the study and test phases, the participants were told that they could not proceed to the next problem if they finished ahead of time, nor could they go back to study or to work on any previous problem. After the participants completed the four test problems, they were asked to answer the subject information sheet and they were informed about the basic purpose of the study. Their questions about the study were answered by the experimenter.

RESULTS AND DISCUSSION

Types of Constructed Problems

All the problems constructed by the participants were encoded verbatim. Each of the 25 participants constructed four analogous problems, so a total of 100 constructed problems were coded and analyzed.

The problems were categorized into several categories. The categories were not preset, and emerged after a preliminary classification of the responses. First, we determined whether the problems were solvable or not. Then, those that were solvable were assessed in terms of whether they were analogous to the original problems or not. Those that were not solvable were also content analyzed in terms of whether they reflected elements of the correct structure of the original problem. From this sorting, nine categories emerged.

The first category was for correct analogs (CA). Answers were included in this category if the problems constructed reflected the same problem structure as the original problem, and was, hence, completely solvable using the solution earlier provided. Out of the 100 problems, 29 were counted in this category, including three problems with minor errors (e.g., the given numbers did not add up correctly). Some exemplars of the category are:

> There are 75 DJs participating for [sic] the DJ's Battle. 30 DJ's are competing in doubles, 30 in exhibition, and 15 in DJ's all around. If a DJ is chosen randomly, what is the probability that the DJ is competing either [in] doubles or exhibition? (Disjunction problem with exclusive events)

> There are 13 players in a basketball team, 8 of them are Grant Hill fans, 2 of them Webber fans and the 3 are Penny Hardaway fans. If someone asks a player who is his favorite basketball star, what is the probability the player idolizes Grant Hill or Penny Hardaway? (Disjunction problem with exclusive events)

> There is [sic] 10 apples in a basket, 3 of which are rotten. And in another basket there are 20 oranges and 7 are rotten. The blind man picks a fruit on [sic] each of the baskets. What is the probability that the blind man picks a rotten fruit from each basket? (Conjunction problem with independent events)

> There are 60 cards in a deck of "Magic The Gathering" cards. 40 are blue cards and 20 are black. If a player was to take 2 random cards, what is the probability of getting a blue card in the first draw, and a black card in the next? (Conjunction problem with dependent events)

The second category was for solvable problems that were not analogous to the original ones; these problems were called solvable non-analogs

(SNA). The question for these problems typically required the computation of a simpler probability (i.e., not a conjunction or a disjunction). Often the given of the problem was analogous to the given in the original problem. Hence, because of the simpler question, much of the given information in these problems was actually extraneous or irrelevant to the problem solution. Of the 100 problems, 21 were coded in this category. The following are examples of such problems:

> There are 60 cards in my deck. 20 of which are rare and 40 of which are commonly found. I accidentally dropped one of them on the muddy floor. What is the probability that the rare card would be the one soiled? (Constructed problem for conjunction problem with dependent events)

> There are 30 applicants applying in [sic] a job, 15 are graduates from UST, 10 are from DLSU, and 5 from CSB, What are the chances of the applicants to be chosen if they are interviewed randomly? (Constructed problem for disjunction problem with exclusive events, UST, DLSU, and CSB are three higher education institutions in Manila.)

The third category was called almost analog (AA) because the constructed problem was virtually almost a correct analog except that one or two problem elements were missing. For example, the problem did not include the value of one of the subsets or of one of the supersets, or the selection was not done randomly. Because of the missing information, the problem was not solvable. There were only five such problems; the following is one of them:

> There are 50 patients in the clinic, 20 are Asians and the rest are non-Asians. 21 non-Asians have AIDS. What is the probability that patient is either Asian or a patient with AIDS. (Constructed problem for disjunction problem with intersecting events; information on total number of patients with AIDS is missing)

The fourth and fifth categories both involved problems with analogous given information, but the questions given rendered the problem unsolvable. For example, the fourth category included problems where the question was not specific enough so that many possible solutions and answers were possible. These problems were called nonspecific questions (NSpQ). Five problems were counted in this category, an example of which is:

> In the school library there are 252 books that can be borrowed out of 402. In the city library there are 981 books out of 1092. In each library, a book is chosen to be the book of the week. What is the probability of a book to be the book of the week? (Constructed problem for conjunction problem with independent events)

In the fifth category, the question had a semblance of a mathematical question (it involved references to the sets and given quantities), but was actually nonsensical. These were called nonsense questions (NSeQ), and there were six such problems. An example of this is:

> There are 60 students who are in a special class. 30 of whom [sic] are Chinese. There are also 15 students in the Filipino class, 4 of whom [sic] are also Chinese. A teacher gives a test to them and picks a leader to collect the test papers. What is the probability that the student picked is from both classes? (Constructed problem for conjunction problem with independent events)

The sixth and seventh categories both involved incomplete or unfinished problems. The problems in these categories all did not include a problem question, and were all unsolvable. For the sixth category, however, the given information provided in the unfinished problem were analogous to the given in the original problem. There were ten such problems, which were called incomplete with analogous given (IAG). One example of this type of problem is:

> There are 100 patients in a clinic; 30 patients are sick with cough and the rest are sick with fever. 50 of the patients, 36 with a cough and 14 with fever are male. If a patient will be treated, what is the probability that the patient... (Constructed problem for disjunction problem with intersecting events)

On the other hand, for the seventh category, the analogous information was not analogous to the original problem. The quantities and quantitative relations in the given information did not parallel the original. Hence, these problems were called incomplete with nonanalogous given (ING). There were only four such problems, one of which is:

> There were 100 different women in the international beauty contest. 30 were from countries in the US, 30 from Asia, and 20 from different nations. If a winner is chosen randomly, what is the probability that the ... (Constructed problem for disjunction problem with intersecting events)

The eighth category of constructed problems was called the nonsense problem (NS). These problems were complete problem texts with given information and a question. However, the information provided was not connected in any meaningful way. It was as if bits of information were heaped together employing no coherent organization. Hence, the problems were all unsolvable. There were 15 such problems, and the following are examples:

> There are 64 gangs in L. A. 34 are affiliated with the Crups and the rest are with Brood. 50 of the gang members, 34 with the Princes and 26 with the

Bishops, if a member is beaten up randomly, what is the probability that the group will punish him? (Constructed problem for disjunction problem with intersecting events)

There are 300 patients, 50% have leprosy. 25% have lung cancer, 25% have skin disease. 10 doctors consulted 35% of the patient [*sic*]. How many were left? (Constructed problem for disjunction problem with intersecting events)

The final category included those cases when the subject did not construct a problem, hence called no answer (NA). There were only five such cases.

Looking at the eight categories (excluding the NA's), one could infer that each one reflects a different level of understanding about the problem structure. For example, we can assume that those who were able to make correct analogs probably had a good understanding of the problem's known and unknown elements and how they relate to each other. The understanding might not be a completely principled, but it is most likely an accurate representation of the most important problem elements and relations. Figure 1 describes a schematic representation of how the student may have represented the problem elements and relations. On the other extreme, those who merely combined pieces of information in a senseless manner (NS) probably were not able to appreciate the same problem elements or comprehend the significant relations between these, as described in Figure 2.

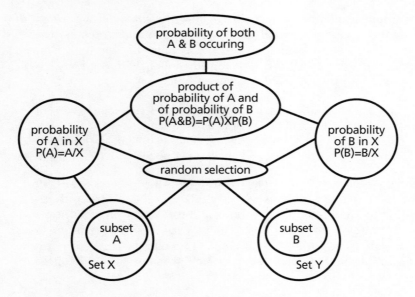

Figure 1.   Schematic diagram of a complete and accurate representation of problem elements and relations for conjunction problem with independent events.

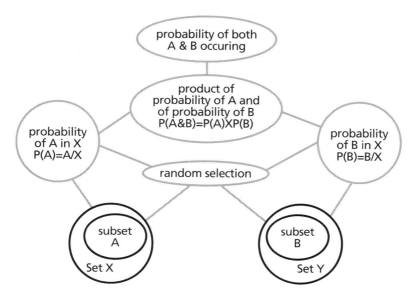

Figure 2. Schematic diagram of disjointed representation of lowest level problem elements. (Broken lines indicate that the concept or relation was not represented correctly.)

In the middle of the continuum, we probably have participants who understood how some pieces of information related to each other but did not have a complete grasp of how all the known and unknown elements were linked. For example, the constructed problem groups under SNA could be indicating that the participants correctly understood and represented all the problem elements and how they related, but they missed on the higher level set relations involved in combining probabilities. Hence, they ended up proposing simpler unknown elements that were nevertheless solvable given the information they provided. Likewise, the problems classified under NSEQ, NSPQ, and IAG might indicate that participants correctly represented some aspects of the problem but were not able to grasp the broader relations among these, hence the difficulty in arriving at the appropriate question defining the unknown element. The problems grouped under AA and ING might have had similar difficulties in grasping the larger relations, moreover, they might have not been properly representing certain discreet elements of the given information. Figure 3 describes a schematic representation of how a subject's representation at these intermediate levels.

We can group the different types of constructed problems in different clusters representing different levels of understanding. This clustering could be as follows:

Highest	Level A:CA
	Level B:SNA
	Level C:NSeQ, NSpQ, and IAG
	Level D:AA, and ING
Lowest	Level E:NS

To further explore the possible implications of the different categories of constructed problems, the participant's transfer performance was analyzed, and these results are described in the next section.

Analogical Transfer

For each of the problems constructed by the subject, they had to later solve an analogous problem. To determine whether some type of constructed problem might indicate higher levels of understanding, performance on the analogous test problems was assessed. The assumption was that transfer would be better if the participant had a better understanding of the similar problem structure underlying the analogous problems (Brown, 1988; Brown & Campione, 1994; Kolodner, 1997; Salomon & Perkins, 1989).

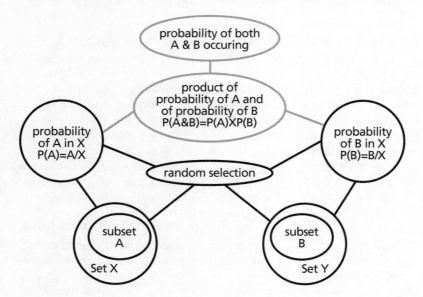

Figure 3.   Schematic diagram of accurate representation of lower level problem elements but incomplete/inaccurate representation of higher level concepts and relations for conjunction problems with independent events. (Broken lines indicate that the concept or relation was not represented correctly.)

For each of the analogous test problems the solutions were coded in terms of two criteria: (a) whether the solution showed that the participant retrieved the correct problem information, and (b) whether the solution showed that the participant correctly instantiated or applied the problem information to the new analogous problem. These two criteria correspond to two of the important elements of analogical transfer: retrieval and application (Holyoak, Novick, & Melz, 1994; Keane, Ledgeway, & Duff, 1994; Reeves & Weisberg, 1994; Ross, 1989). A transfer solution was scored as showing retrieval if the solution showed that the correct solution equation was retrieved. Only 33% of the solutions were scored as showing retrieval. A transfer solution was scored as showing correct application when the retrieved solution was correctly adapted for the new problem given, even if the solution did not lead to the correct or complete final solution. Only 21% of the solutions were scored for application.

For the analysis the proportion of correct access and use was coded for each of the corresponding constructed problems in the five levels of understanding described in the previous section. Table 1 shows the proportion of access and use for each of the levels.

Table 1 shows that retrieval of the correct problem information decreases as the assumed level of understanding of the original problem becomes weaker. This relationship between level of understanding and retrieval of analogous problem was verified computing for the contingency coefficient C, a nonparemetric statistical measure of the relation between two attributes, at least one of which is a categorical variable (Siegel, 1956). For the relationship between level of understanding and probability of retrieval, C (4, $N = 95$) $= .40$, $p < .01$.

Likewise, the correct use of the accessed information also decreased, as the assumed level of understanding becomes weaker. For the relationship between level of understanding and probability of application, C (4, $N = 95$) $= .36$, $p < .01$. If we assume that correct access and use are largely dependent on the subject's understanding of the underlying problem structure, then the categories and levels used to describe the problem structures seem to be viable indicators of the students' level of understanding of the word problems in the domain.

Table 1.   Proportion of Correct Retrieval and Application Across Types of Problem Constructed

Level	Type of Problem Constructed	N	Retrieval	Application
A	CA	29	55.2%	41.4%
B	SNA	21	47.6%	28.6%
C	NseQ, NSpQ, IAG	21	23.8%	14.3%
D	ING, AA	9	11.1%	0.0%
E	NS	15	0.0%	0.0%

CONCLUSIONS

The usefulness of the analogical problem construction procedure and the categories used to describe the student's level of understanding should be further explored. Indeed the categories used to describe students' understandings of the problems in this study were based on how these compared to an "accurate" representation of the problem. It is possible that students' problem representations could be described using other types of categories, which assume different types of mental models. But what this exploratory study shows is that there is some evidence to suggest that the features of the problems constructed by the participants indicate the characteristics of their problem representations.

The practical benefits of using the analogical problem construction as an informal diagnostic or assessment procedure of the teacher are apparent. By looking at the gaps and weaknesses in the structure of the problems constructed by the students, the teacher can infer which aspects of the original problem structure need to be focused on. For example, if the student shows a grasp of the problem elements but cannot seem to link them together (as with the Level C problems), then the teacher can choose appropriate guides and interventions that will allow the student to discover the important higher level relations. On the other hand, if the student does not even appreciate the specific nature of the different known or given elements of the problem (as with Level D and E problems), the teacher can work harder with the student at comprehending the problem information in the text.

Although it is truly difficult to have a complete and accurate understanding of how a student represents any situation at any given time, teachers need to be creative and persistent in trying to arrive at a fair description not only of what their students know and do not know, but how they are representing such knowledge in their minds. Only with such an understanding will teachers be able to design effective instructional tasks, interventions, and environments that aim to develop better representations of the different problem domains in the various subject areas.

APPENDIX

Examples of Probability Problems Used in the Study in Conjunction with Independent Events

There are 76 books in the Science section of the library, 6 of which are new. In the History section, there are 120 books, 15 of which are new. The principal randomly picks a book from each of the two sections.

What is the probability that the principal picks a new book from both sections?

There are 24 schools in District A, 8 of which are public schools. In District B, there are 32 schools, 12 of which are public schools. For each district, a school is randomly chosen to host the district sportsfest. What is the probability that a public school is chosen to host the sportsfest in both districts?

Solution: P(A & B) = P(A) * P(B)

Conjunction with Dependent Events

A total of 40 votes were cast for class president. Dennis received 30 votes and Claudia got the remaining 10 votes. The ballots were tallied one at a time in random order. What is the probability that the first ballot tallied was a vote for Dennis and the second ballot was for Claudia?

There are 45 students riding the bus for a camping trip; 25 students were seniors and 20 were juniors. The students are randomly assigned to a numbered seat in the bus. What is the probability that the first seat is assigned to a senior and the second seat is assigned to a junior student?

Solution: P(A & B) = P(A) * P(B/A)

Disjunction with Mutually Exclusive Events

There are 150 athletes participating in the intramural sportsfest. Sixty athletes are competing in basketball, 60 in volleyball, and 30 in taekwondo. If an athlete is chosen randomly, what is the probability that the athlete is competing either in basketball or taekwondo?

All 210 seniors applied for admission to college. Fifty seniors applied for a premed course, 80 for an engineering course, and 80 for commerce. If a senior is chosen randomly, what is the probability that the senior is applying either for a course in pre-med or commerce?

Solution: P(A or B) = P(A) + P(B)

Disjunction with Intersecting Events

There are 54 councilors in one city; 34 are with the LAKAS party and 20 are with LABAN. Forty of the councilors, 24 with LAKAS and 16 with LABAN, are lawyers. If a councilor is chosen randomly, what is the probability that the councilor is either with LAKAS or is a lawyer?

There are 36 patients in a provincial clinic, 16 of who are adults and 20 are children. Twenty patients, 12 adults and 12 children, are diagnosed with anemia. If a patient is chosen randomly, what is the probability that the patient is either an adult or has anemia?

Solution: $P(A \text{ or } B) = P(A) + P(B) - P(AB)$

ACKNOWLEDGMENT

This study was supported by a Spencer Postdoctoral Fellowship awarded to the author by the National Academy of Education, USA. The final preparation of the article was supported in part by a grant from the College of Education Research Council, De La Salle University—Manila. I thank Nino Jose Mateo, Christopher Cadua, Sendy Mangilit, Annalyn de Guzman, and the administrators and teachers of La Salle Greenhills High School and St. Mary's Quezon City High School for their assistance. Correspondence regarding the article may be sent to the author at the College of Education, De La Salle University, 2401 Taft Avenue, Manila 1004 Philippines, e-mail: claabb@dlsu.edu.ph

REFERENCES

Bernardo, A.B.I. (2001a). Analogical problem construction and transfer in mathematical problem solving. *Educational Psychology, 21*, 137–150.

Bernardo, A.B.I. (2001b). Principle explanation and strategic schema abstraction in problem solving. *Memory & Cognition, 29*, 627–633.

Brown, A.L. (1988). Motivation to learn and understand: On taking charge of one's own learning. *Cognition and Instruction, 5*, 311–322.

Brown, A.L., & Campione, J.C. (1994). Guided discovery in a community of learners. In K. McGilly (Ed.), *Classroom lessons: Integrating cognitive theory and classroom practice* (pp. 229–270). Cambridge, MA: MIT Press.

Holyoak, K.J., Novick, L.R., & Melz, E. (1994). Component processes in analogical transfer: Mapping, pattern completion, and adaptation. In K.J. Holyoak & J.A. Barden (Eds.), *Connectionist approaches to analogy, metaphor, and case-based reasoning* (pp. 113–180). Norwood, NJ: Ablex.

Keane, M.T., Ledgeway, T., & Duff, S. (1994). Constraints on analogical mapping: A comparison of three models. *Cognitive Science, 13*, 295–355.

Kintsch, W., & Greene, J.G. (1985). Understanding and solving word arithmetic problems. *Psychological Review, 92*, 109–129.

Kolodner, J.L. (1997). Educational implications of analogy: A view from case based reasoning. *American Psychologist, 52*, 57–66.

Lesh, R. (1990). Computer-based assessment of higher order understandings and processes in elementary mathematics. In G. Kuhn (Ed.), *Assessing higher order thinking in mathematics* (pp. 81–110). Washington, DC: American Association for the Advancement of Science.

Lipson, J.I., Faletti, J., & Martinez, M.E. (1990). Advances in computer-based mathematics assessment. In G. Kulm (Ed.), *Assessing higher order thinking in mathematics* (pp. 121–134). Washington, DC: American Association for the Advancement of Science.

Nuñez, T., & Bryant, P. (1995). Do problem solving situations influence children's understanding of the commutativity of multiplication? *Mathematical Cognition, 1*, 245–260.

Reeve, R.A., & Pattison, P.E. (1996). The referential adequacy of students' visual analogies of fractions. *Mathematical Cognition, 2*, 137–169.

Reeves, L.M., & Weisberg, R.W. (1994). The role of content and abstract information in analogical transfer. *Psychological Bulletin, 115*, 381–400.

Ross, B.H. (1989). Distinguishing types of superficial similarities: Different effects on the access and the use of earlier problems. *Journal of Experimental Psychology: Learning, Memory, and Cognition, 15*, 458–468.

Salomon, G., & Perkins, D.N. (1989). Rocky roads to transfer: Rethinking mechanisms of a neglected phenomenon. *Educational Psychologist, 24*, 113–142.

Schoenfeld, A.H. (1985). *Mathematical problem solving.* San Diego, CA: Academic Press.

Siegel, S. (1956). *Nonparametric statics for the behavioral sciences* (internationalstudent ed.). Tokyo: Mcgraw-Hill Kogakusha Ltd.

Singer, J.A., & Resnick, I.B. (1992). Representation of proportional relationships: are children part-part or part-whole reasoners? *Educational Studies in Mathematics, 23*, 231–246.

Wenger, R.H. (1987). Cognitive science and algebra learning. In A.H. Schoenfeld (Ed.), *Cognitive science and mathematics education* (pp. 217 251). Hillsdale, NJ: Erlbaum.

CHAPTER 6

THE CHANGING MODEL OF INTELLECTUAL ABILITIES:

EFFECTS ON SCHOOLING IN HONG KONG

Jimmy Chan

ABSTRACT

The development of the concepts of intelligence and emotion will be critically reviewed and discussed in the light of modern theories advanced by various influential psychologists today. The relative importance of intelligence and personality in learning has been the center of interest among educators and psychologists in recent years, not only in Western countries, but also in Mainland China, Taiwan, and Hong Kong itself. The relatively new terms of Emotional Intelligence (Goleman, 1995), Multiple Intelligence (Gardner, 1983), and Successful Intelligence (Sternberg) have become very popular not only in the academic circle, but also among the lay parents, who are always very concerned about their children is learning in schools and their careers after graduation. Hence, this paper will concentrate on the present status of academic results of students in relation to their intellectual and emotional characteristics and on the implications for teaching. It is also hoped to redefine the concept of giftedness in social and cultural contexts in addition to genetic influence.

INTRODUCTION

In this chapter, I will review and discuss the development of the concepts of intelligence and emotion in the light of modern theories advanced by various influential psychologists today. The relative importance of intelligence and personality in learning has been the center of interest among educators and psychologists in recent years not only in Western countries but also in Mainland China, Taiwan, and Hong Kong itself. The relatively new terms of *Multiple Intelligences* (Gardner) and *Emotional Intelligence* (Goleman) are currently very popular, not only in academic circles, but also among the general public and lay parents, who are always very much concerned about their children's learning in schools and their careers after graduation. Undoubtedly, students' learning in Hong Kong is highly related to their intellectual and emotional characteristics. The concept of giftedness can be redefined in theoretical and practical terms as well as in social and cultural contexts in addition to genetic influences, when the changing models of intellectual development are examined.

DEVELOPMENT OF INTELLIGENCE

The human mind is divided into two distinct parts, namely, the cognitive and the conative aspects. The cognitive aspects, such intelligence and aptitudes, concern mainly the intellectual functioning of the brain (i.e., learning abilities or the abilities to know about things). The conative aspects, such as attitudes, interests, motivation, popularity, and personality, mainly deal with the emotional areas (i.e., feelings that affect the learning outcomes). It seems that for successful learning, both abilities and emotions play a significant part to bring about desirable academic results.

The concept of intelligence is probably the oldest among all the concepts in psychology, and the relevant intelligence testing is also the most reliable and consistent among all kinds of psychological testing. The description of intelligence dates back to the time of factorial studies of Spearman (1904), Burt (1940), Vernon (1940), Eysenck (1967), Jensen (1969). Recent formulations by Gardner (1983) and Goleman (1995) are built on Thurstone's (1931) multiple factors theory and Guilford's (1940) emphasis of the emotional abilities. The development of intelligence in Hong Kong has been reported in Chan with others (1980–1997).

Presently, schools in Hong Kong are divided into three main types, namely, grammar, technical, and vocational to cater respectively for academic ability in arts (e.g., languages and history) and sciences (e.g., physics, chemistry, biology), technical ability in subjects such as home economics, art and design, and design and technology, and manual ability in subjects such as shorthand, typing, and drawing. As early as 1950, Vernon pointed out that for learning success, industriousness, personality, motivation, interests, attitudes, and physique are important attributes. Also, performance subjects such as music, singing, and dancing are listed in his intellectual model under aesthetic discrimination.

DEVELOPMENT OF EMOTIONS

There are two main approaches to personality psychology: the trait approach and depth psychology, which can be duly represented by Hans Eysenck (1916–1997) and Sigmund Freud (1856–1939), respectively. Eysenck is a factor analyst and has identified the main dimensions of personality traits that are relevant to academic learning in schools, whereas Freud was more concerned with the abnormal behaviors and mental disorders as well as their underlying causes. It is recognized that a child's development is highly connected with his experiences with his mother. As advocated by Freud and later by John Bowlby (1969) in his attachment theory and the related maternal deprivation theory, a child's emotional development plays an important part in formation of his or her future confidence and self-image. It is also responsible for his success in academic learning and other work.

THE CONCEPT OF IQ

The concept of Intelligence Quotient (IQ) has been widely studied. IQ scores are comparatively more stable than measures of emotional intelligence. Before the advancement of inferential statistics, IQ was measured by dividing the mental age by the chronological age. However, this method of defining IQ is no longer acceptable, as psychologists know that intelligence and age are not linearly related beyond the earlier years of development (say after year 6). Hence, a more appropriate definition is *Deviation IQ*, which relies on the normal distribution of intellectual performance at a particular age level and sometimes for a particular gender group. Nowadays, almost every intelligence test manual contains tables for IQ norms at different age intervals and for separate sexes in some tests.

The biggest factor affecting intelligence is heredity. Westerners often playfully address dull people with "You haven't got the genes," and the reason behind this is the belief that genes play an important role in determining whether a person is bright or not. Many psychometricians after lengthy, systematic empirical studies, concluded that heredity account for about 80% of the variance in intellectual behavior. However, this proportion is meaningless on its own, since without the environment, inherited talents cannot be brought out effectively. In other words, the actualization of inherited abilities relies on the interaction of heredity and the environment.

Take for example, the internal condition (heredity) of a seed, which will affect its growth and development. The seed needs water, air, and warmth (all three come from the environment) for its germination, and without which the seed cannot have an active life. Similarly, without parental care and school education, a child cannot learn properly no matter how potentially gifted he is. Modern education aims to develop the child's potentials effectively by making use of a favorable environment. Intelligence testing is used to identify a child's strengths and weaknesses, so that educators can help him or her develop his or her latent talents. As said in a Confucian proverb, the goal of education is to *"teach all children regardless of their abilities."* Other related work can be found in Kline (1996) and Li (1996).

THE CONCEPT OF EQ

The concept of EQ, very fashionable in the United States, has also been welcomed by Hong Kong people. Advocates of EQ claim that the practice of EQ can increase people's chance of success in life, especially for those in the commercial world. Hence, this concept has many supporters in the business and industry sectors. But, is EQ as magical and wonderful as suggested? It still needs further empirical evidence to demonstrate its effect on academic and job-related successes.

In our daily life, both intelligence and emotion are important for success in study or work. What we do reflects our mental capabilities. The performance of a pupil reflects his or her intelligence, and we cannot expect the same performance from a pupil with lower intelligence as from a pupil with higher intelligence. The function of education is limited by the intellectual level of the pupils. If a less able child has the appropriate personality, he or she can still achieve the same goals as a bright child does. Nonetheless the chance of success for this child is comparatively smaller, and this child no doubt has to pay a much greater effort or price than a bright child.

On the other hand, if a pupil has a poor study attitude, no interest in books, no aspiration for schoolwork, and a lot of emotional problems, he or she will have learning difficulties, even though he or she is intelligent. It is recognized therefore that both intelligence and emotion are important factors for learning. Also, in the work situation, no matter how clever a person is, he or she has to adopt the right attitude if he is to succeed. The development of personality in Hong Kong has been reported in Chan and with others (1978–1998).

Unfortunately, the measurement of emotion is much more difficult than that of intelligence, because people's reactions and behaviors tend to vary according to time, place, and who they are. Hence, attitude, interest, motivation, popularity, and personality are not as stable as intelligence. References on personality and other related concepts can be found in Eysenck (1970–1982), Eysenck and Chan (1982), Fontana (1977), Hayes (1991), Heim (1971), Kline (1997), Lazarus (1963), Semeonoff (1966), Vernon (1953, 1972), and Yang (1986).

It should also be noted that EQ is an inaccurate term, and is only used to counteract the popular and well-known term IQ. The term *emotional intelligence* was originally used by its initiator Daniel Goleman (1995), who has never used the term EQ, possibly because he does not know how to measure it. Hence, EQ can be said to be a misnomer.

EI as advocated by Goleman consists of five main areas, namely, (a) knowing one's own emotions, (b) managing one's own emotions, (c) motivating oneself, (d) knowing others' emotions, and (e) handling interpersonal relationships. In other words, EI is the "ability" of a person to monitor his own emotions as well as other people. Given the same intellectual abilities, if emotions can be directed to their proper use, a better result can be expected as far as learning is concerned.

THE CONCEPT OF MULTIPLE INTELLIGENCES

The concept of *Multiple Intelligences (M.I.)*, which has become very popular and fashionable in recent years in the United States, has also gradually gained momentum in Hong Kong. It has been advocated by Howard Gardner (1983) in the enunciation of his theory of "multiple intelligences," which makes the kinds of intelligences required for different successes in life stand out more clearly in relation to brain structure and daily practice. He identifies the following seven main important intelligences to be: (a) linguistic abilities, (b) logico-mathematical abilities, (c) spatial abilities, (d) musical abilities, (e) bodily-kinaesthetic abilities, (f) interpersonal abilities, and (g) intrapersonal abilities. The theory that stresses people possess different components of intelligence localized in particular areas of the brain. This theory combines both the cognitive and conative aspects of the human mind as well as the physical ability of the human body, and supports the views that every child is gifted in some way, and that success should be measured more comprehensively rather than limited to academic performance alone.

A PILOT MI TEST IN HONG KONG

Motivated by this new concept of intelligence and the current direction of education, a first attempt was made in Hong Kong several years ago to construct a multiple intelligences test for local use for teachers of gifted children to find out the various talents of children between the ages of 6–7. A pilot study has been undertaken to examine the feasibility and usefulness of such a test. Specialists in the assessment of different intelligence components contributed items for the test, which was moderated by kindergarten teachers, psychologists, social workers, and academic experts. Opinions of the parents on these items were also obtained, as parents are more familiar with the children's behaviors and daily activities at home.

The linguistic intelligence subtest consists of items that assess word perception, vocabulary, syntax, and comprehension. The logico-mathematical intelligence subtest measures: counting, subtraction, series, places, time, and buying in accordance with the topics commonly learned in most kindergartens. The spatial intelligence subtest comprises tests of conversion of 3-dimensional to 2-dimensional figures, and joining point patterns to form 3-dimensional figures. The musical intelligence subtest tests recognition of same pitch, different pitches and rhythm, metrical perception, pattern comparison, sonority perception, and intensity perception, and is administered through the use of a recorded cassette tape, which plays the music to the children during testing. The bodily-kinaesthetic intelligence subtest consists of an obstacle course on jumping, springboard jumping, crawling, balancing (on a large bag filled with peas), and meandering running (around a number of inverted large ice-cream cones). The interpersonal intelligence subtest is designed to test human relationship patterns among children with various social interactions in daily life, and their responses are recorded on a 3-point scale. Tests of intrapersonal intelligence require the assessees to be more mature in age, and therefore no attempt is made to assess intrapersonal intelligence.

Item analyses were carried out to determine the test's reliability and validity. Preliminary results showed that the item statistics were generally satisfactory, though considerable improvement is needed in certain areas. The test's reliability is as high as 0.99 (Spearman-Brown) and 0.95 (Cronbach). When all the items were submitted to a principal component analysis with varimax rotation, no general factor was found. The first five factors explained 35.3% of the total variance, indicating that the test measures multiple factors. However, more research is needed to provide evidence to support Gardner's Multiple Intelligences Theory in the Hong Kong context.

HOW ABOUT MQ?

In view of Gardner's theory and the above pilot study, it seems that it is possible to propose the concept of *Multiple Intelligences Quotient, M.Q.* In other words, a multiple regression equation can be formulated to account for success in any academic subject in school using various components of intelligence including physical features and personality as independent variables. In this multiple approach to learning, both physical and mental (cognitive and conative aspects) attributes of a child are used in determining the outcome of learning, and this can be yet another breakthrough in understanding the learning process of the child.

TRENDS OF INTELLECTUAL MODELS

From the above review, it can be said that the human factors that affect learning are basically the same now as before. Educational abilities, comprising physical, cognitive, and conative characteristics were identified by psychologists a long time ago, notably Vernon in 1950, to account for individual differences in learning. The hierarchical approach (e.g., the two-factor theory, the group factor theory of Spearman-Burt-Vernon-Eysenck-Jensen) and the multiple-factor approach by Thurstone-Guilford in the explanation of the learning process are not mutually exclusive. Instead, they are complementary in the understanding of the human mind.

In other words, the emphasis on emotional abilities by Goleman appears to be the result of the special needs of the commercial world where interpersonal skills play a significant part in business success. On the other hand, the comprehensive coverage of both cognitive and conative aspects of intelligence together with physical characteristics by Gardner in recent years is the revival of the traditional educational abilities proposed by early psychologists.

In sum, all these new theories are just old wine in new bottles, merely either a change of emphasis or a revival of old concepts. In this review, I have identified eight trends in the conception of human abilities. They are the trend shift (a) from general to specific; (b) from cognitive to conative; (c) from individual to social; (d) from genetic to environmental; (e) from academic to practical; (f) from simplicity to diversity, (g) from uni-approach to multi-approach; and (h) from factorial to conceptual. After all, learning is a complicated process, is it therefore reasonable to adopt more than one approach to education, be it IQ, EQ, or even MQ?

CONCLUSION

Finally, it is noted that when universities in Hong Kong admit students, given the same academic results, due attention should be given to their personal characteristics, and to the applicants' activities in their school life. Currently, the Hong Kong Examinations Authority is seriously considering a plan to make use of the school's internal assessment in the evaluation of overall student performance, and thus a more all-round approach could be adopted. Both the Hong Kong and Mainland Chinese governments are actively promoting quality education, which has led to extensive use of information technology, with particular emphasis of computer usage in the teaching and learning process at both primary and secondary levels. But it is also pertinent to ensure that children can learn effectively, by developing their intellectual, emotional and physical attributes equally well, in order for them to get the maximum benefit of the present huge investment in education and to meet the principle of cost-effectiveness.

In line with the changing concepts of human abilities, it cannot be over-emphasized that learning in school should be more comprehensive than before, i.e., students should not only concentrate on academic pursuit but also on their emotional growth and physical performance. This would help the development of well-balanced individuals who will contribute to the society at large. This changing model of intellectual abilities will have a profound effect on the education system in Hong Kong, and has yet to be fashioned.

REFERENCES

Bowlby, J. (1969). *Attachment and loss*. New York: Basic Books.

Burt, C.L. (1940). *The backward child*. London: University of London Press.

Chan, J. (1978). Parent-child interaction and personality. *New Horizons, 19,* 44–52.

Chan, J. (1980). Two basic concepts of educational psychology: "Intelligence" and "personality". *New Horizons, 21,* 17–22. (in Chinese)

Chan, J. (1993). Effect of personality on learning and teaching. *New Horizons, 34,* 107–109.

Chan, J. (1995). The use of Eysenck Personality Questionnaire. In H. Kao & L. Ou-Yan (Eds.), *The application of psychology—The symposium of the international congress* (pp. 23–24). Beijing: World Book Publishing Co.

Chan, J. (1996a). Chinese intelligence. In M.H. Bond (Ed.), *The handbook of Chinese psychology* (pp. 93–108). Hong Kong: Oxford University Press.

Chan, J. (1996b). Intelligence, personality, and measurements. In H. Kao (Ed.), *New theories in psychology* (pp. 200–221). Hong Kong: Commercial Press. (in Chinese)

Chan, J. (2001). Chinese value systems in personality testing. *Journal of Psychological Research in Chinese Societies*. (in preparation)

Chan, J. et al. (1996). Personality and education in the classroom. In H. Kao & L. Ou-Yan (Eds.), *Personality and education—The symposium of the international congress* (pp. 15–17). Xian: Shaanxi Normal University Press. (in Chinese)

Chan, J. et al. (1997a). Multiple intelligences and multiple intelligences testing: Experience and prospect. *The symposium of the eighth Chinese academic conference of psychology by the Chinese Psychological Society*. Suzhou: University of Suzhou.

Chan, J. et al. (1997b). *EQ and IQ: Theory and practice*. Paper presented at the Psychology Department of the Peking University. (in Chinese)

Chan, J. et al. (1997c). Multiple intelligences in Hong Kong. *Proceedings of the seventh international conference on thinking*. Singapore: National Institute of Education.

Chan, J., & Lynn, R. (1989). The intelligence of six-year-olds in Hong Kong. *J Biosoc. Sci., 21*, 461–464.

Chan, J., & Ripple, R. (1982). Cross-cultural perspectives in the life span development of divergent thinking abilities. *Proceedings of the sixth congress of the international association for cross-cultural psychology*. Aberdeen, Scotland.

Chan, J., & Vernon, P.E. (1998). Individual differences among the peoples of China. In S. H. Irvine & J. Berry (Eds.), *Human abilities in cultural context* (pp. 340–357). Cambridge: Cambridge University Press.

Chan, J., Eysenck, H.J., & Lynn, R. (1991). Reaction times and intelligence among Hong Kong children. *Perceptual and Motor Skills, 72*, 427–433.

Eysenck, H.J. (1967). Intelligence assessment: A theoretical and experimental approach. *British Journal of Educational Psychology, 37*, 81–98.

Eysenck, H.J. (1970). *The structure of human personality*. London: Methuen.

Eysenck, H.J. (1978). Personality and education. *New Horizons, 19*, 27–43.

Eysenck, H.J. (Ed.). (1981). *A model for personality*. New York: Springer-Verlag.

Eysenck, H.J., & Eysenck, S.B.G. (1975). *Manual of the Eysenck Personality Questionnaire (junior and adult)*. London: Hodder and Stoughton.

Eysenck, H.J., & Eysenck, S.B.G. (1976). *Psychoticism as a dimension of personality*. London: Hodder and Stoughton.

Eysenck, S.B.G., & Chan, J. (1982). A comparative study of personality in adults and children—Hong Kong versus England. *Personality and Individual Differences, 3*,153–160.

Fontana, D. (1977). *Personality and education*. London: Open Books.

Freud, S. (1953–1964). *The complete psychological works* (24 vols., J. Strachey Ed.). London: Hogarth.

Gardner, H. (1983). *Frames of mind: The theory of multiple intelligences*. New York: Basic Books

Goleman, D. (1995). *Emotional intelligence*. London: Bloomsbury Publishing.

Guilford, J.P. (1940). Human abilities. *Psychological Review, 47*, 367–394.

Hayes, J. (1991). *Interpersonal skills*. London: Routledge.

Heim, A. (1971). *Intelligence and personality*. Harmondsworth: Penguin Books.

Jensen, A. (1969). How much can we boost IQ and scholastic achievement? *Harvard Educational Review, 39*, 1–123.

Kline, P. (1996). *Intelligence: The psychometric view*. London: Routledge.

Kline, P. (1997). *Personality: The psychometric view.* London: Routledge.

Lazarus, R.S. (1963). *Personality and adjustment.* Englewood Cliffs: Prentice-Hall.

Li, R. (1996). *A theory of conceptual intelligence: Thinking, learning, creativity, and giftedness.* Westport, CT: Praeger.

Lynn, R., Chan, J., & Eysenck, H.J. (1991). Reaction times and intelligence in Chinese and British children. *Perceptual and Motor Skills, 72,* 443–452.

Lynn, R., Pagliari, C., & Chan, J. (1988). Intelligence in Hong Kong measured for Spearman's *g* and the visuo-spatial and verbal primaries. *Intelligence, 12,* 423–433.

Poon, P., Yu, W.Y., & Chan, J. (1986). A correlation between intelligence and auditory reaction time. *Perceptual and Motor Skills, 63,* 375–378.

Semeonoff, B. (Ed.). (1966). *Personality assessment.* Harmondsworth: Penguin Books.

Spearman, C. (1904). "General intelligence," objectively determined and measured. *American Journal of psychology, 15,* 201–293.

Thurstone, L.L. (1931). Multiple factor analysis. *Psychological Review, 38,* 406–427.

Vernon, P.E. (1940). *The measurement of abilities.* London: University of London Press.

Vernon, P.E. (1953). *Personality tests and assessment.* London: Methuen.

Vernon, P.E. (1972). *Personality assessment—A critical survey.* London: Methuen.

Yang, K.S. (1986). Chinese personality and its changes. In M.H. Bond (Ed.), *The psychology of the Chinese people* (pp. 106–170). Hong Kong: Oxford University Press.

PART II

SELF-REGULATED LEARNING

CHAPTER 7

FROM MOTIVATION TO SELF-REGULATION:

CLUSTERING STUDENTS' MOTIVATIONAL AND COGNITIVE CHARACTERISTICS, AND EXPLORING THE IMPACT OF SOCIAL INTERACTION ON LEARNING

Jennifer Archer

ABSTRACT

This study investigates the chain of events linking students' motivational orientation with their reported use of effective learning strategies. The data
comprise interviews with 54 undergraduate students in their first year and 42
follow-up interviews in the second year.

INTRODUCTION

Models of learning have integrated motivational and cognitive aspects: students are seen to adopt motivational intentions that are brought to fruition
by appropriate study strategies. These models have been fleshed out by the
addition of emotional, metacognitive, volitional and social variables (e.g.,

Pintrich & Garcia, 1991). Self-regulation focuses on students' role in manipulating these various aspects of learning to enhance their learning (e.g., Boekaerts, 1997). The present study makes use of a model of learning and its variables are described in the following paragraphs.

MOTIVATION

Achievement goal theory provides a useful conceptualization of students' motivation (Ames, 1992; Archer, 1994; Dweck, 1986; Maehr, 1984; Meece & Holt, 1993). Students may adopt a mastery goal (I want to understand this work), a performance goal (I want to look competent in front of my peers, or I do not want to look incompetent), or an academic alienation goal (I want to pass by doing as little work as possible). A mastery goal has been associated with a positive approach to learning, uses of effective learning strategies, and perseverance in the face of difficulties. On the other hand, a performance goal, especially in students who lack confidence in their abilities, has been associated with a negative attitude to work, "surface" rather than "deep" study strategies, and anxiety and retreat in the face of difficulties. An alienation goal also is associated with negative attitudes and surface study strategies.

To what extent do students carry goals with them from one situation to another? Can environmental cues change students' goals? How do personal goals and environmental cues interact? Recent work also has been looking at how students manage multiple achievement goals, or balance achievement goals with other goals such as social goals (Wentzel, 1999, 2000). Harackiewicz and her colleagues (Harackiewiez, Barron, & Elliot, 1998; Harackiewicz, Barron, Tauer, Carter, & Elliot, 2000) call for the separation of the performance goal into two goals (performance-approach and performance avoidance) and argue that a performance-approach goal coupled with a mastery goal will enhance both achievement and ongoing interest in a topic.

EMOTIONS AND INTEREST

As Turner, Thorpe, and Meyer (1998) point out, most research has treated emotion as an outcome variable of attributional analyses or orientation toward a goal. For example, a student attributing failure to a lack of ability would feel shame because he lacks a desirable characteristic. Anxiety during test taking also has received considerable attention. The place of emotions within a causal chain remains open to debate. Turner et al. (1998) found that negative emotions following failure mediated performance goals and reported use of strategies, preference for difficult tasks, self-efficacy, and behavior. Boekaerts (1993), on the other hand, argues that emotions influence students' adoption of a goal: a student who experiences pleasure in an academic situation and who feels capable of completing the task will be more likely to adopt a mastery orientation. A student who feels anxious and incapable of completing a task will try to avoid it. Seifert (1997) supports Boekaerts argument that emotions give rise to goals.

Interest is labeled in this study as an emotion. This label is problematic, however, because interest contains not only emotional elements (an interesting activity often, but is not necessarily enjoyable), but also motivational elements (the desire to approach an interesting activity) and cognitive elements (an activity is interesting because it provokes thinking). The link between interest and enjoyment has been well documented (Hidi, 1990). There is also overlap between interest and intrinsic motivation. An interesting activity, like an intrinsically motivating activity, is enjoyable and mentally stimulating whether or not a goal or reward is achieved in the long run.

A distinction is drawn between situational and topic or individual interest (Krapp, Hidi, & Renninger, 1992). Situational interest is the result of particular events, while individual interest refers to relatively enduring preferences for topics or contexts. Hidi and her colleagues argue that individual and situational interest enhances cognitive functioning and thus facilitates learning.

VOLITION

Volition, or self-discipline, refers to the thoughts and behaviors that students use to maintain an intention to achieve a goal in the face of internal and external distractions (Corno & Kanfer, 1993). As Garcia, McCann, Turner, and Roska (1998) point out, volition, like interest, is difficult to categorize because it has both motivational elements (the intention to learn) and cognitive and metacognitive elements (the strategies employed). For example, managing resources effectively has been categorized as a metacognitive strategy though obviously it overlaps with volition. Theoretical and empirical work (Corno & Kanfer, 1993; Kuhl, 1985) show that volition can operate as an independent variable that mediates motivational goals and the cognitive strategies that produce learning.

STUDY STRATEGIES

Both cognitive and metacognitive strategies have been identified (McKeachie, Pintrich, Smith, Lin, & Sharma, 1990; Pintrich & Garcia, 1991; Vermunt, 1998). Cognitive strategies include rehearsal (repeating material verbatim), organization (categorizing or grouping material), and elaboration (giving meaning to new material by linking it with prior knowledge). Organization and elaboration strategies are necessary for high quality learning because they shape knowledge into a coherent whole. Organization would be evident, for example, when a student draws a diagram showing how various aspects of a topic are related, while elaboration would be evident in note-taking when a student makes links to related aspects studied earlier. Metacognitive strategies include planning a course of study, monitoring progress, making changes if necessary, and using the experience when approaching a new task. Effective students use metacognitive strategies by consciously planning, monitoring, and evaluating their work.

SOCIAL ASPECTS OF LEARNING

The social aspects of classrooms operate on at least two levels: meeting social goals, and helping students to learn. To consider social goals first (see Wentzel, 1999, 2000). There is a goal of social responsibility, of wanting to do the "right" thing by others, and a goal of belonging, of wanting to be accepted as a member of a group. There also are goals that combine social and academic aspects, for example, I want to do well so that I am accepted by a group who values high achievement. As Wentzel (1999) and Boekaerts (1993) point out, the link between achievement and social and emotional well-being is well established: students who feel unhappy and disconnected from their peers are unlikely to do well.

The work of Vygotsky (e.g., Wertsch, 1991) highlights the role of social interaction in helping students learn. At a more fundamental level, Vygotsky's view of learning sees context, and the language used within it, as the dominant factor in learning rather than as a backdrop to learning. More recent perspectives in motivation and cognition, for example, Paris and Turner's (1994) *situated cognition*, reflect this shift in emphasis (for a detailed discussion, see Hickey, 1997).

METHODOLOGICAL APPROACH OF THE STUDY

Much of the work integrating motivation and cognition has used linear statistical models to delineate relationships among variables. In addition, some researchers (Ainley, 1993; Meece & Holt, 1993; Pintrich, 1989; Seifert, 1997; Turner et al., 1998) have used cluster analyses to identify groups of students who share relatively similar sets of motivational and cognitive characteristics. Pintrich (1989) argues that the links among the motivational and cognitive aspects of learning probably are more complex and interdependent than they appear in linear models. The strength of linear models lies in their ability to show causal relationships among relatively few discrete variables, whereas models that cluster variables are able to show integration and interdependence among variables (Ainley, 1993). These models can complement each other. Salomon (1991) makes a similar case: research is enhanced by the use of both analytic research (isolating components of causal linear models) and systemic research (analyzing the interdependence of the many variables that produce, for example, a class in operation).

Cluster analysis is able to show how the relative rather than the absolute strength of variables defines groups of students (Turner et al., 1998). Further, it is the interdependence of variables within a cluster that makes students' behavior more or less adaptive. It is difficult to summarize the results of the various cluster analyses because they incorporate different variables into clusters, link the clusters with different variables, and use subjects who range widely in age. Two studies with older students will be examined: Ainley (1993) clustered senior high school students on their ability levels and three approaches to learning (similar to the three achievement goals described earlier). The five clusters identified then were linked with students' reported use of elaboration and rehearsal strategies, and their school achievement. For example, a cluster comprising high ability students who endorsed both mastery and performance goals reported frequent use of elaboration strategies and did well in school. In contrast, another cluster comprising average ability students endorsed an alienation goal, reported using more rehearsal strategies and did not perform as well. Pintrich (1989) identified five clusters of college students using seven variables: intrinsic motivation, valuing of the task, beliefs about control, expectancy of success, cognitive and metacognitive strategies, and expenditure of effort. These clusters linked to achievement in predictable ways.

With the large number of quantitative studies now linking motivation, cognitive, and social aspects of learning, it is timely to complement these with qualitative studies that use similar theoretical frameworks. The first part of the present study analyzes interview data using what might be called a naturalistic cluster analysis, that is, looking for sets of characteristics that define groups of students. The data came from semi-structured interviews with 40 students undertaking a first year university subject in child and adolescent psychology as part of a teacher education degree. Once groups of students were identified, the groups were linked to the grades the students received for the subject. Did the groups show predictable levels of achievement? Moreover, to what extent did the groups display the self-regulatory attitudes and behaviors necessary for effective study? Finally, to what extent did the groups resemble those generated by the quantitative cluster analyses?

The second part of the study used the same interview data, but looked closely at students' reactions to the weekly two-hour tutorial sessions. This allowed examination of the social aspects of learning. Three questions were posed. Is there evidence of motivation being changed by participation in tutorials? What is the connection among emotion, interest, and motivation? How does social interaction help students to learn? Asking students to reflect on their experiences lacks the specificity of a Likert-type questionnaire. On the other hand, relatively open-ended questioning avoids the downside of questionnaires, that they dictate some areas of investigation while ignoring others that may be more salient to students.

METHOD

Participants were 40 students (18 males, 22 females) enrolled in the first year of a Bachelor of Education program in the following specializations: (English/history, 4; physical education, 3; Asian languages, 2; early childhood, 3; art, 2; social sciences, 3; music, 1; primary, 5; mathematics, 5; science, 4; design and technology, 8). The total number of first year students was 354. All first year students were required to take a year-long subject in child and adolescent development, usually referred to as Education 1. The subject was run by a team of eight lecturers, four of whom took turns to present a weekly one-hour lecture attended by all students. In addition, there was a two-hour tutorial held each week for smaller groups of students (about 20 to 25 per group). Each lecturer was responsible for anywhere from one to five tutorial groups, and for marking the work for students in those groups.

Assessment consisted of a major assignment (30%), an end of year examination requiring essay responses (40%), a minor assignment (15%), and a number of small tests (15%). The major assignment was structured to encourage a mastery motivation in students (reported in Archer & Scevak, 1998). Four aspects were addressed. First, the assignment was to be submitted twice: the first submission would be marked out of 10 and returned with written feedback about how it could be improved; the second submission would be marked out of 20, resulting in a mark out of 30. Students also were required to submit a plan with their assignment. Second, students were given a 30-page booklet, prepared specifically for Education 1, explaining how to go about writing an academic assignment. The booklet covered finding references in the library, citing references in the assignment, taking notes, planning the assignment, examining and improving upon a previous essay, and guidelines for expression. Third, students were given a choice of five topics for the assignment, for example, *Discuss the controversy concerning whether or not there is an adolescent identity crisis.* Fourth, students were given the choice of working individually on the assignment or working with one partner. (Note: This last aspect, working with a partner, is not explored here because of the confounding factor of university holidays, that is, many students chose to work alone because they were writing the assignment during holidays when they were too far from possible partners.)

The 40 students participated voluntarily in individually conducted, audio taped interviews with a research assistant. The interviews were conducted toward the end of the year, and later were transcribed. Students were assured of confidentiality and that the grades they received would not be affected by their participation or otherwise in an interview. As part of a longer interview, they were asked about their experiences in Education 1: *Do you enjoy Education 1? Why do you say that? How do you go about studying for Education 1; Do you enjoy the tutorials in Education 1? Why do you say that? How would you compare studying at university to studying at high school? What did you think about having to resubmit the major assignment? Did you use the strategies booklet? Which parts did you use? Did you like having a choice of topics for the major assignment? Why?* In terms of final grades for Education 1, nine of the students received a distinction, twelve a credit, sixteen a pass, and three failed.

RESULTS

Six groups of students were identified by looking carefully for sets of characteristics that separated one group from other groups. Each group displayed relatively similar characteristics in terms of emotions, motivational goals, study strategies, self-discipline, and response to the environmental and assessment aspects of the subject (including the tutorials and the assessment procedures for the major assignment). Obviously, the groups containing smaller numbers of students (Groups 2, 4, and 6) must be accepted with caution. They were included because their distinctiveness suggested a separate grouping. Not all students categorized within a group displayed exactly the same characteristics. Occasionally, too, some students were not asked all the questions because the interviewer forgot to ask a question, or skipped a question because a lot of time had been taken up with a previous question.

Group 1 (*N* = 7)

Emotional responses.   All students spoke of interest and enjoyment.

Motivational goals.   All indicated a mastery goal of doing the best they could do (e.g., I want to do the best I can; I'm competitive with myself; do well yourself and get the best mark you can).

Study strategies:

- *Looking for major themes:*   Virtually all the students made reference to looking for overarching themes (e.g., coming together; connecting is the big thing; getting the whole picture).
- *Relating/elaborating:*   Students spoke about relating new information to prior knowledge (e.g., I saw that happening to someone else; if you put things in real life terms, then it applies to real life and it's relevant; you think about how you would bring up a child).
- *Wide reading:*   All students read widely (e.g., I do cover extra material mainly because I'm interested not because it's on a test; if I find what I'm studying is enjoyable, then I actually shock, horror might go home and read a bit more about it).
- *Purposeful note-taking:*   The students made their own notes in addition to copying down notes presented by lecturers during the massed lectures (e.g., I make summaries with subheadings and points and keywords; cross referencing; I think of an example and then I understand the concept).

Self-discipline.   Students accepted that university required self-discipline (e.g., it's a challenge that you've got to do the work by yourself; now I set my own goals whereas in high school they'd say what you had to do).

Environmental support:

- *Involvement in tutorials:*   They participated fully (e.g., when I'm in a group and I don't understand something, I'll find out within the group; everyone has their own opinion and doesn't mind giving their opinion; you'll hear all these different arguments in the tutorial).
- *Resubmission of major essays:*   This was a way of getting useful information about the quality of their work (e.g., we know what we've done wrong and we can fix it up; essays shouldn't be about the final mark, they should be about what you know; a chance to put a thorough effort in).
- *Essay writing booklet:*   They used the booklet (e.g., it's right there in front of you and you can look at it if you have problems; I was in bed with it).
- *Choice of topics:*   They could choose something of interest (e.g., if you're interested you're more likely to read, to find out more information; you can have an active job in what you do).

Group 2 (*N* = 2)

These two students have been categorized separately from Group 1 because of their strong performance orientation.

Emotional response.   Both enjoyed the tutorials.

Motivational goals.   Both expressed a strong performance orientation. (Competition is just a natural human characteristic, that you like to do better than the next person; I think everything's competition these days, so it's no good sticking your head in the sand and saying that competition doesn't exist), though they acknowledged that understanding was important too (I think teachers should emphasize understanding, people compete naturally so it doesn't need egging on; if you get a good mark, that means you're going to be a really good teacher).

Study strategies:

- *Looking for major themes.*   Both looked for themes (I'll try and find basic themes, you've got to work out your own opinion, how things fit together, rather than just what other people think ... relate them all together).
- *Reading.*   Both said they read a lot. It was a more focused reading than the reading for interest of Group 1 (when it comes closer to exams I put a lot of pressure on myself ... I get as much as I can together, and read through it, try and understand it, then try and memorize it; I find covering extra material is very important ... I know that sort of stuff actually adds to what you're learning and can be the difference between knowing something and not knowing something).
- *Note taking.*   Both took careful notes (I read through the textbook and summarize it ... I'll try and find basic themes; I go through each chapter and answer the questions at the back, and use the study guide ... with the exam coming up ... I tend to write some essays myself and get into the mode of thinking).

Self-discipline.   Both displayed strong self-discipline (I'm a pretty independent sort of person. If there's something I don't understand, I'll try and battle it out for myself. I'll accept the way it's being taught and adjust to it; there's no pressure to perform here at university, it's all self-motivation).

Environmental support:

- *Involvement in tutorial groups.*   Both enjoyed the tutorials (I enjoy them ... he gives us stories, it makes it so much easier ... and everyone wants to tell their stories, it's like a kindergarten class, everyone wants to help encourage each other; we discuss a lot of things ... he brings up experiences he's had, he links what we do in lectures to other things … we discuss between each other and that's always good).

- *Resubmission of major assignments.*   Both were uncomfortable with the resubmitted essay getting twice the marks of the original submission. One also was uncomfortable with lack of consistency in marking across the tutorial groups (They should make the first part worth 30% and the next part 10% and I hope they do average the consistency within the marking between the education tuts … it's probably my biggest grudge … I know other tuts got higher marks than us and a bigger range; if somebody does a really lousy job they might get six the first time, and then really improve their second job, they might get eighteen or nineteen out of twenty. They're getting all the advantage).
- *Essay writing booklet.*   One did not make much use of the booklet because he had done a similar subject the year before, while the other described it as helpful.
- *Choice of topics.*   One was not happy with a choice (I don't like the idea because the lecturers don't take into account that some questions are harder than others when they're marking), but the other one was (you might have a particular interest in one of them, and there'll be more library resources).

Group 3 (*N* = 14)

This group resembled Group 1 in their mastery approach, though the quality of their study strategies was not at the level of that group.

Emotional responses.   All used words such as *interesting* and *enjoy.*

Motivational goals.   Most mentioned a mastery goal (e.g., I don't compete, I work for me; I'm working for me and myself only; don't worry too much about other people, just focus on what you're doing).

Study strategies:

- *Reading.*   All read, However, except for a few (e.g., the wider you read and the more you read in education, the better you understand it), there was no mention of wide reading.
- *Note taking.*   A few mentioned more sophisticated forms of note taking (e.g., I make notes and gradually reduce them as I read through them, sort of stripping them down, so I've got, say a page for each topic, even with just headings) but again this was not as marked as it was for Group 1.
- *Relating.*   A few related new information to previous knowledge (e.g., I relate what I'm studying to things I know about), but not as marked as for Group 1.

- *Discussions not during tutorials:*   A number of students mentioned that they had family or friends with whom they discussed their work (e.g., I try and get my husband involved … he likes to read about the subject too. I get him to ask me questions).

Self-discipline. Most accepted the independent approach required at university (e.g., you're left up to your devices to work things out for yourself … it suits me fine; you have to get yourself motivated to work … it's complete responsibility … I enjoy that kind of thing). Two students, though, missed the more intimate atmosphere of high school (e.g., you don't have that same level of companionship … by the end of Year 12 at high school I knew the teachers reasonably well and I had no qualms about asking them for help … and they were usually keen to help me).

Environmental support:

- *Involvement in tutorials:*   There was enthusiastic participation (e.g., we discuss what we've read. I find that to be invaluable because sometimes I'll come up against something I might not understand, but one of the people in the group might understand better and they can explain it to me, there's a lot of margin for interaction … there's freedom to learn from others). One student said that tutorials were stiff and dull.
- *Resubmission:*   This was an opportunity to learn (e.g., so you're learning from it rather than getting it back, seeing it, and throwing it in the bin; if they hand it back to you, then you try a bit harder to make it a good assignment). The booklet was useful (e.g., I was able to write with the booklet beside me and make sure I was going ahead the right way; our blue bible).
- *Choice of topics:*   They could choose something of interest, with some making a connection between interest and *effort* (e.g., if you're interested in something you work harder at it).

Group 4 (*N* = 4)

This group resembled Group 3, but differed in endorsing an alienation goal. However, at times they displayed a mastery approach.

Emotional response. All enjoyed the tutorials (e.g., you feel comfortable; I'm beginning to enjoy it; I enjoy learning the new material).

Motivational goals. They did not dislike the subject. In fact, they rather enjoyed it, but other aspects of their lives took precedence (e.g., I do what I have to do and that's about all I do … I like to go and see my family because my family's important; I'm paying my way through university, accommodation, everything … so my aim is to get over 50%; I'm trying to juggle two careers at the moment … I may break into a career in baseball).

Study strategies:

- *Reading:*   They all read the required material, though one put off reading till the last moment.
- *Note taking:*   Two described useful note-taking techniques (putting things together logically … if I can relate it to something I know … I think about how I would explain it to others; I read through and highlight and then take notes from the highlights … I try to relate what I'm reading to his stories because his stories make sense) while the other two admitted that they did little note-taking.
- *Discussions outside tutorials:*   One discussed material with his wife (She's almost doing this degree with me).

Self discipline.   They were willing to work independently (e.g., even though I don't like a subject I'll work for it; you have to be more independent here; I think motivation comes from an internal source rather than an external source).

Environmental support:

- *Involvement in tutorials:*   They got a lot out of tutorials (e.g., we get to use our opinions … the discussion helps because it gives other people's views of what they're learning … I think discussion is great because I personally get so much out of it).
- *Resubmission of major essay:*   This gave them a chance to improve their work (e.g., really good because usually you get an essay back that's not so good and that's the end of it; you learn from your mistakes).
- *Essay writing booklet:*   It was useful, particularly the section on referencing.
- *Choice of essay:*   This gave them a chance to choose something of interest.

Group 5 (*N* = 8)

Group 5 and Group 6 are similar, but differ in level of self-discipline.

Emotional response.   They were bored. Some also considered much of it irrelevant because they were required to study development from early childhood to late adolescence. Some of the prospective high school teachers objected to studying infants.

Motivational goals.   The goal was academic alienation or no clear goal (e.g., I think I'd be a bit more enthusiastic to work if I was around people who work a lot more; happy just to be passing; most people I know just try and pass the course).

Study strategies:

- *Reading:*   Most did not enjoy reading about the subject and so did little reading (e.g., I don't enjoy reading so I find difficulty with education; I'm paranoid about covering extra material, it's worthless).
- *Note taking:*   Note taking was mentioned by most students, but no sophisticated methods emerged (e.g., I try and read all my notes and everything like that, but I get very bored with it; I like concise notes because I don't like reading a lot of stuff that doesn't make much sense to me).
- *Relating:*   One student said that he deliberately did not relate new information to prior knowledge (I don't really try and relate it to other things I know. I believe this is something new, I put it into another category).

Self discipline.   There was not much evidence of self-discipline. Most preferred high school to university because there they were told exactly what to do (e.g., the high school teacher always said: this is what we're going to be doing, you have to take these questions down, and at the end of the year these questions have to be handed in … so if you went away or were sick for a week you knew what had to be done at high school, all the information that was on the board was relevant, so you had it up in front of you to learn). Some also admitted that they were easily distracted from study (e.g., I'd be more enthusiastic to work if I was around people that work a lot more; you get things you don't like and you think, no way, I'm not going to study for that).

Environmental support:

- *Involvement in tutorial groups:*   Some enjoyed the tutorials (e.g., she makes things more interesting than they really are), but most did not (e.g., it doesn't propel you to want to learn more; I find the tutorials fairly boring).
- *Resubmission of major essay:*   Most saw this as a way of passing the assignment, rather than as a way of improving their understanding (e.g., it gives you more chance of getting better marks instead of handing one thing in and total failure; if you get a bad mark you've been told where you can fix it up). One did not like having to resubmit (I feel I've done with it and I don't want to do it again).
- *Essay writing booklet:*   Most made use of the booklet, though some did not (e.g., it wasn't concise enough; I didn't use it a lot, but I think it would have been useful).

- *Choice of topics*:   They could choose something of interest, though one preferred no choice (I'd rather be told exactly what to do).

Group 6 (*N* = 5)

What distinguished Group 6 from Group 5 was stronger self-discipline.
Emotional response.   The subject was boring.
Motivational goals.   The goal was academic alienation (e.g., all I want to do is pass; I'm passing at the moment and that's all I want).
Study strategies:

- *Reading*:   They did not enjoy reading but they did what they thought was necessary (e.g., I don't do extra reading ... it's irrelevant if I'm not going to be tested on it; it's get out the textbook, I force myself).
- *Note-taking*:   Notes were taken, but there was no mention of carefully constructed notes. Interestingly, two students indicated that they knew how to take good quality notes, but chose not to do so (*Interviewer*: And do you do your beautiful summaries like you did for rural technology? *Student*: No, I just do summaries of the lectures. I don't use any strategies for this course ... I think you actually have to know what you're talking about before you do that).

Notions about learning.   Some naive ideas emerged (Everyone's got a different view on child development. You'd think they'd get it right! Take Piaget and every other broke, and buy them all, and just pick the norm; if you don't pass tests, that's basically what you're at uni for ... when you go to the tut, you only have about twenty minutes on the actual stuff you have to know for the exam, and the other hour and twenty minutes is on real world sort of situations).
Self discipline.   All indicated a firm resolve to pass, regardless of their lack of interest (I don't quit, they'll have to throw me out first; when the going gets tough, you dig in and slog away; I sort of slug through it; there's a self discipline in what I do).
Environmental support:

- *Involvement in tutorials*:   There was little enthusiasm for tutorials (e.g., even when we're discussing adolescence, they're not relating it back to classroom things; once it started going over my head I just switched off; it gets a bit boring in two hours).
- *Resubmission of the major essay*:   This gave them a chance to correct their mistakes (e.g., gives you a chance to pull up your marks; it helps you see what you did wrong).

- *Choice of essay topics:* Something of interest could be selected, though one student found it difficult to choose the easiest one (it made it hard to decide ... some topics may be harder to research than other topics).

Summary

Group 1 was distinguished by a positive attitude, a mastery motivation, self-discipline, effective cognitive and metacognitive study strategies (including a deliberate search for underlying themes, relating new information to prior knowledge, wide reading, and sophisticated note taking), keen involvement in tutorial discussion, and a mastery response to assessment. Group 2 resembled Group 1 except that Group 2 endorsed a performance goal more strongly than a mastery goal. This performance orientation was evident in their reactions to assessment. For example, they were uneasy with resubmission of assignments, because it unfairly gave weaker students a chance to catch up to high achieving students.

Group 3 was distinguished by a positive attitude, a mastery motivation, self-discipline, study strategies not as sophisticated as those of Groups 1 and 2 (in particular, there was fewer references to looking for underlying themes and wide reading), keen involvement in tutorial groups and a mastery approach to assessment. Group 4 students resembled Group 3 students in most respects. They differed in goal orientation, describing an academic alienation goal of wanting to do no more than pass even though they quite enjoyed the subject, admitting that their interest and their time were directed elsewhere.

Group 5 was distinguished by boredom, an alienation goal of wanting to do just enough to pass the subject because it was boring or irrelevant, minimal reading, unsophisticated study strategies (such as copying lecturers' notes verbatim without taking additional self-generated notes), a preference for the external regulation of high school rather than the greater self discipline of university, generally minimal involvement in tutorial activities, and a positive reaction to environmental supports such as the resubmission of the major assignment in as much as it enabled them to pass the subject. Group 6 resembled Group 5. In both groups, some students indicated naive epistemological beliefs and reasons for study. Group 6, however, indicated a greater degree of self-discipline than Group 5. However boring or irrelevant they found the subject, they were determined to do enough work to pass it.

The six groups then were linked with the grades students received for the subject, using the formula: high distinction = 4; distinction = 3; credit = 2; pass = 1; fail = 0.

Group 1:   mean = 3.00, SD = 0.00 (N = 7)
Group 2:   mean = 3.00, SD = 0.00 (N = 2)
Group 3:   mean = 1.57, SD = 0.51 (N = 14)
Group 4:   mean = 1.75, SD = 0.50 (N = 4)
Group 5:   mean = 0.63, SD = 0.52 (N = 8)
Group 6:   mean = 1.00, SD = 0.00 (N = 5)

If the six groups are reduced to three larger groups by combining Groups 1 and 2, Groups 3 and 4, and Groups 5 and 6, the mean grades are 3.00 (SD = 0.0), 1.61 (SD = 0.50), and 0.77 (SD = 0.44) respectively. That is, the groups represent high, average, and low achievement. These levels of achievement fit well with the motivational, emotional, volitional, and cognitive characteristics of the groups. High achieving students are enthusiastic, mastery-oriented or a combination of mastery and performance-oriented, self-disciplined, and make use of effective study strategies. Low achieving students lack enthusiasm, adopt the goal of doing just sufficient work to pass the subject, generally lack self discipline (though one group was notably self-disciplined) and use ineffective study strategies. Average students generally are enthusiastic, mastery-oriented, though there was one alienated group, self-disciplined, but lacked the more sophisticated study strategies that distinguish the high achievers.

STUDENTS' REACTIONS TO TUTORIALS

Students' descriptions of the tutorials reveal a web of motivational, social, emotional, and cognitive factors. Students' descriptions of 10 tutorials are labeled D1 to D10 in the appendix. Of the 40 students interviewed, 27 enjoyed the tutorials while 13 did not. Breaking this down by group: Group 1, six positive and one negative; Group 2, two positive; Group 3, thirteen positive and one negative; Group 4, all four positive; Group 5, two positive and six negative, and Group 6, all five negative.

There were four reasons for disliking a tutorial: they were stiff and formal with students worried about public humiliation if they gave a wrong answer (e.g., D8); the subject was irrelevant (e.g., D7); the subject was boring (e.g., D9); or the subject was too difficult (e.g., D10). When students enjoyed tutorials, they combined the following aspects (e.g., D1 to D6). There was a lot of interaction between the lecturer and the students and among the students themselves. The atmosphere was easy, relaxed, friendly, and frequently humorous. Students were encouraged to give their opinions and they knew they would not be ridiculed for a wrong answer. Lecturers made the subject interesting by giving personal anecdotes that showed a theory in action, and encouraging students to think of their own pertinent experiences.

Three questions were raised. Can environmental experiences alter students' motivation? What are the links among emotion, interest, and motivation? What is the role of social interaction in learning? These questions are examined separately though it is artificial to do so because these variables operate in a fluid, interconnected manner. Points of connection among the questions are noted in the discussion.

Environmental Influences on Achievement Goals

There is considerable evidence (see Ames, 1992) that it is possible to encourage students to adopt one achievement goal over another by manipulating the environment. In this subject, as noted earlier (Archer & Scevak, 1998), there were measures implemented to encourage students to adopt a mastery goal while they were working on the major assignment. In addition, most tutorials had a pleasant, relaxed atmosphere where students were encouraged to ask questions and to give their opinion without fear of ridicule. Time was allotted for sharing ideas with other students and work was returned privately with no public announcement of marks.

Obviously, these measures were not sufficient to encourage most students in this study to adopt a mastery goal. In fact, more than 40% of the students indicated an alienation goal, and two students in Group 2 showed strong performance goals. Interestingly, all students in Group 4 who endorsed an alienation goal reacted positively to the mastery elements of the tutorials (e.g., D4). It seems that students' goals, if firmly established, are not amenable to environmental manipulation. On the other hand, three students said that their initial misgivings were overturned by their tutorial experiences (*I have to admit that I didn't have a lot of interest in the course to begin with, but now I do in tutorials, it's very interesting; at the beginning I thought this looks like it'll be terrible, but I really like it now ... you have good conversations ... she's very approachable too; at first I didn't like the course and I was worried that it would be boring, but it turned out to be very good ... the lecturer was really helpful and made the class more interesting*).

There was little mention of performance goals in the interviews. Some students who publicly endorsed an alienation goal (all I want to do is pass) in private may have held a performance-avoidance goal (I don't want to look incompetent in front of others). There were few environmental cues for adoption of a performance goal. The subject ran in the first year before most students realized that they would be competing for jobs. There was no quota system whereby only a small number of students would be admitted into the second year. Although grading was expected to conform roughly to a normal distribution, most students were not aware of this. Finally, when students were asked whether or not they felt they were being encouraged to compete with their peers (this section of the interview was not included here), the overwhelming answer was no. The two performance oriented students seem to have brought a competitive spirit with them.

Emotion, Interest, and Motivation

The positive emotions students mentioned when describing tutorials included enjoyment, relaxation, and feeling comfortable (e.g., D3, D4, D5). What was not mentioned explicitly, but which emerged when students described tutorials as *friendly* was a sense of belonging, of being an accepted member of a group (considered in more detail in the next section). Students spoke of the way the lecturer gave personal anecdotes relating to the topic and then encouraged students to respond with anecdotes of their own. Sharing personal stories and jokes can generate an intimate, friendly atmosphere.

What also emerges from this sense of acceptance is the confidence that, with help if necessary, one will be able to do the work. (For example: *if you're having problems with something she'll take the time to help you understand it; it's like she's there to help all of us ... I think she really does worry if we don't get it, she's not getting across to us; in the massed lecture you wonder what they're talking about ... you go to the tut and you understand it.*) This sense of competence fits Bandura's (1993) construct of self-efficacy. Students who lack confidence in their ability to do a task are unlikely to exert effort to complete it. Social interaction can enhance self-efficacy. If students lacking confidence see students similar to themselves involved in discussions, asking for help, and producing acceptable work, then their self-efficacy may rise (Zimmerman, 2000).

As mentioned earlier, interest can be categorized as individual or situational. Here it is likely that students' interest is situational rather than individual because, for almost all of them, this was their first exposure to psychology. Research on situational interest has focused mainly on texts and the characteristics that increase students' interest in them and their ability to recall information from them (Krapp, Hidi, & Renninger, 1992). Two factors appear to contribute to text-based interest: the first is novelty or surprise, unexpected events or ideas; and the second is universal themes of human life. These factors also may explain interest in a "live" context such as a tutorial.

When students were asked why a tutorial was interesting they named the following: the lecturer provided personal anecdotes that tied in with the theory under discussion; the lecturer encouraged students to provide their own; and the lecturer encouraged discussion among students where different points of view would emerge (e.g., D1 to D6). Anecdotes are stories about human life, and possibly include surprise if the anecdote was unusual or concerned a problem resolved in an unexpected way. The interest generated may be more pronounced than it would be in a text because the physical presence of the narrator (and, in the case of the lecturer, a more powerful academic figure) would add intensity to the anecdote. Students frequently mentioned the benefits of hearing other points of view. This aspect could be classified as surprise or incongruity, finding that another student holds a point of view different from one's own. Humor often generates interest through surprising or incongruous endings.

Interest generated in a tutorial may encourage the adoption of a mastery goal. Another interpretation might be that situational interest has changed into individual interest. In the previous section, excerpts from interviews with three students showed them initially expecting to dislike the subject but then adopting a mastery goal because of their tutorial experiences. In each case, the mediating factor was interest. Because interest often is linked with enjoyment, this finding may provide support for Boekaerts' (1993) argument that emotions can precipitate the adoption of a motivational goal. Students' pleasure in a subject may be the result of the stimulation of interest. The interaction among interest, enjoyment, and a mastery orientation undoubtedly is complex and may not easily fit a linear model. There were no instances of students being eager to learn but finding the subject boring and adopting an alienation goal. To complicate matters further, there were students in Groups 4, 5, and 6 who found tutorials interesting but who did not adopt a mastery goal.

Social Context of Learning

Students' descriptions of tutorials allowed an examination of social aspects of learning. It was not possible to explore students' social goals or social-academic goals in detail because the appropriate questions were not asked. Students were asked the more general questions about the attitudes toward tutorials. When students describe tutorials as friendly and relaxed, this suggests the realization of the goal to be accepted as a member of a group (Wentzel, 1999). Because the subject ran in first year, the desire to belong may have been particularly pronounced. In addition, as mentioned previously, the sense of belonging to an academic group may provide a subtle confidence boost to nervous, anxious students who worry about their coping with the work. The friendly atmosphere gives them the courage to ask for help (e.g., D5).

There were many aspects of students' descriptions that fit Vygotsky's notion of assisted learning (Vygotsky, 1987). If students admitted that they were having trouble understanding a concept, the lecturer or a fellow student provided another way of explaining it, frequently using an example that connected more closely with students' prior experience. Discussion raised different points of view and this helped students delineate their own position more clearly. The previous section on interest is pertinent here: what students describe as interesting and therefore memorable are the personal anecdotes relating to the topic and the discussions. Some students commented that the massed lecture confused them, and that it was in the tutorial that things began to make sense.

DISCUSSION

Grouping Students

Categorizing students according to their motivations, emotions, self-discipline, study strategies, and response to environmental support provided in a university subject produced six groups. Even though three of the groups contained small numbers, their distinctiveness and theoretical interest warranted their inclusion. If the six groups are reduced to three larger groups in terms of high, average, and low achievement, the main characteristic defining each group is the effectiveness of their study strategies: from sophisticated cognitive and metacognitive strategies for Groups 1 and 2 to relatively few and unsophisticated strategies for Groups 5 and 6. This makes sense because study strategies are more proximal to achievement than other aspects such as motivation (Pintrich & Garcia, 1991). Also, achievement was related, roughly, to students' university entrance scores. Students in more sought-after areas such as primary, physical education, or English teaching tended to get higher grades than students with lower entrance scores entering mathematics, science, or design and technology teaching.

It is useful to compare the groups identified here with those identified in the quantitative cluster analyses that also use older students. Group 1 of high achieving, mastery-oriented, self-disciplined students who use effective study strategies has much in common with Pintrich's (1989) "good student" cluster. Similarly, Group 5 of low achieving, alienated, ill disciplined students who use few sophisticated study strategies resembles Pintrich's "poor student" cluster. There also are similarities with Ainley's (1993) "disengaged" students. Ainley's "committed" cluster resemble Group 2 in that the cluster contained students who were both mastery and performance oriented, used elaboration strategies, and were high achievers. Finally, Group 3 of mastery-oriented, keen and committed students who lack the sophisticated study strategies that lead to high achievement resembles Ainley's "engaged" cluster.

Group 2 was interesting because it showed two high achieving performance-oriented students displaying the sorts of desirable characteristics (sophisticated study strategies, enthusiasm, self-discipline) generally associated with mastery-oriented students. Harackiewicz et al. (1998) argue that a performance approach goal coupled with a mastery goal is adaptive for learning at the university level. Though undoubtedly the major goal was getting a high grade, both indicated that doing better than others without understanding the content would be pointless. Group 4, another small group, was distinctive because of students' motivation to do no more than was necessary: other parts of their lives were more important, even though they reacted favorably to the mastery aspects of the subject. Both Groups 2 and 4 show evidence of multiple achievement goals, though with one goal stronger than the other.

Groups 5 and 6 both held an alienation goal of doing just enough work to pass the subject because they found it boring or irrelevant. Group 6 was distinguished from Group 5 because these students indicated a high level of self-discipline, that no matter how much they disliked the subject, they would persevere with it. It is interesting to see a high level of self-discipline in a low achieving group because self-discipline usually is associated with high achieving students. However, if a student's goal is to do enough to pass a subject, and he or she takes the steps to achieve it, then there is self-discipline even though poor quality work is produced (Alexander, 1995). Perhaps volition in low achievers may be stronger than in high achievers because they do not have the level of interest that would make the work less onerous.

The other aspect of note is the large numbers of students endorsing an alienation goal. In the absence of a strong performance climate and in the presence of a "mild" mastery climate, it seems that students adopt either a mastery or an alienation goal. Academic alienation goals need further investigation both alone and in concert with other goals. In addition, it may be useful to distinguish two types of alienation goal: wanting to get by with little effort because of competing non-academic goals, and wanting to get by because the subject is irrelevant or boring.

Students' Reactions to Tutorials

The social aspects of the tutorials attract students and fulfill two purposes. First, they provide a place to find friends and a place to be with friends. Second, social interaction helps students to learn. The role of the lecturer in stimulating learning is pivotal. He or she must create an atmosphere where students feel relaxed and comfortable about voicing their opinion and asking for help (see Seifert, 1997). This can enhance students' confidence that they can pass the subject. Personal anecdotes give color to topics, and hearing others' points of view helps students to sort out their own position. This picture of highly interactive tutorials brings to mind Volet's (1991) study of computer programming students. Students in tutorials dominated by whole group discussion about a common computing problem, compared with students working independently on individual problems, performed better on more demanding examination questions and went on to take more advanced subjects in computer programming.

Interest emerged as an important variable. It was mentioned frequently, usually in conjunction with enjoyment. There was evidence of interest precipitating the adoption of a mastery goal, and this supports Boekaerts' (1993) and Seifert's (1997) argument that positive emotional experiences can encourage the adoption of a mastery goal. Obviously, interest generated within a tutorial needs to be carried over to personal study (catch and hold). As students remarked, it is easier to study something interesting than something dull. An attributional study with the same group of students as the present study (Scevak & Archer, 1995) produced noteworthy results. When the students were asked to explain why they did well or did poorly in a subject in high school or at university, interest and lack of interest emerged as the most common attributions, usually in conjunction with effort (e.g., I found it so interesting that I spent a lot of time studying it). Interest figures strongly in students' understanding of the world. As noted earlier, researchers have acknowledged the need to delineate more clearly the distinctive characteristics of interest, intrinsic motivation, and a mastery goal.

Examination of achievement goals within tutorials presented complex results. There was evidence of goals being changed because the subject turned out more interesting than expected. On the other hand, some students maintained an original alienation goal even though they reacted positively to the mastery elements of the tutorials. As Dweck (1986) argues, it is likely that the strength of one's personal goal (for example, the strong performance orientation of two students in a climate that did not encourage a performance goal) influences the extent to which environmental cues can effect a change in motivation.

Limitations of the Study

Three points should be noted. First, there was no analysis of students' responses by tutorial lecturer. This would have allowed analysis of the influence of the lecturer on students' approach to study. This did not occur because of the uneven distribution of students and lecturers: some lecturers took up to five tutorial groups while others took only one or two tutorials. That led to wide variation in the interview data so that a few lecturers were referred to frequently while others were referred to only once or twice. It is interesting to note, however, that for the lecturer who took the tutorial sessions of nine of the 40 interviewed students, these students were categorized into four groups. It appears that a lecturer (even a vivacious and experienced lecturer) does not exert a major influence on students' choice of goals. Second, the relatively small sample size means that the results of the study must be accepted with caution, particularly so for the groups that contained small numbers of students.

Third, though not necessarily a limitation, the sociocultural context of the study should be noted. The students were attending an Australian university and studying to become teachers. As discussed earlier, the subject under study did not have the strong competitive atmosphere that often characterizes university study. The subject was compulsory for all students, and it had a strong career focus (that is, understanding how students change as they age will help student teachers to become professional teachers). Students from other cultures, students further advanced in university study, or students less sure of their career path may react differently.

CONCLUSION

Analysis of interview data with first year university students produced six groups that varied according to their emotions, motivations, self-discipline, study strategies, and response to the environmental and assessment aspects of a university subject. Four of the groups were similar to groups identified in quantitative cluster analyses. Two smaller groups did not fit previously identified clusters but they warrant further attention. One of these groups displayed multiple achievement goals (academic alienation and mastery) while the other was notable for its combination of alienation, negative emotions, poor strategies, but strong self-discipline.

Academically alienated students do not respond readily to attempts to improve their motivation. For example, consider resubmission of the assignment following useful feedback. This did not work as intended to increase the mastery orientation of alienated students. Rather, they saw it as a means of reaching their original goal (it gives me the chance to bring a failing piece of work up to a passable standard). The students who reacted positively were those who already were mastery oriented. Similarly, it was these students who welcomed other mastery-oriented aspects such as a strategies-booklet and informative tutorial sessions.

The examination of context has shown the benefits of social interaction. Tutorials can satisfy social goals while simultaneously improving understanding of subject matter. For some students, too, social interaction may help increase their confidence in the subject. For tutorials to work well lecturers must generate interest in the subject matter, bringing it to life with personal anecdotes, and involving students in discussions about it. Because most research on situational interest has focused on texts, more work needs to be done on the way in which interest is generated in social situations, and the connection between situational interest and the adoption of a mastery goal.

All students can benefit from mastery-oriented social interaction. The ones who probably benefit the most are mastery-oriented students who lack the understanding and study strategies that characterize high achieving students. These high achievers usually have the skills and self-discipline to learn relatively independently. In an era when university study is increasingly on-line (note the courses that do not require attendance on campus), it is pertinent to remind ourselves of the benefits of social interaction.

APPENDIX

Students' Descriptions of Tutorials, Labeled D1 to D 10.

D1:   I find the lecturer really good, entertaining … it's got a friendly atmosphere … everyone has their opinion and doesn't mind giving their opinion, no-one's worried if they're wrong … she explains it in really simple terms, step by step, and gives examples … makes it relevant. (Group 1)

D2:   We have a fair bit of fun and we get a fair amount of work done … he has the practical knowledge, brings up the experiences he's had … he links what we do in lectures to other things … we get our input and our various perspectives. (Group 2)

D3:   If somebody puts up a wrong answer she doesn't say, no that's wrong, She tries to figure out why they've come up with that answer, and see what their point of view is … she treats us as individuals … she's very approachable … willing to help. (Group 3)

D4:   We get to talk, we get to use our opinions. And it's a lot more informal than a lecture. You feel comfortable because there's not a lot of people and the lecturer's willing to listen to what you've got to say … she uses practical examples of the theory which helps us to understand it ... and the discussion helps because it gives other people's views of what they're learning. (Group 4)

D5: We get the opportunity to sit in our little groups ... we discuss what we've read. I find that to be invaluable because there's sometimes I'll come up against something that I might not understand, but one of the people in the group might understand better and they can explain it to me ... if she asks for an answer and you're wrong, it's OK ... people in her workshop are not frightened to answer because they know if they're wrong they're not going to be put down and feel like idiots ... she'll draw on her own experiences and give them to the students in a way that is really quite wonderful ... if the lecturer makes it interesting then you'll go out and read more. (Group J)

D6: The group work is good, it's more casual, you don't feel restricted ... the lecturer's funny ... she uses things from her own experience which is really interesting and then you think, oh yeah, I remember the time that happened to me, and you reflect on your own thing. And that's probably what makes it most interesting, actually, when she brings up things that happened to her. (Group 3)

D7: Tutorials are OK, but sometimes I fail to see the relevancy of the things we do because we're going to be high school teachers ... our course has been centered around birth to pre-adolescent ... we don't get them till they're thirteen years old, so why go through the child psychology ... we go off into little groups each week and we discuss what we've learned in the mass lectures ... and that helps us enjoy the course. It helps you to understand it more if you're discussing it with someone else in the course, rather than just writing it down and reading through it because you get their ideas on things. (Group 6)

D8: Our class is really stiff, we really don't say much, but when people do you can get things from it. It's sort of selected on the roll, some people have to prepare questions for next week ... even me, when I get up there ... you're so nervous ... it's sort of painful watching people out there ... the hot flushes people get, the nerve rashes ... everyone wants to get the best mark ... it's high expectations but the pressure gets too much sometimes. (Group 1)

D9: You could have good discussions with him ... but once it started getting over my head I just switched off ... he'll relate it back to an experience he's had in real life, so you could see where he's coming from. (Group 6)

D10:   I think they're good. Some things I don't understand though. Words and things just go straight over my head ... she makes things more interesting than what I see they really are ... I understand things like stories and little examples of things, and she uses a lot of them ... I have problems writing essays and things like that which probably puts down my marks. (Group 5)

REFERENCES

Ainley, M. (1993). Styles of engagement with learning: Multidimensional assessment of their relationship with strategy use and school achievement. *Journal of Educational Psychology, 85*, 395–405.

Alexander, P.A. (1995). Superimposing a situation-specific and domain-specific perspective on an account of self-regulated learning. *Educational Psychologist, 30*, 189–194.

Ames, C. (1992). Classroom: Goals, structures, and student motivation. *Journal of Educational Psychology, 84*, 261–271.

Archer, J. (1994). Achievement goals as a measure of motivation in university students. *Contemporary Educational Psychology, 84*, 261–271.

Archer, J., & Scevak, J.J. (1998). Enhancing students' motivation to learn: Achievement goals in university classrooms. *Educational Psychology, 18*, 205–223.

Bandura, A. (1993). Perceived self-efficacy in cognitive development and functioning. *Educational Psychologist, 28*, 117–148.

Boekaerts, M. (1993). Being concerned with well-being and with learning. *Educational Psychologist, 28,*149–167.

Boekaerts, M. (1997). Self-regulated learning: A new concept embraced by researchers, policy makers, educators, teachers, and students. *Learning and instruction, 7*, 161–186.

Corno, L., & Kanfer, R. (1993), The role of volition in learning and performance. *Review of Research in Education, 19*, 301–341.

Dweck, C.S. (1986). Motivational processes affecting learning. *American Psychologist, 41*, 1040–1048.

Garcia, T., McCann, E.J., Turner, J.E., & Roska, L. (1998). Modeling the mediating role of volition in the learning process. *Contemporary Educational Psychology, 23*, 392–418.

Harackiewicz, J.M., Barron, K.E., & Elliot, A.E. (1998). Rethinking achievement goals: When are they adaptive for college students and why? *Educational Psychologist, 33*, 1–21.

Harackiewicz, J.M., Barron, K.E., Tauer, J. M., Carter, S. M., & Elliot, A.E. (2000). Short-term and long-term consequences of achievement goals in the college classroom: Maintaining interest and making the grade. *Journal of Educational Psychology, 92*, 316–330.

Hickey, D.T. (1997). Motivation and contemporary socio-constructivist instructional perspectives. *Educational Psychologist, 32*, 175–193.

Hidi, S. (1990). Interest and its contribution as a mental resource for learning. *Review of Educational Research, 60,* 549–571.

Hidi, S., & Harackiewicz, J. M. (2001). Motivating the academically unmotivated: A critical issue for the 21st century. *Review of Educational Research, 70,* 151–179.

Kuhl, J, (1985). Volitional mediators of cognition-behavior consistency: Self-regulatory processes and action versus state orientation. In J. Kuhl & J. Beckmann (Eds.), *Action control: From cognition to behavior* (pp. 101–128). New York: Springer-Verlag.

Maehr, M.L. (1984). Meaning and motivation. In R. Ames and C. Ames (Eds.), *Research on motivation in education: Student motivation (Vol. 1).* New York: Academic Press.

McKeachie,W.J., Pintrich, P.R., Smith, D.A.F., Lin, Y.G., & Sharma, R. (1990). *Teaching and learning in the college classroom.* Ann Arbor, MI: National Center for Research to Improve Postsecondary Teaching and Learning.

Meece, J.L., & Holt, K. (1993). A pattern analysis of students' achievement goals. *Journal of Educational Psychology, 85,* 582–590.

Murphy, P. K., Alexander, P. A. (2000). A motivated explanation of motivation terminology. *Contemporary Educational Psychology, 25,* 3–53.

Paris, S.G., & Turner, J.C. (1994). Situated motivation. In P. Pintrich, D. Brown, & C. Weinstein (Eds.), *Student motivation, cognition, and learning. Essays in honor of Wilbert J. McKeachie* (pp. 213–237). Hillsdale, NJ: Lawrence Erlbaum.

Pintrich, P.R. (1989). The dynamic interplay of student motivation and cognition in the college classroom. In M. L. Maehr and P. R. Pintrich (Eds.), *Advances in motivation and achievement: Motivation enhancing environments* (Vol. 6) (pp. 117–160). Greenwich, CT: JAI Press.

Pintrich, P.R., & Garcia, T. (1991). Student goal orientation and self-regulation in the college classroom. In M. L. Maehr & P. R. Pintrich (Eds.), *Advances in motivation and achievement: Goals and self-regulatory processes* (Vol. 7) (pp. 371–402). Greenwich, CT: JAI Press.

Renninger, K. A., Hidi, S., & Krapp, A. (Eds.)(1992). *The role of interest in learning and development.* Hillsdale, NJ: Lawrence Erlbaum.

Salomon, G. (1991). Transcending the qualitative-quantitative debate: The analytic and systemic approaches to educational research. *Educational Researcher, 20* (6), 10–18.

Scevak, J., & Archer, J. (1995). *Exploring success and failure with university students: Layers of attributions, and the highlighting of interest as a motivational variable.* Paper presented at the annual meeting of the Australian Association for Research in Education, Hobart, Tasmania, November 26–30. Published at www.aare.edu.au/index.htm (archj.305).

Seifert, T.L. (1997). Academic goals and emotions: Results of a structural equation and a cluster analysis. *British Journal of Educational Psychology, 67,* 323–338.

Turner, J.C., Thorpe, P.K., & Meyer, D.K. (1998). Students' reports of motivation and negative affect: A theoretical and empirical analysis. *Journal of Educational Psychology, 90,* 758–771.

Vermunt, J.D. (1998). The regulation of constructive learning processes. *British Journal of Educational Psychology, 68,* 149–171.

Volet, S.E. (1991). Modelling and coaching of relevant metacognitive strategies for enhancing university students' learning. *Learning and Instruction, 1,* 319–336.

Vygotsky, L.S. (1987). *Mind in society: The development of higher psychological processes.* Cambridge, MA: Harvard University Press.

Wentzel, K. R. (1999). Social-motivational processes and interpersonal relationships: Implications for understanding motivation at school. *Journal of Educational Psychology, 91,* 76–97.

Wentzel, K. R. (2000). What is it that I'm trying to achieve? Classroom goals from a content perspective. *Contemporary Educational Psychology, 25,* 105–115.

Wertsch, J. V. (1991). *Voices of the mind. A sociocultural approach to mediated action.* Cambridge, MA: Harvard University Press.

Zimmerman, B. J. (2000). Self-efficacy: An essential motive to learn. *Contemporary Educational Psychology, 25,* 82–91.

CHAPTER 8

MOTIVATION AND SELF-REGULATION:

A CROSS-CULTURAL COMPARISON OF THE EFFECT OF CULTURE AND CONTEXT OF LEARNING ON STUDENT MOTIVATION AND SELF-REGULATION

Farideh Salili, Ho-ying Fu, Yuk-yue Tong, and Diana Tabatabai

ABSTRACT

This study compared motivational orientation and self-regulation of Chinese students in Hong Kong, Chinese Canadian students and Canadian students of European origin studying in Montreal Junior Colleges (CGEP). The results showed that Hong Kong students spent more time studying than Canadian students, but had lower marks, were more anxious, perceived themselves to be less competent, and engaged in less appropriate self-regulatory activities than their Canadian counterparts. Differences between Canadian Chinese and Hong Kong Chinese in motivational orientation reflected differences in learning and teaching methods used in the two different educational contexts as well as cultural differences.

INTRODUCTION

The goal of education has traditionally been to equip students with the skills necessary to deal with problems in everyday life. However, in an increasingly complex information age, the skills and knowledge that we gain in schools become obsolete as new information is introduced on an almost daily basis. Thus, it is important to equip students with an adaptive pattern of learning motivation and self-regulatory skills to enable them to be lifelong learners. Such learning motivation and skills however, do not develop in a vacuum. Educators must provide learning contexts that help students acquire skills that enable them to learn for themselves (Maehr, 1996; Salili, 1995; Volet, Renshaw, & Tietzel, 1994; Zimmerman, Bonner, & Kovach, 1996).

This chapter will examine the significance of learning contexts on student motivation and self-regulation by comparing students in two different contexts of learning namely, Grades 12 and 13 Chinese students in Hong Kong, and Chinese and European Canadian students in Canada. More specifically, this chapter will report on the differences in the motivational beliefs, self-regulation, actual effort (actual time spent studying), and performance between these groups. In addition the relationship between motivational beliefs and self-regulation will be examined to see if previous findings in the West are applicable to a different culture?

THEORETICAL BACKGROUND

Self-Regulation

The role of self-regulation of cognition in learning has been the focus of much research in recent years. According to Zimmerman, Bonner, and Kovach (1996) "Academic self-regulation refers to self-regulated thoughts, feelings, and actions intended to attain specific educational goals, such as analyzing a reading assignment, preparing to take a test, or writing a paper" (p. 2). Three components of self-regulation are particularly important in learning and performance (Pintrich & De Groot, 1990): The first component is the metacognitive strategies used in planning, monitoring, and if necessary modifying one's own cognition. The second component is control and management of effort in learning or in performing an academic task (Zimmerman & Pons, 1988). A student could, for example, persist at a difficult task, or maintain cognitive engagement by blocking out distractions (Corno & Snow, 1986). The third aspect of self-regulated learning is the actual cognitive strategies used by the students to learn, understand, and remember the learning material (Zimmerman & Pons,

1988). Strategies such as rehearsal, elaboration and organizational strategies help learners sustain active cognitive engagement and have higher levels of achievement (Pintrich & DeGroot, 1990). However, Pintrich and De Groot (1990) reported that in a factor analysis of the Motivated Strategies for Learning Questionnaire (MSLQ), metacognitive strategies and effort management strategies appeared as one factor rather than two independent factors. Pintrich et al. renamed this factor "self-regulation strategies."

Self-regulation is closely linked with motivation. Research evidence has shown that highly motivated students engage in self-regulatory activities that help them achieve their goals. Such activities in turn promote learning, self-competence and motivation (Schunk, 1991).

Zimmerman and Kitsantas (1997) proposed a social cognitive approach to the development of self-regulatory skills involving four phases. The first phase, "cognitive-motor skill observation," involves observational learning by hearing or observing a model with the expertise to be learned. The second phase is imitation—in this phase, the learner imitates cognitive or motor skills personally and receives feedback or guidance from a teacher. The third phase is self-control in which the learner performs cognitive-motor skills automatically. To develop to this automatic level, the learner needs to practice by herself/himself without relying on the model. During this phase, strategies that focus on efficient execution of important skills such as process goals and self-monitoring, will help the learner attain automaticity (Zimmerman & Kitsantas, 1997). In the final phase, the student learns to adapt his/her skills to a dynamic and changing environment. The learner can perform skills automatically without intentional thought, and is able to shift attention to the outcome goal without detrimental consequences. According to Zimmerman et al., the important distinction between the self-control and self-regulation phase is the need for the learner to focus first on performance processes when they practice on their own instead of outcome goals. For a novice learner focusing on the outcome goal is problematic, because the learner makes a "maladroit process adjustment" before he or she learns self-evaluative skills. Once fundamental processes are mastered, students can benefit from shifting their goals to learning outcomes. The novice learner can avoid the frustrations of trial and error by focusing on the practice of strategic processing observed from an expert model. The process goals not only help students learn the key techniques, but also enhance their self-efficacy beliefs about future success and their self-perceptions of progress, hence, increasing student motivation.

From the above account, two important conclusions can be derived: first, the social cognitive approach to self-regulation implies that social factors reflected in the culture and the context of learning are very important in learning self-regulatory skills. Second, there is a close link between self-regulation and motivation. As Zimmerman et al. noted, process goals appear to be very similar to the learning goal orientation described by Dweck (1986) and outcome goals appear to be similar to performance orientation goals. From Zimmerman et al.'s perspective, however, process and outcome goals are related to different phases of self-regulatory development, whereas from the point of view of goal theory, goal orientations are guided by the learner's purposes for learning. In the following section, the literature on goal orientation theory will be discussed. In the study presented in this chapter, we examined the relationship between self-regulation and goal orientations.

Learning Motivation

Student motivation is often explained through the expectancy by value theory of motivation (Eccles, 1983). The theory proposes three components of motivation. The expectancy component includes belief about one's ability or competence to perform a task. In the present study we used self-efficacy belief as a measure of expectancy. Perception of self-competence or self-efficacy refers to a student's belief in how well he or she could perform in a learning task and how responsible they are for their own performance (Bandura, 1994). Students' perceptions of self-efficacy have been associated with both motivation and the strategies that they use in learning. Students who believe in their own ability to do well in tasks engage in "more metacognitive strategies, and are more likely to persist at a task than students who do not believe they can perform the task" (Pintrich & De Groot, 1990, p. 34).

A second component is the value, goal or interest that a student has in learning the task. We used goal orientation as our value component. Motivational theories in recent years have used goal orientation theory to explain achievement behavior. Goal orientation refers to "different ways of approaching, engaging in, and responding to achievement situations" (Ames, 1992b, p. 261). It reflects students' reasons, purposes and goals for achieving in school (Ames, 1992a; Urdan & Maehr 1995). While all students in a class may strive to do well, the underlying reasons or goals for their behaviors could be different. As an example, the goal of one student may be to master the subject matter, while another student may strive to outperform other students. Research on goal theory has shown that goal orientations are related to behavioral indicators of motivation such as effort, persistence and task choice (Wolters, Yu, & Pintrich, 1996). Empirical evidence also shows that goal orientation has an effect on the kind of cognitive strategies students use in learning and the way they monitor and regulate their own learning (Wolters et al., 1996).

Among many goal orientations, learning goal (also referred to as task goal) and performance goal (also referred to as ego, competitive, or relative ability goal) orientations have been the focus of much research. Studies have found that students with learning goal orientation engage in learning activities that are directed at the deep knowledge, competence, and understanding of the subject matter (Ames, 1992b). Learning goal oriented students are good at regulating their own learning activities, they are less anxious, enjoy a high level of perceived self-competence (Pintrich & De Groot, 1990) and generally perform well in academic tasks. This pattern of learning is considered adaptive by western educators (Dweck & Leggett, 1988; Nichols, 1990).

Performance goal, on the other hand, is focused on ego-enhancement. Students with performance goal are concerned with how others judge their abilities as compared to their peers. They seek to prove their abilities by outperforming others. Depending on the situation, these students tend to engage in achieving strategies (Biggs, 1992) or surface learning and rote memorization (Ames, 1992b). Since their self-esteem is tied to the judgment of their abilities by others, they may avoid challenging tasks and failure (Ames, 1992b; Covington, 1992). In addition, students high in the performance goal are found to have high test-anxiety and low self-efficacy (Pintrich & De Groot, 1990; Wine, 1971).

Research has found that students' goal orientation is influenced by perception of the classroom goal structure, teaching method, and assessment practices (Ames, 1992a). A classroom context that emphasizes mastery of the subject matter, uses analytical or problem-based approaches to teaching, and criterion-referenced assessment will encourage students to adopt learning goals. On the other hand, a classroom structure that emphasizes competitive examinations will promote performance goal orientation.

There is some debate on whether learning and performance goals are independent of one another. One study (Nicholls, Cheung, Laurer, & Patashnick, 1989) reported that the correlation between task orientation and ego orientation was sufficiently low for these goal orientations to be considered more or less orthogonal. Similar findings were reported by other studies (see Kaplan & Maehr, 1996; Midgely, Anderman, & Hicks, 1995; Midgely & Urdan, 1995). However, some researchers have argued that students may have both learning and performance goals at the same time and indeed the integration of these two goal orientations may enhance academic performance by providing students with the flexibility to perform effectively in different learning contexts (Dweck & Leggett, 1988). Some support for this idea is found in studies conducted among Asian students (Biggs, 1993; Volet, Renshaw, & Tietzel, 1994). Biggs reported a study in which he found positive correlation between deep and achieving approaches (roughly the same as learning and performance goals respectively in American studies) among Asians. It is speculated that the culture and the context of learning in East Asian countries promote both goal orientations. This is necessary in order to cope with the demands placed on students both for academic excellence and self-improvement in a very competitive education system such as Hong Kong's (see Salili, 1995). Hence, in the present study we expected a positive correlation between learning and performance goals for the Chinese, but not for the European Canadian students.

Finally, the third component of the proposed model of academic motivation is affective response. According to Hill (1972, cited in Phillips, Pitcher, Worsham, & Miller, 1980), test-anxiety is an affective reaction to evaluative situations, especially, in testing situations. From a motivational perspective, high-test anxiety has been equated with fear of failure and motive to avoid failure. Hill found that while both motive to avoid failure and approach success are stronger in highly anxious students, these students are more motivated to avoid criticism than to seek praise. Low anxious children, on the other hand, "are more concerned about succeeding and obtaining approval" (p. 326). Many studies have found that differences in anxiety levels are at the root of differences in performance achieved by high and low anxious students (Wine, 1971). Low anxious students are more task-oriented and less concerned with external evaluation than high-anxious students (see Phillips et al., 1980 for a review of research on test-anxiety). Test anxiety is also linked to low self-efficacy (e.g., Nicholls, 1976), extrinsic motivation/ performance goal orientation, and difficulties in effort management (e.g., Tobias, 1985). However, the research evidence on these relationships has not always been consistent. Some research showed, for example, that highly anxious students and low anxious students are equally persistent on a task, but use different strategies (Pintrich et al., 1990). Hence, in our study, we also explored the relationship between test anxiety, motivational beliefs, effort and performance.

Culture and Context of Learning

The context of learning not only influences students' goal orientations, but also has a profound impact on students' self-regulation, continuing motivation, self-efficacy and sense of well-being (Biggs, 1992; Salili, Maehr, & Sorenson, 1976; Volet et al., 1994).

In one early study, we (Salili, Maehr, & Sorenson, 1976) compared the performance and continuing motivation of grade five Iranian students on a language related task following three evaluation conditions (teacher, self, and peer-comparison). In addition, the relationship between causal attributions for achievement, achievement motivation and students' responses to evaluation were also explored. The results of this study showed that while evaluation conditions had no effect on performance, they had a major impact on continuing motivation. Students in self-evaluation conditions had the highest level of continuing motivation while students under teacher-evaluation had the least continuing motivation and those in peer-evaluation condition fell in the middle.

The results also showed that when students attributed their achievement to themselves, they were more likely to exhibit continuing motivation.

More recent studies have confirmed these earlier findings. Stipek (1998), for example, reported several studies in which instructional environments and grading practices had negative effect on young children's self-perception of ability and competence (see also Stipek & Mac Ivar, 1989 for a review). These studies have also found that classroom contexts that arouse students' intrinsic motivation promote self-efficacy in students.

Relationship Between Cultural Values and Learning Context

In any society, the context of learning is shaped by the cultural values that are shared by the participants of that culture (Volet, 1999). These shared values are critical in determining what is perceived as appropriate to learn and how to go about learning it. The difference in cultural values and beliefs between Chinese and Canadians is also reflected in their educational context. Chinese culture is characterized by social orientation and collectivism (Salili, 1994). Under the influence of Confucian philosophy, the Chinese place great importance on filial piety, hard work, and education. Filial piety means loyalty and obedience toward one's parents and by extension, authority figures such as teachers. One way for children to fulfill their filial duties is to work hard and excel in academic work so as to make their parents and families' proud. Education is considered important in building character and in securing a good future (Salili, 1995). In ancient China, only the most knowledgeable scholars were assigned government and administrative positions. This was achieved through competitive civil examinations—a tradition which is believed to influence education systems in Chinese societies even today (Chen, Stevenson, Hayward, & Burgess, 1995).

The Chinese believe that the best way to learn a subject is through repeated practice and memorization (Liu, 1986). A typical classroom in a Hong Kong Chinese school is highly structured and teacher-centered. Teachers provide instructions, often in the form of lectures, while students take notes or listen quietly. This is often followed by assignments and exercises, as well as memorization of factual material. Students are given enormous amounts of homework and frequent tests and examinations (Salili, 1995). Evidence from Western studies suggests that such learning contexts promote performance goal and discourage students from adapting a learning goal (Ames, 1992b).

European Canadian culture on the other hand is based on the individualistic Western tradition, where individual achievement is not tied to the family. Stevenson and Lee (1990) explored values related to achievement in the United States and in Asia (i.e., Japan and Taiwan). They reported that Western parents were not as concerned with academic excellence so much as the all-round development of their children. The education context in Canada is more child-centered and less structured than in Hong Kong. The methods used in Western societies are often more project-oriented and analytical with less emphasis placed on evaluation than in Hong Kong.

Based on the above literature, we hypothesized that Canadian students would spend less time studying, but would be more learning goal oriented, and that they would have higher levels of self-regulation than their Hong Kong Chinese counterparts. It was also hypothesized that Hong Kong students would be higher on performance goal orientation than Canadian students. Since Chinese Canadian share Hong Kong students cultural heritage but have different education contexts, it was assumed that differences between these two groups would be largely the result of differences in their learning environment, while differences between Chinese and European Canadians would be the result of their cultural differences.

METHOD

Participants

Participants were 571 grade 12 and 13 students aged 17–19 senior high school students in Hong Kong ($N = 217$), Canadian students of Chinese origin (Chinese Canadian, $N = 66$) and Canadian students of European origin (European Canadian, $N = 288$) studying in junior colleges in Montreal Canada. All students were predominantly from middle socioeconomic backgrounds.

Measures and Procedures

Several of the measures of motivation administered, relevant to the present paper, were items relating to goal orientation (e.g., performance goal: "The main reason I would do an extra project is to get better grades"; learning goal: "The main reason I do my work in school is because I like to learn"), self-efficacy (e.g., "I am certain I can master the skills taught in school this year") and test anxiety (e.g., "I have an uneasy, upset feeling when I take a test") adapted from Patterns of Adaptive Learning Survey (PALS, Midgley, Maehr, & Urdan, 1993). We also included a direct measure of motivation, namely the amount of time students spent studying during a typical week (effort). The Items related to cognitive strategy and self-regulation were adapted from MSLQ (Pintrich & De Groot, 1990) and used to measure cognitive strategies (e.g., "When I study for a test, I try to put together the information from our class and from the book") and self-regulation (e.g., "I ask myself-questions to make sure I know the material I have been studying"). Both PALS and MSLQ have been used with Chinese students and found to be valid and reliable both in China and the United States. Students were asked to rate the relevant statements on 7-point scales, with 1 indicating that the statement is not at all/seldom true and 7 indicating that the statement is very true for them. They were also asked to indicate the amount of time they spent studying each day. Several measures of academic performance were also collected, including students' last mark for math, English and social science tests/projects as well as average performance in the last term's examinations. The results related to these measures were all similar. Hence, in this chapter, we included only the results concerning the average marks. The questionnaire was administered in a group setting in English for Canadian students and in Chinese for Hong Kong students. The Cronbach alpha reliability in this study ranged from .72–.89.

RESULTS

Exploratory Factor analysis performed on PAL showed roughly the same factors as originally described by Midgley, Maehr, and Urdan (1993), namely self-efficacy, test anxiety, learning goal, performance goal as well as other goal orientations not included in this chapter. Similar analysis performed on items from MSLQ relating to self-regulation and cognitive strategies showed much overlap between self-regulation and cognitive strategies. To be able to compare our results with the findings of previous studies, we decided to use the two theoretical factors for the purpose of further analyses after removing the problematic items.

Self-Regulation and Cognitive Strategies

As can be seen from the Table 1, one-way between-subject ANOVAs showed significant differences between the three groups on all variables. Hong Kong students scored significantly lower on self-regulation and cognitive strategies than both groups of Canadian students. To explore a common belief that Chinese students' predominant mode of learning strategy is memorization, we conducted a one way ANOVA on memorization strategies (i.e., memorization items extracted from cognitive strategy scale) with culture as the independent variable. The results showed significant differences between the three groups of students, F (1, 553) = 94.27, $p < .0001$. Hong Kong students scored highest on the use of memorization strategies ($M = 4.00$), followed by Canadian Chinese ($M = 3.50$) and European Canadian students ($M = 3.19$). However, ANOVA on average performance with culture and memorization strategies as independent variables showed that memorization has no effect on performance.

Table 1.   Mean (And Standard Deviations) for Cognitive Strategy, Self-Regulation, Test Anxiety, Goal Orientations, Time Spent Studying and Grades For Hong Kong Chinese, Canadian Chinese and European Canadian Students

	Hong Kong Chinese N = 217	Canadian Chinese N = 66	European Canadian N = 288	F-Ratio
Cognitive Strategy	4.19[a] (.75)	4.67[b] (.87)	5.02[b] (.87)	77.33***
Self-Regulation	3.99[a] (.63)	4.47[b] (.88)	4.57[b] (.87)	34.6***
Test Anxiety	4.16[a] (.10)	3.81[b] (.17)	3.67[b] (.08)	7.37**
Learning Goal	3.91[a] (.07)	4.26[a] (.12)	4.45[b] (.06)	19.08**
Performance Goal	4.53 (.07)	4.86 (.13)	4.64 (.06)	2.59
Academic Self-Efficacy	3.99[a] (.06)	4.47[b] (.12)	4.76[b] (.06)	40.38**
Time Spent Studying (Effort)	5.51[a] (.11)	4.57[a] (.20)	4.17[b] (.09)	50.37**
Average Mark in Last Term Exam	2.47[a] (.10)	6.39b (.18)	6.02[b] (.09)	408.26**

Note: Group means, in each raw, with different superscript letters (i.e., a & b) indicate significant difference between groups. ** $p < .001$, *** $p < .0001$

Motivational Variables

The results showed that Hong Kong students worked harder by spending significantly more time studying, but were more anxious, felt less competent and had received lower marks than Chinese Canadian and European Canadian students (see Table 1). No significant differences were found between Canadian Chinese and European Canadian students on these variables, although Chinese Canadian students spent more time studying.

Hong Kong Chinese students were also significantly less learning goal oriented than European Canadian students and non-significantly so compared with Chinese Canadians. No differences were found between the groups on performance goal. Interestingly, performance goal was rated higher than learning goal by all the groups, especially by the Chinese Canadian students.

Relationship Between Self-Regulation and Motivational Variables

Zero-order correlation among the variables (Tables 2, 3, & 4) showed that self-regulation and cognitive strategies correlated positively with effort, self-efficacy, and learning goal for all three groups of students. Self-regulation also correlated significantly with performance goal for Hong Kong students and with average performance for Chinese and European Canadian students. However, cognitive strategies correlated significantly with average performance for European Canadian students only. There was a moderately high correlation between self-regulation and cognitive strategies for all three groups of students.

Self-efficacy positively correlated with learning and performance goals for all three groups of students. Self-efficacy was also significantly and negatively related to test anxiety and positively with time spent studying for Chinese Canadian and European Canadian students but not for Hong Kong Chinese students. Finally, self-efficacy was significantly correlated with average performance for all three groups.

Learning and performance goals were both positively and significantly related with average mark for the Canadian European students and non-significantly so for Canadian Chinese students. However, learning goal correlated negatively with average mark for Hong Kong students. As expected, learning and performance goals were positively correlated for Hong Kong students only.

The correlation between time spent studying and average mark was positive and significant for both Chinese Canadian and European Canadian students, but was negatively correlated for Hong Kong students.

Table 2. Correlations between Self-Regulation, Cognitive Strategy, Test Anxiety, Self-Efficacy, Goal Orientations, Amount of Time Spent Studying and Average Grade in Last Term Examinations for European Canadian Students.

Variable	2	3	4	5	6	7	8
Self- Regulation	$.61^{***}$	$-.09$	$.42^{***}$	$.35^{***}$	$.23^{**}$	$.48^{***}$	$.40^{***}$
Cognitive Strategy		$.03$	$.32^{***}$	$.31^{***}$	$.19^{*}$	$.32^{***}$	$.17^{*}$
Test Anxiety			$-.23^{*}$	$-.12$	$.22^{**}$	$.06$	$-.18^{*}$
Self-Efficacy				$.30^{***}$	$.29^{***}$	$.27^{***}$	$.35^{***}$
Learning Goal					$-.06$	$.22^{**}$	$.17$
Performance Goal						$.23^{**}$	$.18^{*}$
Time spent Studying							$.41^{***}$
Average Grade in Last Exam							

Note: $^{*}p < .01$, $^{**}p < .001$, $^{***}p < .0001$

Table 3. Correlations between Self-Regulation, Cognitive Strategy, Test Anxiety, Self-Efficacy, Goal Orientations, Amount of Time Spent Studying and Average Grade in Last Term Examinations for Canadian Chinese Students.

Variable	2	3	4	5	6	7	8
Self- Regulation	$.41^{***}$	$-.17$	$.42^{**}$	$.32^{**}$	$.08$	$.34^{**}$	$.32^{**}$
Cognitive Strategy		$.08$	$.25$	$.26$	$.20$	$.13$	$.15$
Test Anxiety			$-.49^{***}$	$-.29^{**}$	$.29^{*}$	$.06$	$-.29^{**}$
Self-Efficacy				$.49^{***}$	$.17$	$.35^{**}$	$.46^{***}$
Learning Goal					$-.10$	$.37^{***}$	$.18$
Performance Goal						$.23$	$.06$
Time spent Studying							$.35^{**}$
Average Grade in Last Exam							

Note: $^{*}p < .01$, $^{**}p < .001$, $^{***}p < .0001$

As expected, test-anxiety was negatively correlated with learning goal for the Canadian students and significantly so for Canadian Chinese students. It was, however, positively related with learning goal for Hong Kong students. Test anxiety was also negatively and significantly correlated with average mark, and positively and significantly related with performance goal for all three groups of students.

Table 4.   Correlations between Self-Regulation, Cognitive Strategy, Test Anxiety, Self-Efficacy, Goal Orientations, Amount of Time Spent Studying and Average Grade in Last Term Examinations for Hong Kong Chinese Students.

Variable	2	3	4	5	6	7	8
Self- Regulation	$.33^{***}$	.10	$.47^{**}$	$.30^{**}$	$.35^{**}$	$.31^{**}$	.05
Cognitive Strategy		$.26^{**}$	$.39^{**}$	$.39^{***}$	$.32^{***}$	$.26^{***}$	$-.02$
Test Anxiety			.03	.15	$.27^{***}$	$.18^{*}$	$-.17$
Self-Efficacy				$.21^{**}$	$.40^{***}$	.09	$.19^{*}$
Learning Goal					$-.26^{***}$	$.19^{*}$	$-.14^{*}$
Performance Goal						$.24^{**}$	.13
Time spent Studying							$-.20^{**}$
Average Grade in Last Exam							

Note: $^{*}p < .01,$ $^{**}p < .001,$ $^{***}p < .0001$

DISCUSSION AND CONCLUSION

This study set out to investigate the impact of learning context on student motivation, self-regulation and performance in three groups of students namely, Hong Kong Chinese, Canadian Chinese and European Canadian students. Student motivation was assessed by measures of perceived self-efficacy, goal orientation, test-anxiety, and actual time spent studying. It was hypothesized that any differences in these measures between Chinese students in Hong Kong and Chinese students in Canada could be attributed mainly to their learning environment based on their similar cultural background, whereas, differences between European Canadian and Chinese Canadian students would be the result of their cultural differences since their learning contexts were largely the same.

The results showed interesting differences between the groups. Hong Kong students spent much more time studying but received the lowest marks among the three groups. They used less appropriate cognitive and self-regulatory strategies and engaged more in memorization strategies than their Canadian counterparts. However, their higher scores in memorization did not have any effect on their performance. Our results also showed that Hong Kong students were more anxious and perceived themselves to be less competent than Canadian Chinese and European Canadian students. The profile of Hong Kong students revealed in this study is very different from the overwhelming research evidence (see Stevenson, 1992; Stevenson & Stigler, 1992; Sue & Okazaki, 1990) that showed that Chinese students outperformed Western students on standard achievement tests. One reason for this is that the samples used in those studies were often from Chinese students who were already in Western countries or were planning to study abroad and these were compared with typical American students. Chinese students abroad are usually among the brightest and most highly motivated students. A second and important reason is that in Hong Kong, the standard of achievement is set very high and geared toward the brightest and the highest achieving students. When transferred to international schools, it is common knowledge that students who fail or perform poorly in Chinese schools often outperform students in their new learning environments. In addition, since these students are preparing for matriculation exams, the teachers set the exams at extremely difficult levels to ensure that students will not get good marks. This is because Chinese teachers in Hong Kong believe that receiving bad marks encourages the students to work even harder toward their public examinations. Successive examinations of this nature would make students very anxious and in time, lead them to doubt their own competence—no matter how hard they work, they will not be able to achieve good results. These findings clearly showed how teaching methods and assessment practices could affect students' motivation and self-confidence.

The findings also show that the direction of ratings, for Chinese Canadian students are more similar to that of European Canadian students despite the fact that these students were first generation Canadian Chinese. This may suggest that the context of learning is more powerful than cultural values in influencing students' motivation. However, Chinese Canadian ratings were always between the ratings of the other two, showing a residual influence of their cultural background. Although non-significant, Chinese Canadian students rated higher on time spent studying, average mark, and performance goal, while they were lower on learning goal and self-efficacy than their European Canadian counterparts. This pattern of ratings clearly shows the cultural values placed on effort and academic excellence among Chinese communities. Chinese families living in their new countries may feel that the most secure way of ensuring good futures for their children is for them to have strong academic credentials. This may explain why these students had the highest ratings on performance goal compared to other groups and a higher average mark than their European Canadian counterparts. European Canadian families on the other hand, tend to be more concerned with all-round education of their children and place more importance on the child's sense of self-confidence than academic results. This is reflected in the students' higher ratings of learning goal and self-efficacy.

The results, however, also showed that regardless of culture and context of education, all students seem to have higher ratings for performance goal than learning goal. This finding was contrary to our expectation that Hong Kong Chinese would be significantly higher on performance goal than other groups. However, upon reflection, it is not surprising since all the students were preparing for university entrance. It is well known that acceptance to a good university can be very competitive and depends among other things, on who has the highest marks. This suggests that students' goal orientation may not only depend on the immediate learning context but also on other more general goals and requirements for succeeding, such as gaining admission to a prestigious university.

One interesting finding of this study concerns the relationship between motivational variables and self-regulation. In Western literature, learning goal, self-efficacy, academic achievement and self-regulation are positively associated with each other and negatively with test-anxiety (see, e.g., Pintrich & De Groot, 1990). We found this pattern to hold true generally for both groups of Canadian students, but not always true for Hong Kong Chinese students. This suggests that the relationship between these variables is influenced by the context of learning. In the case of Hong Kong, self-efficacy was related significantly with both learning and performance goals but unrelated to effort. Self-efficacy was also significantly related to achievement level, suggesting that having confidence in one's competence and abilities is perhaps the most important factor in achieving academic excellence for Hong Kong students.

We found that for Canadian students as a whole, self-regulation was correlated with average performance but not so for the Hong Kong group. This again suggests that no matter what strategies students employ or how much time they spend in preparation for their examinations, they cannot receive good grades because of an extremely high standard of achievement imposed by the schools and teachers. This may be related to the cultural belief that shaming students for not getting good marks achieves better results than encouragement. Shame, however, could have undesirable consequences. In our study not only did Hong Kong students have lower self-efficacy than their counterparts in Canada, but they were also lower in self-esteem (which was not included in this chapter), and had higher levels of test-anxiety.

Finally, we found that learning and performance goals were moderately correlated for Hong Kong students. This finding has been reported in Hong Kong students by other researchers (see Biggs, 1993) and in other East Asian students who began their studies in Australia (Volet, Renshaw, & Tietzel, 1994). As stated above, we believe both learning and performance goal orientations are needed to meet the demands of the education system in Hong Kong and in other Chinese societies. On the one hand, Chinese cultural values encourage students to study hard for the sake of gaining knowledge and for self-improvement, while on the other hand, it places great emphasis on academic excellence and competitive examinations (Salili, 1995). In such conditions, both learning and performance goals are necessary to accomplish one's goals. Additionally, performance goal in some situations (e.g., gaining admission to a good university), may have a short-term beneficial effect in motivating students to perform well as suggested by our results. In the long-term, however, it could be detrimental to self-efficacy and the psychological well being of the students.

One limitation of our study is that we could not separate different components of learning context (e.g., teaching method, assessment and other classroom factors). Furthermore, although Chinese Canadian students were new immigrants the extent to which Canadian culture in general affected them is not clear. Further studies are needed to clarify these points and to confirm our findings.

REFERENCES

Ames, C. (1992a). Achievement goals and the classroom motivational climate. In D.H. Schunk & J.L. Meece (Eds.), *Student perceptions in the classroom* (pp. 327–348). Hillsdale, NJ: Lawrence Erlbaum Associates, Inc.

Ames, C. (1992b). Classrooms: Goal, structures, and student motivation. *Journal of Educational Psychology, 84,* 261–271.

Bandura, A. (1994). *Self-efficacy: The exercise of control.* New York: Freeman.

Biggs, J.B. (1992). *Why and how do Hong Kong students learn? Using the Learning and Study Process Questionnaires.* University of Hong Kong: Education Papers, No 14.

Biggs, J.B. (1993).What do inventories of students' learning process really measure? A theoretical review and clarification. *British Journal of Educational Psychology, 63*(1), 3–19.

Chen, C., Stevenson, H.W., Hayward, C., & Burgess, S. (1995). Culture and academic achievement. In M.L. Maehr & P.R. Pintrich (Eds.), *Advances in motivation and achievement: Culture, motivation and achievement* (pp. 73–118). Greenwich, CT: JAI Press.

Corno, L., & Snow, R. (1986). Adapting teaching to individual differences among learners. In M.C. Wittrock (Ed.), *Handbook of research on teaching* (3rd ed., pp. 605–629). New York: Macmillan.

Covington, M.L. (1992). *Making the grade: A self-worth perspective on motivation and school reform.* New York: Cambridge University press.

Dweck, C.S., & Leggett, E.L. (1988). A social-cognitive approach to motivation and personality. *Psychological Review, 95,* 256–273.

Dweck, C.S. (1986). Motivational processes affecting learning: *American Psychologist, 41,* 1040–1048.

Eccles, J. (1983). Expectancies, Values and academic behaviors. In J.T. Spence (Ed.), *Achievement and achievement motives* (pp. 75–146). San Francisco: Freeman.

Hill, K. (1972). Anxiety in the evaluative context. In W.W. Hartup (Ed.), *The young child* (Vol. 2, pp. 225–283). Washington, DC: National Association for the Education of Young Children.

Kaplan, A., & Maehr, M.L. (1999). *Achievement motivation: The emergence, contributions, and prospects of a goal orientation theory perspective.* Unpublished paper, Leadership and Learning Laboratory, University of Michigan, Ann Arbor.

Liu, L.M. (1986). Chinese cognition. In M.H. Bond (Ed.), *The psychology of Chinese people* (pp. 73–102). Hong Kong: Oxford University Press.

Maehr, M.L., & Midgley, C. (1991). *The motivation factor: A theory of personal investment.* Lexington, MA: Lexington Books, D.C. Health.

Midgley, C., Anderman, E., & Hicks, L. (1995). Differences between elementary and middle school teachers and students: A goal theory approach. *Journal of Early Adolescence, 15,* 90–133.

Midgley, C., Maehr, M.L., & Urdan, T. (1993). *Pattern of Adaptive Learning Survey* (PALS). Ann Arbor: University of Michigan, Combined Program in Education and Psychology.

Midgley, C., & Urdan, T., (1995). Predictors of the use of self-handicapping strategies in middle school. *Journal of Early Adolescence, 15,* 389–411.

Nicholls, J.G. (1990). What is ability and why are we mindful of it? A developmental perspective. In R.J. Sternberg & J. Kolligian (Eds.), *Competence considered* (pp. 11–40). New Haven, CT: Yale University Press.

Nicholls, J., Cheung, P., Lauer, J., & Patashnick, M. (1989). Individual differences in academic motivation: Perceived ability, goals, beliefs, and values. *Learning and Individual Differences, 1,* 63–84.

Phillips, B.N., Pitcher, G.D., Worsham, M.E., & Miller, S.C. (1980). In I.G. Sarason (Ed.), *Test-anxiety: Theory, research and applications* (pp. 326–343). Hillsdale, NJ: Lawrence Erlbaum.

Pintrich, P.R., & De Groot, E.V. (1990). Motivational and self-regulated learning components of classroom academic performance. *Journal of Educational Psychology, 1,* 33–40

Pintrich, P.R., & Schunk, D.H. (1996). *Motivation in education: Theory, research, and application.* Englewood Cliffs, NJ: Prentice-Hall.

Salili, F. (1994). Age, sex, and cultural differences in the meaning and dimensions of achievement. *Personality and Social Psychology Bulletin, 20*(6), 635–648.

Salili, F. (1995). Explaining Chinese motivation and achievement: A sociocultural analysis. In M.L. Maehr & P.R. Pintrich (Eds.), *Advances in motivation and achievement: Culture, motivation and achievement* (Vol. 9, pp. 73–118). Greenwich, CT: JAI Press.

Salili, F., Maehr, M.L., & Sorenson, R.L. (1976). A cross-cultural analysis of the effects of evaluation on motivation. *American Educational Research Journal, 13,* 85–102.

Schunk, D.H. (1991). Self-efficacy and academic motivation. *Educational Psychologist, 26,* 207–231.

Stevenson, H.W. (1992). Learning from Asian schools. *Scientific American, 267*(6), 70–76.

Stevenson, H.W., & Lee, S. (1990). Context of achievement. *Monograph of the Society for Research in Child Development* (Serial no. 221, Vol. 55, Nos. 1–2).

Stevenson, H.W., & Stigler, J. (1992). *The learning gap: Why our schools are failing and what can we learn from Japanese and Chinese education.* New York: Summit Books.

Stipek, D. (1997). *Motivation to learn: From theory to practice.* Needham Heights, MA: Allyn & Bacon.

Stipek, D. (1998, June). *Classroom effects on young children's motivation.* Paper presented at the International Conference on Application of Psychology to the Quality of Learning and Teaching, Hong Kong.

Stipek, D., & Mac Ivar, D. (1989). Developmental change in children's assessment of intellectual competence. *Child Development, 60,* 521–538.

Sue, S., & Okazaki, S. (1990). Asian American educational achievement: A phenomenon in search of an explanation. *American Psychologist, 45*(8), 913–920.

Tobias, S. (1985). Test anxiety: Interference, defective skills, and cognitive capacity. *Educational Psychologist, 20,* 135–142.

Urdan, T., & Maehr, M.L. (1995). Beyond a two-goal theory of motivation: A case for social goals. *Review of Educational Research, 65,* 213–244.

Volet S.E. (1999) Motivation within and across cultural-educational contexts: A multi-dimentional perspective. In P. Pintrich & T. Urdan, (Eds.), *Advances in Motivation and Achievment, Vol. 11.* London: JAI Press.

Volet, S.E., Renshaw, P.D., & Tietzel, K. (1994). A short-term longitudinal investigation of cross-cultural differences in study approaches using Biggs SPQ questionnaire. *British Journal of Educational Psychology, 64,* 301–318.

Wine, J. (1971). Test anxiety and direction of attention. *Psychological Bulletin, 76,* 92–104.

Wolters, C.A., Yu, S.L., & Pintrich, P.R. (1996). The relation between goal orientation and students' motivational beliefs and self-regulated learning. *Learning and Individual Differences, 8,* 211–238.

Zimmerman, B.J., & Kitsantas, A. (1997). Developmental phases in self-regulation: Shifting from process goals to outcome goals. *Journal of Educational Psychology, 89,* 29–36.

Zimmerman, B.J., & Pons, M. (1988). Construct validation of a strategy model of student self-regulated learning. *Journal of Educational Psychology,* 284–290.

Zimmerman, B.J., Bonner, S., & Kovach, R. (1996). Developing self-regulated learners: Beyond achievement to self-efficacy. *Psychology in the classroom: A series on applied educational psychology.* Washington, DC: American Psychological Association.

CHAPTER 9

WHY PURSUE A COLLEGE EDUCATION?

THE INFLUENCE OF EARLY REFLECTION AND GOAL ORIENTATION ON ADJUSTMENT DURING THE FIRST SEMESTER

Regina Conti

ABSTRACT

Students planning to attend a small private liberal arts college were mailed the College Goals Questionnaire (CGQ), which assessed their underlying reasons for choosing to attend college. The CGQ asked students to choose the four goals that were most important to them and then to respond to a series of items that assessed the degree to which they reflected on these goals, and the degree to which these goals were autonomous (freely and voluntarily chosen) or controlled by expectations. The Student Adaptation to College Questionnaire (SACQ; Baker, & Siryk, 1989) was administered to these students twice during the first semester. At the start of the second semester a subset of students were interviewed along with their same-sex closest friends. Regression analyses showed a similar pattern across the three assessments. Students who reflected on their goals showed better academic adjustment, and students who felt controlled reported poorer emotional adjustment. These results suggest that this sampling of students may have a motivational advantage if they are actively engaged in the process of setting long-term goals when planning for college.

INTRODUCTION

Higher education has long been thought of as a crucial element in the formula for achieving the American Dream. Earning a college degree is thought of as the first step a young adult can take toward a successful and happy life. Those achieving a college degree enjoy a wider array of career opportunities and higher salaries (Murphy & Welch, 1989) and, as a result, the proportion of graduating high school students pursing a college education has steadily increased in the United States from less than 50% in the early 1970s to more than 60% today (National Center for Educational Statistics, 1995). With a majority of the population attending college, a bachelor's degree has become an expectation rather than an achievement for upper-middle and upper class young adults in the United States.

Rather than seeing college as an opportunity to pursue their dreams for the future, today's high school students may think of college as simply the next logical step in their lives. These recently developed cultural expectations eventually benefit those young Americans who profit from a college education, and who otherwise may not have sought one. But, initially students who pursue an education at a residential college without much forethought may be at risk for adjustment problems. They are likely to be shocked by the dramatic and stressful changes that face them. They are confronted with demanding academic work, a new social environment, an expanded array of activities to pursue and, for many, their first experience living away from their families. While students who have a clear sense of purpose will have the direction and focus they need to navigate these changes, students without a sense of why they are in college are likely to be overwhelmed by the decisions and challenges ahead.

Several lines of psychological theory and research support the notion that students' underlying reasons for going to college will influence their first year adjustment. Young adults who have considered what college has to offer and who make an informed and autonomous choice to attend will have an advantage over those who enroll because their parents expect them to, because they feel like they "should," or because they cannot find an appealing alternative. There are two major differences between the former group of students and the latter. The first difference is the degree to which the student has engaged himself or herself in reflection about his or her goals for the future. The second difference is the degree to which the student feels autonomous or independent in his or her choice to attend college and, alternatively, the degree to which he or she feels controlled or pressured (concepts proposed by Deci & Ryan, 1989, 1991). Students with a "dream" that college will help to fulfill have reflected and feel autonomous, while students who "drift" into college have not reflected and are more likely to feel controlled (the distinction between "dreaming" and "drifting" was originally drawn by Daniels, 1981).

DREAM VERSUS DRIFT

College years are often the time when the "dream" of what one would like to become as an adult begins to be translated into reality. The set of central life aspirations that form the "dream" has been described as a crucial element of successful adjustment during young adulthood (Levinson, 1977). Whether students pursue a course of study to prepare themselves for a long desired professional goal or make efforts to form a much anticipated close relationship, they are taking action on an intention that brought them to college. Students may come to college with very specific objectives in mind or students may have broad, long-range ideas of what they will gain from higher education. Regardless of their level of specificity, these ideas give shape to the students' initial college experiences. They help the student to prioritize and make choices from among many academic, social and extra-curricular alternatives. A student who aspires to become a pediatrician, for example, may lean toward science courses, have high goals for their grades, and perhaps become involved in outreach activities with children. The much more abstract goal of becoming a well-educated person might lead a student to take a wide variety of courses, to integrate what he or she is learning in different courses, and to take advantage of the intellectual opportunities on campus. Even though the "dream" may evolve over time and bear little relation to what the individual eventually becomes, it serves the important purpose of giving coherence to the individual's experience.

Not all students come to college equipped with a "dream," however. Without aspirations for the future, these young people "drift" into the role of student as the course of least resistance. The contrast between "dreaming" and "drifting" was first drawn by Daniels (1981) in her analysis of generativity in women's careers. From this account, the "dreamer" has a clear advantage in his or her direction and focus, but the "drifter" may benefit from greater flexibility. While a student with a clear conception of what they would like to gain from their college experience may be sorely disappointed if college does not provide the hoped-for opportunities, the student who enters college without such a conception may be better able to take advantage of the opportunities available. A "drifter" may be more likely to take the advice of a faculty member, join an exciting extracurricular activity on a whim, or pursue an entirely unfamiliar field of study.

Although there may be practical advantages of "drifting," a review of the self-regulation literature suggests that they are outweighed by the motivational advantages of "dreaming."

REFLECTING ON GOALS

Research on goal-setting has shown over and over again that having a deliberately-set goal leads to better performance than not having a goal (Latham & Locke, 1991). Although the goals that have typically been studied are more circumscribed than those that the present research is investigating, several lines of inquiry have shown that reflecting on complex goals will enhance performance, as well (Gollwitzer & Moskowitz, 1996). Gollwitzer (1996; Gollwitzer & Schaal, 1998) proposes that effortful action begins with a goal intention. Giving greater thought to a goal intention leads to forming implementation intentions, or specific plans for action, which facilitate successful performance. Research on mental simulation has similar implications in this context. Taylor and her colleagues (Taylor & Pham, 1996; Taylor, Pham, Rivkin, & Armor, 1998) have found that imagining the process of pursuing a goal facilitates obtaining that goal. Perhaps most relevant to the present study, Cantor et al. (1987; Cantor & Langston, 1989), found that students high in plan reflectivity, a measure of the degree to which students think through their plans, performed better academically during their first semester than students low on plan reflectivity. Having a clear sense of what one is working toward has motivational benefits. Reflecting on one's reasons for going to college may have advantages for young adults preparing for this transition.

GOALS AS AUTONOMOUS AND CONTROLLED

In its truest form a "dream" is more than simply a clear idea of what you are working toward; a "dream" is intensely personal and meaningful (Daniels, 1981; Levison, 1977). While a student's sense of their college pursuit may have this quality, it may also be influenced by the expectations and demands of others. Despite the independence that college brings, students may still feel substantial pressure to meet the expectations of parents, teachers, or, more generally, the adult world. Thus, students may reflect on their future in college with these expectations in mind rather than the genuine development of their interests and abilities. Thus, their choice of goals may be controlled by these expectations. Recent research on personal goals suggests that these controlled goals, although internalized and personally chosen, may not be truly personal, in that they are not integrated with the student's sense of self (Sheldon & Elliot, 1997; Sheldon & Kasser, 1995). Because students do not fully identify with goals that are pressured by expectations, they will not invest themselves as fully in attaining these goals, and, hence will have more difficulty in reaching them.

Just as students' aspirations can range from barely considered to well formulated, students' aspirations can range from fully autonomous to fully controlled. Autonomous endorsement of a goal is characterized by an inner endorsement and personal willingness to pursue that goal. The prototypical autonomous goal is one that is intrinsically motivated. For example, a student who joins a university tennis team because of her long-standing love of the sport is intrinsically motivated. Even a goal that is not intrinsically satisfying can be autonomously regulated if it is pursued with a full sense of choice and willingness. A student enrolled in a tedious and difficult course may pursue his coursework autonomously because of the genuine value he places on the skills and knowledge that will result from his hard work. Controlled endorsement instead is motivated by a need to meet rigidly imposed standards (Deci & Ryan, 1987, 1991). Although controlled endorsement can result from direct pressure imposed on the student by parents or others, students may also impose goals on themselves. A student pursuing a high GPA because she feels like she should, or because her parents place a high value on grades, would be controlled in her self-regulation.

Research shows that autonomous goals are better attained than controlled goals (Sheldon & Elliot, 1997), perhaps because autonomous goals are more pleasant and satisfying to work toward than controlled goals. Controlled regulation is associated with feelings of pressure, tension and guilt (Deci & Ryan 1987, 1991), while autonomous regulation is associated with positive affect and well-being (Sheldon & Kasser, 1995). Because adjustment has as much to do with satisfaction with college life as with performance, the level of autonomy and control associated with students' college goals are expected to be important predictors of college adjustment during the first semester.

ADJUSTMENT TO COLLEGE

Students need to feel successful and satisfied in their classes, and in their lives outside of class in order to adjust well to the college environment. Generally, I expected that those students who have reflected on their college goals and whose goals are more autonomous and less controlled would adjust more easily. However, these variables may influence one area of adjustment more powerfully than others. Academic adjustment, one important area, is influenced by students' impressions of the quality of their courses and their performance in courses. Students' success in forming friendships, seeking out social activities on campus and living with roommates are determinants of social adjustment. Emotional adjustment reflects students' feelings; students who are emotionally distressed and dissatisfied during their first semester are experiencing poor emotional adjustment. Students having trouble emotionally are likely to be experiencing stress in either academic or social pursuits and homesickness (Baker & Siryk, 1984). Although both academic and social adjustment are crucial to overall adjustment, the demands of these two domains create difficult choices for students (Cantor & Blanton, 1996).

Academic goals are consistently rated as more difficult and stressful to achieve than social goals (Cantor et al., 1987). Courses may not all be of students' choice or liking. Even with carefully chosen courses, college students are challenged to develop academic skills and demonstrate mastery of new areas of knowledge. Students are continuously evaluated on their academic progress with grades and many are disappointed to learn that they have not performed as well as they had anticipated. Perhaps for these reasons, students feel a low level of control over academic goals and report limited progress toward them (Cantor et al., 1987). Because academics are such a difficult area for students, having direction and focus is especially important. In the present study, students who spend more time reflecting on their goals for college are expected to report substantially higher levels of academic adjustment than those who spend less time reflecting.

Achieving social goals may not require as much direction and focus as do academic goals. Most students enjoy socializing (Cantor & Blanton, 1996). Social goals are self-chosen and feedback is often ambiguous. For these reasons, most students may have the sense that they are making good progress toward their social goals. In fact, the majority of college students think of themselves as above average in social skills (Dunning, Meyerowitz, & Holtzberg, 1989). Perhaps because social goals are an area where confidence is high, students may use social connections to bolster their efforts in other areas. Morris and Reily (1987) reported that students found spending time with friends an effective way to improve their mood. Because students generally do not experience much stress in relation to social goals and because social goals are rarely experienced as pressured, social adjustment may be influenced less by students' underlying reasons for coming to college than the other two areas of adjustment.

Emotional adjustment reflects how students are coping with the stresses of college life. Students who are strongly influenced by pressures and expectations may have a particularly difficult time coping with stress during their first semester. Controlled self-regulation leads to feelings of guilt, pressure and tension, while autonomous self-regulation is associated with a more positive emotional experience (Deci & Ryan 1987, 1991). Thus, endorsing controlled reasons for attending college is expected to substantially undermine students' emotional adjustment, while endorsing autonomous reasons is expected to enhance emotional adjustment.

In sum, the present research sought to explore the connection between students' underlying reasons for attending a private, selective liberal arts college in the Northeast United States and their adjustment during the first semester. The summer preceding their first semester, students were mailed the College Goals Questionnaire (CGQ), a questionnaire that assessed the degree to which they reflected on their goals, the degree to which their goals were autonomously chosen and the degree to which their goals were chosen for controlled reasons. To assess adjustment, students attended two follow-up questionnaire sessions during their first semester. A subset of students volunteered to bring a close friend to the laboratory for an interview session at the start of their second semester. I hypothesized that in this sample (1) students who reflected on their goals would show better adjustment, especially academic adjustment, (2) students who endorsed autonomous reasons for choosing their goals would report better adjustment, especially emotional adjustment, and (3) students who endorsed controlled reasons for choosing their goals would report poorer adjustment, especially emotional adjustment.

METHOD

Participants

Participants were entering first year students at a small liberal arts college in the Northeastern United States. Three hundred and eighty-two students volunteered to participate by responding to a questionnaire mailed to the homes of 731 incoming students in July of the summer preceding their first year at college. Fifty-two percent of the sample was female and 48% was male. All were between the ages of 17 and 22. Of those who volunteered, 200 were invited to participate in two follow-up assessments during the fall semester of their first year. One hundred and fifty-nine students participated in the first follow-up, making our initial participation rate 79.5%. Eighty-six participated in the second follow-up session for a continued participation rate of 43%. Those students who participated in the second follow-up were invited to bring their closest same-sex friend into the laboratory for an in-depth interview during the spring semester. Twenty-five pairs of students participated in the interview sessions.

Measures

College Goals Questionnaire (CGQ).   This Instrument was developed to assess the degree to which students reflected on their goals before coming to college and the level of autonomy and control associated with their goals (see Appendix A). The CGQ first asks respondents to rate the importance of 35 goals. These goals represent the central motives that lure young adults to college (e.g., securing a good job, becoming well educated, establishing enduring friendships); the list was developed during undergraduate student focus groups. The second section of the questionnaire asks students to list their four most important goals and then to rate five reasons for choosing these goals as most important. These reasons were based on the autonomous and controlled reasons used by Sheldon and Elliot (1997). One autonomous reason read "Because I genuinely believe that this is an important goal to strive toward. I endorse it freely and value it wholeheartedly." One controlled reason read "Because it is important to the people closest to me, achieving this goal would make them happy and proud." The final section of the questionnaire was designed to measure the degree to which students reflected on their goals. Four items asked students to indicate where they fell on a continuum where one end represented not reflecting at all (e.g., "I very rarely think about the goals I will pursue in college") and the other represented reflecting a great deal (e.g., "I spend a good deal of time thinking about the goals I will pursue"). The CGQ was prepared in two different orders to ensure that the order of items did not influence the results.

The CGQ yields scores for autonomy, control and reflection. The autonomy score is computed by averaging students' ratings of autonomous reasons (Cronbach's alpha = .77); the control scale is computed by averaging the controlled reasons (Cronbach's alpha = .78); the reflection scale is computed by averaging the four bipolar items asking about reflection (Cronbach's alpha = .55). The control and reflection measures were normally distributed, but the autonomy scale was markedly positively skewed and showed limited variance. For these reasons, results related to autonomy should be interpreted with caution. In this sample, control and autonomy were positively correlated ($r(382) = .17$, $p < .01$), as were autonomy and reflection ($r(382) = .19$, $p < .01$).

Student Adaptation to College Questionnaire (SACQ).   The SACQ (Baker & Siryk, 1989), measures adjustment to college. Academic adjustment, social adjustment and emotional adjustment are of particular interest for this study. Each of these scales has shown high inter-item reliability in previous research (Cronbach's alphas ranged from .82 to .87 for academic adjustment, from .83 to .89 for social adjustment, and from .73 to .79 for emotional adjustment) and in the present sample (Cronbach's alphas for 1st follow-up = .86, .91, and .77, for 2nd follow-up = .86, .92, and .79 for academic, social, and emotional adjustment respectively). Validity has been established by examining the relationship of these subscales with other relevant variables including attrition, first year grade point average, social activity participation, and the seeking of psychological support services.

Social Desirability Scale (SDS). This scale is widely used to assess the extent to which participants are prone to endorsing socially desirable responses (Crowne & Marlow, 1960).

Procedure

Incoming students were mailed the CGQ in the second week of the July preceding their first year in college. Along with the CGQ was a letter explaining the procedures and general purpose of the study (to better understand the reasons that people choose to go to college). Recipients were asked to respond to the questionnaire and return it if they were interested in participating.

In September of their first year, 200 of the students who responded to the CGQ were contacted by phone and asked to participate in a follow-up session. Those students who agreed were scheduled for group sessions, early in October, during which they responded to the SACQ, and the Marlow-Crowne. The same procedure was used to recruit participants for the late November follow-up.

The late-November follow-up sessions ended with a partial debriefing and a request to participate in an in-depth interview during the spring semester. Students were asked to invite their closest same-sex friend to accompany them to the interview. By personally interviewing both participants and their closest friends, we hoped to gain additional measures of adjustment to college that would validate the questionnaire measures taken during the first semester. We also hoped that the personal experiences that students shared during the interviews would add a qualitative dimension to the quantitative results gathered from the questionnaire sessions.

Senior undergraduate students were trained to conduct the interviews. First, the participant's friend was interviewed individually; then the participant was interviewed individually; finally both persons were interviewed together. Each portion of the interview lasted about 20 minutes. They were conducted in a sound proof room and, for the first two portions, interviewees were ensured that their friends could not hear them. The interview protocol asked about the participants' experiences during their first semester in college in three areas: academic, social, and emotional adjustment. Academic questions focused on the student's experiences with his/her courses and with completing the work required for these courses. The social questions focused on relationships at college with roommates, other students in the dormitory, and other students in the participant's classes and from extracurricular activities. The emotional adjustment questions focused on whether the participants experienced homesickness and depression, and the degree to which they felt comfortable and happy with college life.

Interviews were rated by two undergraduate students who were blind to the hypotheses and had not met any of the participants. These raters viewed videotapes of the interviews and rated the interviewees' responses to each question on seven point scales according to the level of academic, social or emotional adjustment that they indicated. Correlations between raters were positive and uniformly high (r's ranged from .66 to .91). Raters' responses were combined by averaging them. Because scores for questions corresponding to each dimension were also highly intercorrelated (Cronbach's alphas for friend interviews =.74, .78, and .73, and for participant interviews = .93, .73, and .90, for academic, social and emotional adjustment, respectively), averages were computed to form one score for each area of adjustment for each interviewee. Thus, interviews yielded 6 averaged adjustment scores: friends' reports of academic, social, and emotional adjustment and participant's reports of academic, social, and emotional adjustment.

RESULTS

Hierarchical multiple regression analyses were conducted to examine the relationships between the three predictor variables measured by the CGQ and the outcome variables measured by the SACQ during the two follow-up sessions. The three college goal variables (reflection, autonomy and control) were entered on the first step of each analysis. Three control variables, social desirability score, high school GPA, and SAT score were entered on the second step. Results of the first step of these analyses are summarized in Tables 1 and 2. The relationships between the college goals variables and the outcome variables were not substantially changed when control variables were entered.

Several hypotheses were supported. Academic adjustment was predicted by the degree to which students reflected on their goals. Emotional adjustment was negatively predicted by the degree to which students endorsed controlled reasons for adopting their goals. This pattern was observed during both follow-up assessments. Social desirability scores significantly predicted all three types of adjustment, but did not account for the relationships among control, reflection, and adjustment. High school GPA and SAT scores were not significant predictors.

Table 1.   Summary of Multiple Regression Analyses for College Goals Variables Predicting College Adjustment at the First Follow-Up (N =159)

Variable	B	SE B	b
Academic Adjustment (R^2 = .06*)			
Reflection	.25	.11	.18*
Autonomy	.26	.19	.11
Control	−.09	.09	−.08
Social Adjustment (R^2 = .01)			
Reflection	.16	.15	.09
Autonomy	−.05	.24	−.02
Control	−.07	.12	−.05
Emotional Adjustment (R^2 = .06*)			
Reflection	.01	.12	.00
Autonomy	.20	.21	.08
Control	−.31	.10	−.24**

Note. * $p < .05$; ** $p < .01$.

Table 2.   Summary of Multiple Regression Analyses for College Goals Variables Predicting College Adjustment at the Second Follow-Up (N = 86)

Variable	B	SE B	b
Academic Adjustment (R^2 = .09*)			
Reflection	.37	.16	.27*
Autonomy	.23	.29	.09
Control	.01	.13	.01
Social Adjustment (R^2 = .04)			
Reflection	.00	.24	.00
Autonomy	.33	.43	.09
Control	−.32	.20	−.19
Emotional Adjustment (R^2 = .11*)			
Reflection	.00	.18	.00
Autonomy	.39	.34	.13
Control	−.42	.16	−.31**

Note. * $p < .05$; ** $p < .01$.

Correlations were computed between ratings of friends' and participants' reports of college adjustment during the interview sessions. These correlations were consistently positive and statistically significant, despite a small sample. For academic adjustment $r(25) = .49$, for social adjustment $r(25) = .78$, for emotional adjustment $r(25) = .55$. The agreement between friends and participants is encouraging and points to the validity of participants' self-reports. Friends and participants scores for each dimension was averaged to form overall adjustment scores for the interviews.

To assess the degree to which reports of adjustment during the interviews were related to autonomy, control, and reflection, hierarchical multiple regression analyses were conducted using the same procedure as was used for the questionnaire analyses. The results of the first step of each analysis are summarized in Table 3.

Table 3.   Summary of Multiple Regression Analyses for College Goals Variables Predicting College Adjustment From Interviews
($N = 25$)

Variable	B	$SE\ B$	b
Academic Adjustment ($R^2 = .31$)			
Reflection	.63	.26	.56[*]
Autonomy	.25	.48	.12
Control	.03	.22	.03
Social Adjustment ($R^2 = .40$)			
Reflection	.27	.37	.18
Autonomy	−.18	.68	−.07
Control	.54	.32	.42
Emotional Adjustment ($R^2 = .29$)			
Reflection	−.14	.38	−.09
Autonomy	1.04	.69	.35
Control	−.59	.32	−.43[m]

Note. [m] $p < .10$; * $p < .05$; ** $p < .01$.

These results replicate the pattern observed for the questionnaire data. Reflection significantly predicted academic adjustment and control was a marginal negative predictor of emotional adjustment. Although these relationships were no longer significant when control variables were entered, their direction and magnitude did not change substantially. Given the limited sample size, these results are encouraging.

DISCUSSION

Taken together, the findings from this study provide consistent support for two predictions. Students who reflect on their goals prior to attending college feel more comfortable and confident in the academic arena during their first semester. This effect is not due to stronger academic skills; it was obtained even with high school GPA and SAT scores controlled. Students who chose goals for controlled reasons experience more emotional difficulties. This effect does not seem to be related to problems with academic or social adjustment. Although the effect sizes for these findings are small, the same pattern was obtained at three points in time, using two different methodologies. Both of these findings make contributions to the self-regulation literature and have practical implications.

Students who reflect on why they are pursuing a college education approach their first semester with a clearer sense of direction. They know what is important to them and can use these priorities to make decisions and plans. One interviewee, for example, came to college with a desire to learn more about other cultures. He had always been close to his Italian American family. When a cousin from Italy visited during his junior year of high school, he was struck by the cultural differences between his cousin's community and his own. During his first semester, he sought out friends from different cultural backgrounds, enrolled in an Italian course and a Western Traditions course in an attempt to learn more about his culture. Although this interest did appear to have some effect on his social life, it arose again and again when he was describing what he had gained from his courses. By reflecting on what he might learn in college, this student was able to choose courses that satisfied a personal curiosity. In doing so, he paved the way for a satisfying academic experience. This example and others give a glimpse of the mechanisms by which students' reflections support their academic adjustment. Ultimately, these mechanisms need to be explored empirically.

The work of Taylor, Pham, and their colleagues (Taylor & Pham, 1996; Taylor et al., 1998) on mental simulation provides one promising avenue. Mental simulation allows people to begin to tackle daunting future tasks by envisioning them and working through the cognitive and emotional challenges that they entail. In one study (Pham & Taylor, 1994), they found that when students envisioned the process of studying for an exam, performance on the exam was bolstered. However, simply envisioning receiving a high score did not have the same impact. By measuring several potential mediators, they learned that the process simulation had its effects by facilitating planning and reducing anxiety. Similar work investigating the various ways in which students reflect on their college goals could begin to reveal the mechanisms by which reflection has its positive effects on academic adjustment.

The connection between controlled regulation of goals and emotional adjustment adds to the already extensive literature supporting self-determination theory (Deci & Ryan, 1987, 1991). In this study, controlled regulation apparently did not interfere with attaining academic or social goals, but did influence students' ability to cope during this stressful transition. One example that illustrates this pattern comes from the interview of a young woman whose most important goal was to develop her academic potential. When asked why she chose that goal as most important she said, "I think it is something that my parents have tried to instill in me. They are well-educated people and they want me to be one, too." This woman had a first semester filled with tension and stress. In her case, the emotional distress she experienced was not linked with academic and social problems. But, most interviewees who reported poor emotional adjustment also reported difficulties with academic and social pursuits. The fact that the quantitative results did not show a link between controlled regulation and academic or social adjustment is puzzling. From these findings it is difficult to know whether more controlled goals were attained as successfully as less controlled goals or whether students' progress toward their goals was not captured in the measures of academic and social adjustment that were used. Future research should assess students' progress toward each of their primary goals individually. These more precise measures of students' academic and social progress would help to resolve this issue.

Autonomous regulation of goals did not show the anticipated positive effects on college adjustment. Autonomy scores from the CGQ were positively skewed and showed limited variance. Students may have unanimously endorsed autonomous goals because they are highly valued by the independently oriented culture of the United States. This suspicion is supported by the strong correlation between autonomy scores and social desirability scores. For these reasons, it is difficult to interpret the findings related to autonomous regulation of goals.

Generally, these results support the notion that "dreamers" are better prepared for the transition to college than are "drifters." The additional reflection that "dreamers" engage in seems to support their academic adjustment. Because "dreamers" are less likely to endorse controlled goals, they are likely to show better emotional adjustment. These results point to the need for developmental research targeted at understanding how the "dream" develops. Marcia's (1966, 1967) classic work on identity suggests that a crisis needs to occur before a truly autonomous dream for the future can develop. Students who seem to be "drifting" may have been experiencing such crisis at the time of the study, which may account for the greater adjustment difficulties they reported.

These results were obtained using a relatively homogeneous sample from one institution in the Northeastern United States. Most participants were upper-middle class or upper class and Caucasian. A strong cultural expectation that able young adults will pursue a college education exists in this population. This expectation may lead more students to "drift" into their first year of college without much direction or purpose, rather than exploring the possibilities for their future and developing a "dream." Perhaps it is this phenomenon that explains why the college completion rate in the United States has remained steady at about 27%, despite rising enrollments (National Center for Educational Statistics, 1995).

The dynamic explored here may not occur in other cultures within and outside of the United States. In fact, there is evidence that the factors that influence achievement in African-American, Hispanic-American and Asian-American students in the United States are substantially different from those that influence Caucasian students (Steinberg, Dombusch, & Brown, 1992). In cultures where the pursuit of higher education is not expected, "drifting" into college should not occur. In collectivist cultures, where an individual's sense of self is closely connected with his or her social roles, social expectations may take on a different meaning (Markus & Kitayama, 1991; Markus, Kitayama, & Heiman, 1996). Choosing goals because they are expected by others, especially family members, may be more normative and personally satisfying. For these reasons, in collectivist cultures, controlled goals may not be associated with emotional adjustment difficulties in college. Social goals are better defined and of greater importance in collectivist cultures, Perhaps stronger results in relation to social adjustment would be found in these cultures. Although we can speculate about the role of culture in the present study, cross-cultural research is needed to establish the influence of cultural norms on students' motives for enrolling in college and their subsequent adjustment.

Results of the present study have practical implications. High schools where most students are expected to attend college should consider interventions that support students in developing a "dream" that can begin to take form during the college years. Encouraging these high school students to reflect on their goals for college could have positive effects on their academic satisfaction during their first year. High schools might consider focusing writing assignments, projects or class discussions on students' aspirations for the future. Guidance counselors might facilitate reflection through individual work with students. While encouraging reflection, teachers and counselors could help students to evaluate their underlying reasons for wanting to pursue a college education. Discussion of controlled and autonomous reasons for attending college might help students to better integrate their goals with their developing identity. In doing so, students will be freed from the sense of pressure and expectation that can interfere with emotional adjustment. While preparing for college, developing students' hopes and dreams for the future may be as important as developing their intellectual skills.

APPENDIX
COLLEGE GOALS QUESTIONNAIRE

How important is it to you to...

	not at all		extremely				not at all		extremely	
Become a well-educated person?	1	2	3	4	5	Decide what you value in life?	1	2	3	4	5
Explore topics that are new to you?	1	2	3	4	5	Earn high grades?	1	2	3	4	5
Live away from your family?	1	2	3	4	5	Develop as an athlete?	1	2	3	4	5
Develop enduring friendships?	1	2	3	4	5	Develop as an artist or musician?	1	2	3	4	5
Prepare for a fulfilling career?	1	2	3	4	5	Learn more about yourself?	1	2	3	4	5
Increase your earning potential?	1	2	3	4	5	Assume a leadership position on campus?	1	2	3	4	5
Learn more about your culture?	1	2	3	4	5	Join a fraternity/ sorority?	1	2	3	4	5
Learn more about other cultures?	1	2	3	4	5	Enjoy the social life on campus?	1	2	3	4	5
Meet new and interesting people?	1	2	3	4	5	Increase your ability to solve problems?	1	2	3	4	5
Secure a good job after graduating?	1	2	3	4	5	Develop your academic potential?	1	2	3	4	5
Make independent decisions?	1	2	3	4	5	Explore career options/alternatives?	1	2	3	4	5
Develop strong writing skills?	1	2	3	4	5	Make contacts for your career?	1	2	3	4	5
Begin an intimate relationship?	1	2	3	4	5	_____ _____	1	2	3	4	5

	not at all			extremely			not at all			extremely	
Pursue admission to graduate program?	1	2	3	4	5	_____	1	2	3	4	5
Prepare yourself to contribute to society?	1	2	3	4	5	_____	1	2	3	4	5

Of the goals listed on the first page, please choose the four that are most important to you and list them in the boxes on the next four pages. Then, for each goal, respond to the 5 items below by circling **one** number that corresponds to how true that statement is for you.

> **Most important goal (choose from list on page 1):**

Why is this goal important to you?

	not at all true for me			very true for me	
Because it is important to the people closest to me, achievement of this goal would make them happy and proud.	1	2	3	4	5
Because it is important to society. I will receive tangible benefits and be considered a more valuable person if I achieve this goal.	1	2	3	4	5
Because if I didn't, I would feel guilty, ashamed, or anxious. I feel as though it is a goal I ought to have.	1	2	3	4	5
Because I genuinely believe that this is an important goal to strive toward. I endorse it freely and value it wholeheartedly.	1	2	3	4	5
Because working toward this goal will be personally satisfying and enjoyable. My primary reason is my interest in the experience itself.	1	2	3	4	5

Second most important goal (choose from list on page 1):

Why is this goal important to you?

	not at all true for me			very true for me
Because it is important to the people closest to me, achievement of this goal would make them happy and proud.	1	2	3	4	5
Because it is important to society. I will receive tangible benefits and be considered a more valuable person if I achieve this goal.	1	2	3	4	5
Because if I didn't, I would feel guilty, ashamed, or anxious. I feel as though it is a goal I ought to have.	1	2	3	4	5
Because I genuinely believe that this is an important goal to strive toward. I endorse it freely and value it wholeheartedly.	1	2	3	4	5
Because working toward this goal will be personally satisfying and enjoyable. My primary reason is my interest in the experience itself.	1	2	3	4	5

Third most important goal (choose from list on page 1):

Why is this goal important to you?

	not at all true for me			very true for me
Because it is important to the people closest to me, achievement of this goal would make them happy and proud.	1	2	3	4	5
Because it is important to society. I will receive tangible benefits and be considered a more valuable person if I achieve this goal.	1	2	3	4	5
Because if I didn't, I would feel guilty, ashamed, or anxious. I feel as though it is a goal I ought to have.	1	2	3	4	5
Because I genuinely believe that this is an important goal to strive toward. I endorse it freely and value it wholeheartedly.	1	2	3	4	5
Because working toward this goal will be personally satisfying and enjoyable. My primary reason is my interest in the experience itself.	1	2	3	4	5

Fourth most important goal (choose from list on page 1):

Why is this goal important to you?

	not at all true for me		very true for me
Because it is important to the people closest to me, achievement of this goal would make them happy and proud.	1 2	3	4 5
Because it is important to society. I will receive tangible benefits and be considered a more valuable person if I achieve this goal.	1 2	3	4 5
Because if I didn't, I would feel guilty, ashamed, or anxious. I feel as though it is a goal I ought to have.	1 2	3	4 5
Because I genuinely believe that this is an important goal to strive toward. I endorse it freely and value it wholeheartedly.	1 2	3	4 5
Because working toward this goal will be personally satisfying and enjoyable. My primary reason is my interest in the experience itself.	1 2	3	4 5

Please respond to each of the following sentence stems by circling the one number that best corresponds to how you felt while filling out the first two parts of the questionnaire.

Which statement describes how you feel?

A   1 2 3 4 5   **B**

A	B
I found that I had already thought about the kinds of goals listed on the first page.	I had not yet given detailed thought to the goals I will pursue at Colgate.
I found it very easy to decide which goals (on page 1) are important to me.	I found it difficult to decide which goals are important to me.
I knew, right away, <u>why</u> the goals I chose are important to me (pages 2 & 3).	I had to reflect before deciding why the goals I chose are important.
I spend a good deal of time thinking about the goals I will pursue.	I very rarely think about the goals I will pursue at Colgate.

I deliberated, toward the end of high school, about whether to attend college.	I have always known that I would attend college.
I had a difficult time deciding which college to attend.	I decided which college I would like to attend quickly.
I found filling out this questionnaire useful in clarifying my college goals.	I did not find filling out this questionnaire useful.

I am interested in receiving a summary of the findings from this study when the study is complete (August 1997).

Please use the space below to write any comments or questions that you had while responding to the questionnaire.

ACKNOWLEDGMENTS

I am grateful to Caroline Keating and Kennon Sheldon for their helpful comments on an earlier version of this article. I would also like to thank Paula Crivelli, Amy Grennan, Bethany Klynn, Carla Maine, Michelle Park, Katharine Pitula, Kelly Rourke, Danielle Schade, Jill Smith, and Eliza Whoriskey for collecting and entering the data reported here and Kathryn Rollings for proofreading the manuscript.

My participation in the *International Conference on the Application of Psychology to the Quality of Learning and Teaching* was made possible by a grant from Colgate University's Council for Faculty Development.

Correspondence regarding this research may be sent to Regina Conti, Department of Psychology, Colgate University, Hamilton, NY 13346 or RConti@Mail.Colgate.edu.

REFERENCES

Baker, R.W., & Siryk, B. (1984). Measuring adjustment to college. *Journal of Counseling Psychology, 31,* 179–189.

Baker, R.W., & Siryk, B. (1989). *Student Adaptation to College Questionnaire (SACQ) Manual.* Los Angeles, CA: Western Psychological Services.

Cantor, N., & Blanton, H. (1996). Effortful pursuit of goals in daily life. In P.M. Gollwitzer & J.A. Bargh (Eds.), *The psychology of action: Linking cognition and motivation to behavior* (pp. 338–364). New York: The Guilford Press.

Cantor, N., & Langston, C.A. (1989). Ups and downs of life tasks in a life transition. In L.A. Pervin (Ed.), *Goal concepts in personality and social psychology* (pp. 127–167). Hillsdale, NJ: Lawrence Erlbaum.

Cantor, N., Norem, J.K., Niedenthal, P.M., Langston, C.A., & Brower, A.M. (1987). Life tasks, self-concept ideals, and cognitive strategies in a life transition. *Journal of Personality and Social Psychology, 53.*

Crowne, D.P., & Marlowe, D. (1960). A new scale of social desirability independent of psychopathology. *Journal of Consulting Psychology, 24,* 349–354.

Daniels, P. (1981). Dream vs. drift in women's careers: The question of generativity. In B. Goldman & B. Forisha (Eds.), *Outsiders on the inside: Women and organizations.* Prentice Hall.

Deci, E.L., & Ryan, R.M. (1987). The support of autonomy and the control of behavior. *Journal of Personality and Social Psychology, 53,* 1024–1037.

Deci, E.L., & Ryan, R.M. (1991). A motivational approach to self: Integration in personality. In R. Dienstbier (Ed.), *Nebraska symposium on motivation: Vol. 38. Perspectives on motivation.* Lincoln: University of Nebraska Press.

Dunning, D., Meyerowitz, J.A., & Holtzberg, A.D. (1989). Ambiguity and self-evaluation: The role of idiosyncratic trait definitions as self-serving appraisals of ability. *Journal of Personality and Social Psychology, 57,* 1082–1090.

Gollwitzer, P.M. (1996). The volitional benefits of planning. In P.M. Gollwitzer & J.A. Bargh (Eds.), *The psychology of action: Linking cognition and motivation to behavior* (pp. 287–312). New York: The Guilford Press.

Gollwitzer, P.M., & Moskowitz, G.B. (1996). Goal effects on action and cognition. In E.T. Higgins & A.W. Kruglanski (Eds.), *Social psychology: Handbook of basic principles* (pp. 361–399). New York: Guilford.

Gollwitzer, P.M., & Schaal, B. (1998). Metacognition in action: The importance of implementation intentions. *Personality and Social Psychology Review, 2,* 124–136.

Latham, G.P., & Locke, E.A. (1991). Self-regulation through goal setting. *Organizational Behavior and Human Decision Processes, 50,* 212–247.

Levinson, D.J. (1977). *The seasons of a man's life.* New York: Ballantine Books.

Marcia, J.E. (1966). Development and validation of ego-identity status. *Journal of Personality and Social Psychology, 3,* 551–558.

Marcia, J.E. (1967). Ego identity status: Relationship to change in self-esteem, "general maladjustment," and authoritarianism. *Journal of Personality, 35,* 118–133.

Markus, H.R., & Kitayama, S. (1991). Culture and the self. Implications for cognition, emotion, and motivation. *Psychological Review, 98,* 224–253.

Markus, H.R., Kitayama, S., & Heiman, R.J. (1996). Culture and basic psychological principles. In E.T. Higgins & A.W. Kruglanski (Eds.), *Social psychology: Handbook of basic principles* (pp. 957–913). New York: Guilford.

Morris, W.N., & Reilly, N.P. (1987). Toward the self-regulation of mood: Theory and research. *Motivation and Emotion, 11,* 215–249.

Murphy, K., & Welch, F. (1989). Wage premiums for college graduates: Recent growth and possible explanations. *Educational Researcher,* May, 17–26, U.S. Department of Commerce, Bureau of the Census.

National Center for Educational Statistics. (1995). *The condition of education.* U.S. Department of Commerce, Bureau of the Census.

Pham, L.B., & Taylor, S.E. (1993). From thought to action: Effects of process-versus outcome-based mental simulations on performance. *Personality and Social Psychology Bulletin, 25,* 250–260.

Sheldon, K.M., & Elliot, A.J. (1997). Not all personal goals are personal: Comparing autonomous and controlled reasons for goals as predictors of effort and attainment. *Personality and Social Psychology Bulletin, 24,* 546–557.

Sheldon, K.M., & Kasser, T. (1995). Coherence and congruence: Two aspects of personality integration. *Journal of Personality and Social Psychology, 68,* 531–543.

Steinberg, L., Dombusch, S.M., & Brown, B.B. (1992). Ethnic differences in adolescent achievement: An ecological perspective. *American Psychologist, 47,* 723–729.

Taylor, S.E., & Pham, L.B. (1996). Mental simulation, motivation and action. Chapter in P.M. Gollwitzer & J.A. Bargh (Eds.), *The psychology of action: Linking cognition and motivation to behavior.* New York: The Guilford Press.

Taylor, S.E., Pham, L.B., Rivkin, I.D., & Armor, D.A. (1998). Harnessing the imagination: Mental simulation, self-regulation, and coping. *American Psychologist, 53,* 429–439.

CHAPTER 10

MOTIVATIONAL CHANGE IN THE TRANSITION FROM PRIMARY SCHOOL TO SECONDARY SCHOOL

Judith MacCallum

ABSTRACT

This chapter explores motivational change in mathematics and English across the primary-secondary school transition in Australia. It is part of a longitudinal project examining the nature of motivational change and its relation to the contexts in which change occurs. The chapter highlights the different views of motivational change gained through analysis of group and individual data. It uses goal theory as the conceptual framework, and extends the approach by examining the relationship between a range of motivation variables over time and the motivation of students with particular motivational goal patterns.

INTRODUCTION

When teachers and motivation researchers talk of motivating students or enhancing motivation in an educational context they usually have a particular idea in mind about why and for what students ought to be motivated.

For instance, statements like "doing what the teacher wants," being "interested to learn new things" or being "motivated to learn" each conjure up particular attitudes and behaviors (Ames, 1992; Brophy, 1983; Harter, 1981). These "motivations" also imply that questions about enhancing motivation are not necessarily questions about whether or not a student is motivated, or even how much motivation a student has, but what form the motivation takes. Thus enhancing motivation may involve not only increasing motivation in a quantitative sense, but also changing motivation in a qualitative sense, and this is ultimately intertwined with the contexts of motivation and learning. This raises two important and interrelated issues: what is the nature of motivational change, and how is it related to changing contexts.

In order to enhance motivation, then, it is necessary to understand not only the nature of motivation but also the nature of motivational change. This involves examination of quantitative and qualitative changes in motivation, how motivation changes with time (age or development), how motivation changes with different educational (or achievement) contexts (i.e., sociocultural change), and the nature of the person-context relationship in motivation. Although the literature on motivation is vast, it is evident from recent reviews (Blumenfeld, 1992; Eccles, Wigfield, & Schiefele, 1998; Pintrich, 1991) that to date little motivation research has addressed these issues. The main emphases have been on short term change and prediction of achievement, viewed through a diverse and rarely connected plethora of motivation constructs (Eccles, 1991).

A recent approach, goal theory (Ames & Archer, 1988; Dweck, 1986; Nicholls, 1989), considers student motivation in terms of qualitatively different motivational goals or purposes for learning. It offers a means of organizing a number of diverse approaches and hence provides a conceptual framework for examining change in student motivation. From this approach it is the meaning the students ascribe to their experiences that is crucial for motivation and motivational change. Students with different personal goals employ different concepts and interpret situations so as to serve their different goals. These can be described both in terms of personal goals or definitions of success (Nicholls, 1989), which are centered in the person, and in terms of students' perceptions of the psychological dimensions of the classroom (Ames, 1992; Ames & Archer, 1988), which are centered in the environment. These can be viewed as complementary aspects of goal orientations. Nicholls has identified three different types of motivational orientations toward learning: task orientation, ego orientation and avoidance of work, whereas Ames has characterized two goals: mastery goals and performance goals.

To incorporate different facets of motivation that may change differentially, a number of motivational constructs were included in the present framework. Nicholls' motivational orientation or students' personal goals and Ames' classroom perceptions or students' perceptions of their teacher's goals formed the centerpiece of the framework. Students' beliefs about the causes of academic success were included as particular beliefs or attributions for success have been found to be related to particular goals (Ames & Archer, 1988; Dweck & Bempechat, 1983; Nicholls, 1989) and as important cognitive mediators in motivation (Weiner, 1986). Students' beliefs about the causes of success may be intermediary between their personal goals and their perceptions of the environment (Nicholls & Thorkildsen, 1987). Affective responses have been components of many conceptualizations of motivation (e.g., Atkinson, 1964) and have also been associated with particular goal orientations (Duda & Nicholls, 1992; Dweck, 1986).

Perceptions of competence have been shown to be important for some students and play an integral part in the conceptualization of motivation in many studies (e.g., Eccles et al., 1989; Harter, Whitesell, & Kowalski, 1992). Thus, students' self-perceptions of competence, and an achievement measure were also included. Students' perceptions of the importance of different aspects of knowledge (substantive and conventional) which are not usually considered to be motivational in nature, were also introduced to tap sociocultural differences in students' perceptions of the subject areas. These latter constructs were informed by Nicholls and Thorkildsen's (1989) finding that students distinguish between substantive and conventional aspects of school work and perceive conventional matters to be less important. As students distinguish between different subject areas (Gottfried, 1985; Jackson & Harter, 1991), between activities within the one discipline area (Eccles, Wigfield, Harold et al., 1993) and between conventional and substantive aspects of knowledge and their importance (Nicholls & Thorkildsen, 1989), these should be distinguished and treated separately in issues of competence. Change can also be conceptualized in different ways and different conceptualizations reveal information about different aspects of change with respect to groups and individuals. Motivation research has rarely considered different aspects of change (MacCallum, 2001a). When investigating change, motivation research typically has adopted a dimension focus and engaged with a few particular, and often not clearly defined aspects of change, using a limited range of motivation variables (e.g., Graham & Golan, 1991; Nottelman, 1987). Cross-sectional studies have examined change across age or grade (e.g., Eccles, Wigfield, Harold et al., 1993), and longitudinal studies have usually examined mean level change in variables or longitudinal stability (e.g., Block & Robbins, 1993; Meece & Miller, 2000).

A comprehensive study of change needs to consider more than one understanding of change, to distinguish between different facets of change, and to include "context" as a crucial part of the conceptualization of change. Researchers have had less difficulty defining stability than change. As stability is a special case of change, that is, no change (Baltes & Nesselroade, 1979), different definitions of stability can assist in constructing a framework for the conceptualization of change. A number of authors have offered definitions of stability (Caspi & Elder, 1988; Kagan, 1980; Wohlwill, 1973) or change (Baltes & Nesselroade, 1979; Nesselroade, 1991) or concepts incorporating both stability and change (Asendorpf & Weinert, 1990; Lerner, 1986; Wohlwill, 1973, 1980), which provide a useful starting point. A comparison of the definitions highlights the possible different areas of focus with respect to change, such as absolute change versus relative change, change in the dimension versus change in the individual, quantitative change versus qualitative change, univariate analysis versus multivariate analysis, context-free change and context-specific change, and change in individual differences versus individual patterns of change.

Each different way of conceptualizing change takes account of a different aspect of change. In isolation, each way can only tell part of the story of change, but in combination a fuller account of change can be generated. The aspects most useful for examining the different facets of change (and stability as one aspect of change) in students' motivation are listed in Figure 1 (see MacCallum, 2000 for a review of how the motivation literature addresses these different aspects of change).

Change cannot be considered apart from the context in which it occurs. The studies that have incorporated different contexts, such as school contexts before and after a transition or different subject areas, have shown the importance of these dimensions of contexts in change in self-concepts and achievement values (Eccles et al., 1989; Nottelmann, 1987; Simmons & Blyth, 1987). The contexts within which change occurs, however, appear to be multidimensional and need to be more clearly specified and described in motivation research. They need to include not only the normal points of transition, such as from primary to secondary school and from one school year to the next, different points in the course of a normal school year and different subject area contexts, but also the social contexts of the school and classroom, which include interactions with teachers and peers.

Thus, the aim of this research was to explore the nature of motivational change and how is it related to different school contexts. This was achieved through an examination of students' goals and beliefs about success, their perceptions of their classroom contexts and their self-perceptions of competence over and across, as well as within different and changing achievement settings.[1] The data are constructed mainly from self-reports of students, as it is argued motivation is based on reality as perceived by the students (Berliner, 1989; Dweck, 1985; Eccles & Blumenfeld, 1985; Nicholls, 1989; Nolen & Haladyna, 1990; Weinstein, 1989). Thus, the start-

Intraindividual change over time
Dimension focus:
Change in the mean level (direction and intensity) of an attribute (variable)
Change in the pattern of mean levels for a number of variables
Change in the nature of an attribute
Change in the relationship among attributes
Individual focus:
Change in the direction or intensity of a variable for an individual
Change in the relationship among motivation variables for an individual

Change in interindividual differences
Change in relative position or rank of students relative to others (change in individual differences)

The determinants of change
Change as a result of a discernible event

Interindividual patterns of intraindividual change
Differences and similarities in the patterns of change between individuals or specific groups of individuals (individual differences in change)

Intraindividual differences in change (intraindividual variability) across contexts
Differences and similarities in the patterns of change within one context when compared to the patterns of change within another context for an individual or a group

Intraindividual-in-context change
Differences and similarities in the student-context interrelationship over a period of change

Figure 1.   Conceptualizations of change.

ing point of the investigation is the subjective meaning of the self in a particular achievement situation and the subjective meaning of the achievement situation to the individual. Comparing the subjective meanings in two or more achievement situations for each student can provide a basis for examining several aspects of change. At the whole group level it enables intraindividual change over time and interindividual patterns of change to be examined at different levels of context, and at the individual or small group level it enables more detail of the person-context relationship to be explored.

Two views of the data, and hence motivational change, are described in this chapter, *intraindividual change for the student group as a whole and intraindividual-in-context change.*[2] These give complementary views of change and enable the dimension vs. individual, and quantitative vs. qualitative aspects of change to be examined with context included in different ways.

The exploration of these views of change was guided by five research questions. The first three research questions focus on intraindividual change for the student group as a whole and hence examine change in the motivation variables over and within different school contexts.

- How does student motivation change over and within different school contexts?
- How does the relationship among students' goals, beliefs and perceptions change over and within different school contexts?
- Are changes in students' goals, beliefs and perceptions similar in different school contexts?

Ecological approaches stress the mutuality and reciprocal nature of the relationship between students and their contexts (Rogoff, 1982; Valsiner, 1987, 1990). A focus on individual students would enable the relationship to be explored more fully. The final two research questions examine intraindividual-in-context change.

- In what ways do students with different patterns of motivational goals explain the changing contexts and changes in their own motivation?
- What interactions within the social contexts of school and classroom do students perceive as important for motivational change?

METHODOLOGY

The exploration of the different views of change required the use of both quantitative and qualitative methodologies. Quantitative methods were used to examine change at the whole group level and qualitative methods to explore individual change in context. Using a longitudinal design, data were collected on three occasions over two school years. The participating students initially attended one of six primary schools "feeding" a secondary school in a predominantly middle class suburban area of Perth, Western Australia. There were two cohorts of students: the main cohort ($N = 66$) making the transition from Year 7 (the last year of primary school) to Year 8 (the first year of secondary school); and the second cohort ($N = 137$) making a transition from Year 6 to Year 7 (the last two years of primary school). There were approximately equal numbers of males and females.

Students completed survey questionnaires referring to each of the mathematics and story writing classroom contexts, in the September preceding the transition and in the May and September following the transition.[3] A small group of students ($N = 10$) exhibiting particular motivational patterns, some of which differed between the subject areas, were selected for interviews over the period of the transition.

The measures of motivation used were: Motivational Orientation scales modified from Nicholls (1989); Beliefs about the Causes of Academic Success modified from the original set of 13 items used separately by Nicholls (1989) and as scales by Thorkildsen (1988), dealing with students' beliefs about how to be successful in the relevant class; Perceived Teacher's Goals, modified from the classroom goals questionnaire of Ames and Archer (1988) and perceived teacher goals questionnaire of Nolen and Haladyna (1990) designed to find out students' perceptions of their teacher's main focus; and Enjoyment as an affective response. Students' Perceptions of the Importance of Substantive and Conventional Aspects of Knowledge were also measured. Students and their teachers rated Students' Competence with measures mirroring the substantive and conventional aspects of knowledge. This provided a context specific measure of achievement. The questionnaires followed the Likert format, participants responding on a five-point scale. Scales were formed on the basis of previous research and theoretical considerations and confirmed by factor analysis. Alpha coefficients were calculated for each variable on each occasion and were generally in the range of .65 to .85. Details of the scales are given in the Appendix.

The main data set is essentially self-report data and as such relies on the students participating to complete the questionnaires carefully and as honestly as possible. The inclusion of semi-structured interviews with a small number of the students addressed some issues of the validity of questionnaire data. Data gained through informal observations of classroom and school contexts and discussions with teachers were also used as sources of evidence for validating the self-report data.

Intraindividual change over time, reported as *whole group change*, was measured in a number of ways in order to examine the different facets of change. The research design allowed a comparison between the two cohorts and examination of the effects of school context (primary school vs. secondary school) and time of the school year (four months into the year vs. eight months into the year).[4] Group change in the mean level of motivation variables was examined by analyzing change in direction and strength in the mean scores of each of the scales using repeated measures analysis of variance, and relative change in the ordering of the means within each construct. Change in the relationship between different aspects of student motivation was explored by a comparison of Pearson product-moment correlation coefficients over time. In order to assist the interpretation of the change in relationships, the change in interindividual differences (longitudinal stability of each variable) was examined by Pearson product moment correlations of students' scores at different times. A nominal significance level of .05 was selected for all analyses and applies to all results where change or a relationship is indicated.

The analysis of intraindividual-in-context change, reported as *individual change* focused on the contexts of motivation of ten students, considered to be motivationally "at-risk" on the basis of their motivational orientations before the transition to secondary school. It examined the students' explanations of their experiences of change over the transition, and their perceptions of the changes within themselves and aspects of the school environment necessary for motivational change. These can be interpreted as students' critiques of school (Thorkildsen & Nicholls, 1991). Each student's perceptions are then linked to their theories of success and a model accounting for differences in the students' perceptions is presented which relates the students' concerns to the contexts they perceive to be important in their own motivational change.

One of the problems of presenting the results of a study of this kind is the sheer quantity of data and analyses, and the complex nature of the findings. In order to give the reader an overview of the main findings, the account is predominantly descriptive and discussion is interwoven with the results. Further details of the statistical analyses are available from the author. Whole group changes, intraindividual change over time, are presented and discussed first, followed by a discussion of motivational change at the individual level, intraindividual-in-context change, for ten of the students.

WHOLE GROUP CHANGE

Change in Mean Level

At the group level, change in the mean level was found in over half of the motivation variables examined but the direction and amount of change differed across motivation variables, resulting in different patterns of change.[5] Table 1 highlights the different patterns of change, referred to as Increasing, Stable, Decreasing, Highest at Time 2, and Lowest at Time 2. The table indicates which motivation variables showed each of the patterns of change. The results are reported separately for each cohort and for each subject area. Note that for some variables the patterns of change differed depending on whether the transition was to secondary school (year 7/8) or within primary school (year 6/7).

For the group that experienced the transition from primary school to secondary school, increases in mean level for both subject areas were found in work avoidance goals and beliefs about success being caused by extrinsic factors, such as the teacher liking them, having neat work and behaving nicely in class. Work avoidance also showed moderately high longitudinal stability (.68 and .66 in writing and mathematics, respectively) revealing that the increase in work avoidance goals was a general trend for most students. Although this could be considered indicative of some of the negative responses to the transition found in previous research (Eccles, Wigfield, Midgley et al., 1993), increasing work avoidance goals is a recurring finding (Meece & Miller, 2000; Rogers, Galloway, Armstrong, Jackson, & Leo, 1994) and not only across transitions (Meece & Miller, 2000). For the group experiencing the transition within primary school, the only

Table 1. Pattern of Whole Group Change in Motivation Variables over Time

Pattern of Change	Cohort	Subject	Motivational Orientation			Beliefs about the Causes of Success						Perceptions of the Teacher's Goals					Perceptions of Competence		Enjoyment	Importance of Mistakes	
			T	E	WA	IE	SU	C	SA	EF	L	MA	PE	PR	TS	CF	CO	S		CO	S
Increasing	Yr 6/7	SW																*			
		M																			
	Yr 7/8	SW		*	*					*											
		M		*	*					*										*
Stable	Yr 6/7	SW			*											*	*		*		
		M	*	*							*				*	*	*				
Stable	Yr 7/8	SW	*	*		*		*	*		*					*	*	*	*		*
		M	*	*		*		*	*		*						*				*
Decreasing	Yr 6/7	SW		*	*	*	*	*	*	*							*			*	
		M							*				*	*	*				*	*	
	Yr 7/8	SW					*					*	*	*	*				*	*	
		M										*	*	*	*						
Highest Value at Time 2	Yr 6/7	SW	*									*						*			
		M				*	*	*				*					*		*		
	Yr 7/8	SW				*															
		M																			
Lowest Value at Time 2	Yr 6/7	SW									*		*								
		M											*								
	Yr 7/8	SW				*	*					*	*		*	*	*	*			*
		M															*				

Note. * denotes change in the variable. Results for the Year 7/8 transition group are shaded. SW = Story Writing; M = Mathematics; T = Task; E = Ego; WA = Work Avoidance; IE = Interest and Effort; SU = Strategies and Understanding; C = Collaboration; SA = Superior Ability; EF = Extrinsic factors; L = Luck; MA = Mastery; PE = Performance; PR = Presentation; TS = Think for selves; CF = Conformity; CO = Conventional; S = Substantive increase in mean level was in students' self-perceptions of competence in the substantive aspects of mathematics.

There were decreases in the mean level of students' perceptions of the teacher's goals over the secondary school transition. One interpretation of this finding is that students were less able to work out the teacher's goals. Not withstanding that possibility, students' perceptions of the teacher's goals as mastery- and presentation-oriented decreased more than other goals. These changes may reflect a change in the relationship between teacher and students, with students in secondary school perceiving less emphasis on the teacher helping them to understand and prepare work in a specific way. Feldlaufer, Midgley, and Eccles (1988) and Epstein and McPartland (1976) identified perceptions of change in the teacher-student relationship as important differences between primary school and middle or secondary school. Over the transition within primary school, the decreases were in a range of beliefs about success and perceptions of the teacher's goals as presentation-oriented. A decrease over time was the most common change for this group, suggesting that decreases in some aspects of motivation occur before the transition to secondary school.

Change was not always in the same direction within the school year as it was over the transition. Differences in change over different times of the year were indicated by a quadratic trend in the analysis of variance (e.g., higher mean level at Time 2 than at Time 1 and Time 3). Several variables usually associated with task goals showed a decreasing trend within the school year but not over the transition from one year to the next (higher mean levels in the first half of the year than the second half). For the within-primary school transition group these were mainly task-related variables such as task orientation, mastery perceptions and substantive competence in writing, and mastery perceptions, beliefs about success caused by interest and effort, strategies and understanding, and collaboration in mathematics. For the secondary school transition group, this type of change was only evident in the task-related beliefs about success in mathematics. Meece and Miller (2000) found a similar pattern of change over the school year in the task and ego goals of younger students in language arts. The within-year changes are consistent with the decreases in students' perceptions of teacher behavior and student engagement that Skinner and Belmont (1993) reported within an elementary school year. One interpretation of this boost in the task-related variables is that students generally perceive each new school year as an opportunity for a fresh start motivationally, but it does not last into the second half of the school year. It may be significant that the first formal report of student achievement in both primary and secondary school is sent home at the end of first semester. For the present group of students this boost in task-related variables in the first half of each new school year was waning in early secondary school. Several variables showed quadratic trends which were not significant, which suggests if the boost occurs in secondary school it might occur earlier in the year or not to the same extent as in primary school.

There was also a pattern showing a decrease over the transition but not over the school year (lowest mean level in the first half of the year). This was mainly evident in the students' perceptions of the teacher as performance-oriented in mathematics. After receiving their school reports students perceived their teachers as more performance-oriented than earlier in the year. In writing, the increase during the school year did not occur. These findings suggest the students in the present study did not perceive the increase in evaluation and performance to the same extent as students in studies conducted in the United States (Feldlaufer et al., 1988; Harter et al., 1992). One reason could be that Australian students do not sit standardized tests of achievement, rather evaluation tends to be criterion referenced and specific to the setting.

Some motivation variables remained stable or at least did not change significantly. For the secondary school transition group this was the case for task goals, ego goals in mathematics and the remainder of the beliefs about the causes of success. A stable finding for task orientation was not expected, given a moderate correlation between task goals and intrinsic motivation (Meece, 1994) and the generally decreasing trends in previous research on intrinsic motivation (e.g., Gottfried, 1985; Harter, 1981, 1992). However, the context, the particular measures used and the timing of data collection may be critical as Rogers et al. (1994) found task orientation increased slightly over a secondary school transition in the UK, whereas the percentage of students exhibiting a mastery style decreased. The increasing trend in ego orientation in writing in the present study was more in line with expectations (Rogers et al., 1994).

Change in Interindividual Differences

The change in individual differences also showed different patterns of change for different variables. As expected from previous research (Alsaker & Olweus, 1992), the stability coefficients were generally higher for the within-school year times (.34 to .68 in writing and .03 to .72 in mathematics) than across the transitions (.09 to .48 in writing and .15 to .51 in mathematics), but the stability of different motivation variables differed over time. The extent of "disruption" over the transition varied between variables. In general, students' self-perceptions of competence and motivational goals tended to change least relative to each other and students' perceptions of the teacher's goals changed the most. Students' beliefs about the causes of success and their perceptions of the importance of mistakes were variable and intermediate. These findings are not surprising given that the goal orientations and self-perceptions of competence are centered in the person and the perceptions of the teacher's goals are centered in the environment, and support the claims of previous researchers that self-perceptions are relatively stable, although there is some disruption across school transitions (Eccles et al., 1989; Nottelmann, 1987).

Change in Relationships Among Variables

There were strong relationships among task orientation and the "task-related" beliefs about the causes of success, and ego orientation and beliefs about superior ability as expected from the work of Nicholls and his associates (Nicholls, 1989; Nicholls, Cobb, Wood, Yackel, & Patashnick, 1990; Thorkildsen, 1988) and between task orientation and mastery perceptions, as would be expected from Ames' work (Ames & Archer, 1988). The correlation coefficients ranged from .30 to .79. The finding of no relationship between ego orientation and performance perceptions ($r < .30$), but a weak but significant relationship between beliefs about superior ability and performance perceptions (correlation coefficients ranged from .24 to .34), suggests the interrelationships between ego orientation and the "ego-related" beliefs and perceptions differ in some way from that of the task-related variables. The apparently changing conceptualization of ego orientation over the transition may be a factor, but the possibility of different mechanisms of interrelationship is worth further investigation.

The finding of a relationship between task orientation and students' perceptions of competence and enjoyment (correlation coefficients ranged from .28 to .68) are similar in some ways to Harter's findings of a relationship between intrinsic motivation and perceived competence (Harter et al., 1992), except that in the present study self-perceptions of competence are not synonymous with achievement. It was not possible to address the relationship with achievement in secondary school as grades students received were not comparable across courses and students were not given a standardized achievement test.

In general, the direction of change was similar for writing and mathematics.[6] Change differed between subject areas for the self-perceptions of competence and enjoyment, with competence perceptions and enjoyment showing a decrease in mathematics and remaining stable in writing. The gender differences found were complex and not always consistent over time. This suggests that the interindividual differences being tapped are only partly due to gender, or are influenced by another factor or factors that has gender influences.

Examining change in motivation for the whole group provides an overview of change over the transition from primary school to secondary school. It is a backdrop for sketching the motivational change of smaller groups of specific students that is explored in the following section.

INDIVIDUAL MOTIVATIONAL CHANGE

This section examines the contexts of motivational change of ten students through their stories of motivational change in the transition from primary school to secondary school. The students' comments and critiques were analyzed in three stages. Firstly, students' responses to the interview questions were systematically compared with their motivational goals obtained from the questionnaire data. In this way, students' different combinations of goals could be related to their broader theories of success. Comments, which matched the motivational patterns as well as those that differed from expectations were noted. Students expressing ego goals would be expected to see success in terms of performance, especially in reference to others, and to seek some kind of recognition or acknowledgment of their performance. Students expressing task goals would be expected to emphasize understanding, interest and trying to improve, while students expressing work avoidance goals would be expected to seek ways to limit the amount of effort needed to get by. Secondly, students' responses relating to their perceptions of the differences between primary school and secondary school, their stories of motivational change and their perceptions of the differences between writing and mathematics were collated and then compared with the students' initial motivational goal patterns and changes in their wanting to learn and improve.

The third stage of analysis involved an exploration of the contexts that each student implicated in their perceptions of difference and change collated in stage 2. Not only did the students have different views about what success entailed, as would be expected from their different patterns of goals, but they also differed in their perceptions of what was different about secondary school, and in their stories about motivational change. The differences related to the importance of different contexts or different interactions with others within these contexts. Here contexts refer to the contexts in which interaction and change occurs and can be thought of as spheres interacting with the self in the center, and include peers, teacher, subject area, school organization and family. The spheres may be overlapping, but are drawn here as concentric circles for clarity in reporting the findings (see Figure 2).

Although the students chosen had low task orientation scores in at least one subject area relative to the other students in their year group, examination of their scores in all three motivational orientations revealed several different patterns of goals. For each student, some goal or goals predominated. From this multiple goal perspective the students could be arranged into three groups based on the pattern of their initial motivational goals. Marnie, Kim, and Anna had predominantly ego goals, Elise, Paul, Andrew, and Brad had combinations of ego and task goals (usually with higher task or ego goals in one subject area), while work avoidance goals predominated for Shari and Shane, and for Mia in mathematics. A fourth group, "no goals," could have been formed of the students whose scores on each goal were low (i.e., did not endorse the goal) as well as low relative to their peers. Andrew and Brad fitted this pattern in writing, but were included in the task and ego combination group as they expressed a similar but stronger pattern in mathematics.

The students "clustered" together talked about being motivated in ways that would be expected from their goal emphases, but also gave responses that could be categorized under other goal emphases as shown in Table 2. Even within the expected goal emphasis there were subtle differences in

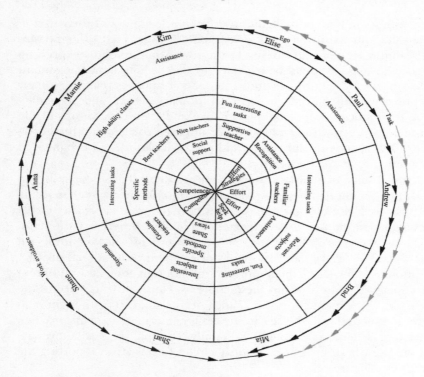

Figure 2.   The contexts of students' motivational change. Circles represent (from center) self, peers, teacher, subject area, school organization and family.

Table 2. A Comparison of Students' Goal Emphases and Motivational Reponses

Initial Goal Emphasis	Motivational Responses			
	Ego	Task	Work Avoidance	Social
Ego				
Marnie	*Perform* at top; *Recognized* as smart formally (AEP). *Compare* work and grades between classes.		*Limit effort;* enough to keep top performance.	*Impress* a wide audience; Accept *responsibility* of high achiever; *Status* as high achiever.
Kim	*Perform* well.		*Limit effort,* work if liked subject.	*Please* parents; *Support* of parents and peers.
Anna	*Perform* at reasonable standard.	*Interest* in new tasks.	*Limit effort,* work because like subject.	*Impress* teachers; *Status* as different.
Task and Ego				
Elise	*Perform* well; Conscious of teacher's *expectations.*	*Strategies* to improve, concentration, work hard.		*Status* as different, liking maths.
Paul	*Perform* at high standard.	*Seek help* if needed; *Effort* to understand and improve.		*Support* of parents, teachers, and peers.
Andrew	*Perform* best in class.	*Seek help* if needed; *Interest* in some aspects of subjects.	*Limit effort,* work if not too hard.	
Brad	*Recognized* as smart informally by teachers.		*Limit effort,* work in the future.	Anxiety about *lack of support* of older peers.
Work Avoidance				
Shari		*Interest* in different and new ideas	*Limit effort,* work if relevant.	*Support* of peers.
Shane	*Perform* to not appear dumb.		*Dislike effort,* all school work; *Limit effort,* work if wanted to.	*Dislike academic support* of peers.

the focus of students' concerns. Also, it was clear that many of the students' responses had a social aspect that needed to be accounted for. Thus, a social category was added. In a recent interview study with Australian students aged 12 to 14 years, Dowson and McInerney (1997) also found students expressed a number of social goals, as well as academic goals, that were important for success at school.

The differences in the students' stories about motivational change related to the importance of different contexts or different interactions with others within these contexts.[7] Many of the stories the students told about incidents that influenced their motivation, can be related to their motivational goal patterns. The incidents are summarized in Figure 2 showing the contexts of change depicted in the students' stories. Each context is discussed in turn.

Self

Few students implicated the self in motivational change. This may be due to a characteristic of this group of students, as initially low in task orientation. In secondary school, Paul had the most task goals especially in relation to his work avoidance goals (which were very low). He saw a poor result in a test or inability to understand something as a signal to work harder and, if necessary, seek help from a peer, teacher or parent. This meant he tended to put himself in control of his motivational change. These strategic types of actions in the face of difficulties are frequently cited as characteristic of a learning or task goal (Dweck, 1985; 1986; Nicholls, Cheung, Lauer, & Patashnick, 1989).

Other students spoke about having feelings of competence that increased the likelihood of their wanting to learn. For example, Shane equated feeling successful, liking and being good at something and thought all students felt the same way he did. In responding to a question about what made him want to learn in mathematics he said:

S: That I get it right. That it's something interesting that I like doing.

I: Maths isn't interesting?

S: Not really, not usually, like when you do some things I like doing and some things I don't.

I: What do you like doing?

S: Things that are fun.

I: What kinds of things?

S: Things that I know how to do, like what I've already done, like addition, subtraction, all them, times.

Anna's comments were very similar to Shane's in that she was motivated to learn if she liked something she thought she was doing well at it. For Anna and Shane this didn't appear to be an "if-then" relationship, rather that liking and feeling competent were mutually reinforcing. It is clear that not all students felt this way about liking as Marnie, who had high ego goals, made it clear she did not have to like something to feel successful and Paul, who tended to have more prominent task goals, appeared to think liking was preferable but not essential. Anna and Shane both maintained high work avoidance goals, although Anna held high ego goals as well. It appears that how these two students felt about their competence and the schoolwork they were asked to do, affected their motivation and the possibility of motivational change.

Peers

Peers were only briefly mentioned in students' stories about motivational change and tended to be as supporting change or maintaining motivation. A number of students with social goals preferred to have friends in class for motivational support. Also, Paul saw peers as helpful in finding the easiest or fastest way to do something:

P: If they can get along with students they may be able to discuss their ideas between each other and they will be able to come up with the easiest one.

Only one student really talked about peers in the sense of working together as a means of enhancing motivation. Shari was quite animated when she talked of discussing ideas with peers in English, and was disappointed she was not in a particular class that spent more time interacting in this way. Shari's task and ego goals increased relative to her work avoidance goals in writing in year 8.

Teacher

All the students mentioned teachers in one way or another and this suggests that teachers are very important in students' perceptions of wanting to learn. Wentzel (1998) found that the students' relationships with the teacher accounted for student achievement over and above parent and peer influences. In the present study, different relationships with the teacher were evident. Some students focused on what the teacher could do for them, others on their understanding or interpreting of the teachers' explanations or instructions, or on their liking of the teacher or the teacher liking them. The students with more prominent or increasing task goals were less inclined to be critical of the teacher and highlighted the positive aspects of interactions. Students with prominent ego or work avoidance goals or both, tended to be critical of the student-teacher inter-action and most had ideas of how they thought it should be.

Paul told a little story about a teacher-initiated incident in primary school that encouraged him to work harder and improve.

> **P:** One day I came in from going to the dentist, my story, the begin-ning of my story was up on the board, and I really liked that. He [the teacher] thought it was an excellent beginning and I liked that. If you are better than others then it gives you more confidence and you think, well, oh, you're really good at it and you try harder.

This incident did make Paul try harder and encouraged him to find out how to do direct speech properly so that the rest of the story was as good as the beginning. It was an ego-involving situation, in this case public acknowledgment of superior performance that motivated him, gave him confidence and faith in himself to try to improve his perceived weakness—using direct speech in a story. Many researchers (Ames, 1990; Butler, 1992; Deci & Ryan, 1985) suggest that public acknowledgment of superior achievement and social comparison in classrooms decreases task involve-ment and intrinsic interest, but in this situation the opposite was the case.

Paul also considered teachers and parents as sources of assistance. Teachers and sometimes parents could help you to understand. Elise thought that if the teacher believed in you, motivation and achievement would follow. This statement expresses the sentiment contained in stu-dents' valuing of the teacher wanting them to do well.

For Shane, there was one teacher that seemed to have sparked in him a desire to learn. He had a new mathematics teacher for term 3.

> **S:** This teacher, like he wants to get us better, like that teacher last term he didn't really care, he just did it as a job to get paid.
>
> **I:** Oh so that's what you thought?
>
> **S:** That's what everyone thought.
>
> **I:** I see, but this term you think you are going to learn more?
>
> **S:** Mm.
>
> **I:** What makes you think the teacher is more concerned about whether you understand or not?
>
> **S:** Oh he told us. He said he wants to get us high marks in the test.

I: All right and how has he gone about that?

S: He's explained all the stuff to us and given us quizzes to see how well we are going, and um just helped us along.

I: So you find that helpful if you have quizzes?

S: Yeah, because you know what you know, and you know if you do know how to do something and you know if don't know how to do something, but if you just keep doing exercises it just gets a bit boring.

I: Right, OK so you like to have feedback?

S: Mm.

He was not sure about "learning more" or getting "feedback" but he was pretty sure he was going to get a higher mark for mathematics. Even though Shane professed to not wanting to do much work he actually liked certain kinds of work and responded positively to a teacher he considered sincere and wanted to help his class learn.

A number of Anna's comments about being motivated to learn revolved around the teacher. Impressing the teacher and performing well, at least better than some others, was very important to Anna. Her goals suggested she was performance or ego oriented and most of her comments confirm this. She thought that if she got on well with the teacher, she worked harder, but said that she was not afraid of trying new things or trying different ways of doing things. Wanting to learn new things and trying things in different ways are usually associated with task goals. In Anna's case, this could be interpreted in terms of her goal to impress the teacher, if a teacher liked things in certain ways she would try that. Another incident Anna related, more clearly fitted with her expressed ego goals. Anna did not like group work when the teacher arranged English classes in this way, which had been the case in term 2. She found it difficult as "the teacher didn't know who had done the work," making the task of impressing the teacher hard. The term 3 teacher preferred individual work and Anna said that this encouraged her to want to learn. So, it is not new things per se in this case as Anna likes new things, which further her goals, not new things, which interfere with them. Later Anna mentioned that she liked working with some of the relief teachers and was beginning to think that sometimes it was better to work with teachers who did not know you. This may have been connected to other comments she made that she didn't like teachers looking too closely at whether she was improving or not. In Anna's terms, if she was not improving the teacher would not be impressed.

Subject Areas

Examination of Figure 2 shows that it was not only the students who expressed task goals that thought interesting tasks make them want to learn. The students who expressed high work avoidance goals wanted tasks and topics to be more interesting, varied and relevant. Perhaps this says something about students' perceptions of the majority of tasks students are required to do in each subject area.

Anna expressed what appeared to be an intrinsic interest in the topics in Year 8 English, which she liked and found new and interesting (media, advertising and more books to read) and this may have encouraged her to want to try new things. Anna, however, seemed to be able to turn everything around to performance terms, as she thought if you liked something you felt successful because you think you are "doing good."

For many of the students, particularly Andrew, the aspects about subject areas that enhanced their motivation to learn were related to specific aspects of that subject area and not to their motivational goals.

School Organization

Marnie, who expressed high ego goals, focused on the way the school needed to be organized and the teachers needed to perform to maximize her performance in the eyes of others, including those in the wider community. As discussed previously, Anna also critiqued the way English classes were organized for individual or group work as important in her wanting to learn.

Marnie had applied for and been accepted into the Academic Extension Program (AEP) at the secondary school. She was very critical of it as the AEP had not lived up to her expectations. With respect to change, Marnie focused on the school and the advertised programs. She expected the teachers in AEP to be excellent and the work offered to be harder than what the other classes did, or at least extended. Marnie's critique is about the school and her perception that the school was not fulfilling its part of an agreement. In one sense, she perceived the school to be inhibiting her achievement. Perhaps it was. She was prepared to "play the game," to go to school, work as hard as necessary, achieve well, even if she did not enjoy it. Later in the interview she came back to the issue of the extension program and it seemed she had given it some thought and wanted to talk about it, maybe as a forum for her disappointment.

M: in this brochure it says well get a better education and everything, but we're not, we do exactly the same as everyone else and they get better marks too than what we do, and they say they'll give us the best teachers, as well, but the teachers we get are real losers, and they are not very good at explaining things.[8]

I: Oh, do you wish you weren't in that program?

M: Nup I wish I wasn't in it.

I: Is this the school you'd have come to anyway?

M: Yeah.

I: So you'd rather have not been in it?

M: Oh it's good to put on your application form that you're in an extension, but then they think, extension does that mean she's dumb? and needs extended work. So I don't know.

The school streamed students in English and mathematics on the basis of achievement. Shane mentioned the effect the streaming had on him, not so much as enhancing his motivation directly, but in terms of enhancing his perceptions of competence, which had implications for his motivation. Shane only put in as much effort as was necessary and was pleased that he had been transferred to the "normal" English class instead of the "really high" one he was put in initially. He thought that if you were in a low class you would do well and if in a high one you could "stuff it up." He did not want to be in a position where he might display lack of ability, even in responses to the interview questions.

S: Well one class was harder and now I've gone into an easier class.

I: Why do you think that is?

S: I went into the top class and I got a C, I went back down to a normal class again.

I: Are you pleased about that or not pleased?

S: I'm not bothered.

Actually his answers to others questions revealed he was much more comfortable in the "normal" English stream.

I: Last time I talked to you, you definitely thought that it would depend on which classes you got put in this year how well you'd do at school.

S: Yeah well it does. If you get in a really low class and you know how to do everything of course you'll do well, but if you get put in a really high class and you don't know how to do anything of course you'll stuff it up.

I: So which classes do you prefer to be in then?

S: Just the normal classes, there's low, medium and really high.

I: So you were in the really high one for English were you?

S: Yeah, that wasn't that hard but, um I'm all right at English, it's one of my better subjects.

I: Is it?

S: Yeah.

Family

Only two of the students, Paul and Kim, mentioned a desire to have assistance from parents and these were students who had increasing task goals. Like peers, parents were couched in a supporting role.

Summary

Overall, these students perceived motivational change to occur in various ways and to involve different contexts. In some ways the students' stories about motivational change or what would have to happen for them to want to learn, covered a range of different views about motivation and motivational change. They also help to illustrate the relationship between goal theory and the other ways of conceptualizing motivation. For students like Shane and Anna, perceptions of competence were foremost and they were keen to protect their self-worth (Covington, 1992), whereas Andrew's concern with competence was more specific in nature (Schunk, 1991). Shari wanted to be self-determining in some aspects of schoolwork (Deci, Vallerand, Pelletier, & Ryan, 1991). Paul and, to a lesser extent, Elise depicted the mastery-oriented strategic learner, whereas Marnie depicted the performance-oriented confident achiever (Ames & Archer, 1988; Dweck, 1986; Nicholls, 1989; Nolen, 1988). None of the students were predominantly intrinsically motivated and Brad appeared to rely on extrinsic motivation (Harter, 1981). Interesting and relevant tasks played a part in the motivational change of most of the students (Wigfield & Eccles, 1992). Kim's motivation had a social flavor (Dowson & McInerney, 1997; Urdan & Maehr, 1995) and Mia's motivation, more than that of the other students, combined several perspectives.

The ten students' perceptions of motivational change explored in this paper differ from each other in a number of ways. Their patterns of motivational goals mean they focus on different aspects of the learning contexts, engage in different interactions with others and respond in different ways. Specific aspects of the subject areas make the picture more complex, at least for some students. The view of motivational change gained from the analysis of the whole group gives little insight into the motivation of these students or insights into ways that their motivation might be enhanced. In order to understand the nature of motivational change both the whole group change and individual change need to be explored in the same study.

CONCLUSIONS

Student motivation is extremely complex and this research points to the usefulness of examining a range of motivation variables in conjunction with a longitudinal design to elicit greater understanding of motivational change. The finding of different levels of change in different aspects of motivation suggests that some facets of motivation may be more important in enhancing or limiting the motivation of particular groups of students. There are subtle differences in students' motivation in different contexts pointing to the need for more in-depth research to elaborate the interrelationship of students' goals and perceptions and the contexts in which they learn. The changes over the transition to secondary school suggest that schools must examine the differences in emphases that students attend to, but they also point to the need for motivation research to take account of more levels of context at the same time, from the broad policy of the school to curriculum issues within different subject areas and to the micro contexts of interrelationships among students and between teachers and students.

APPENDIX

The motivation variables used in the study, showing the stem of the questionnaire items and sample items for each scale.

Motivational Orientations: "I feel successful in—if ..."

Task Orientation (8 items)
  something I learn really makes sense to me
  a lesson makes me think about things
Ego Orientation (6 items)
  I do the work better than other students
  I show people I am smart

Work Avoidance (10 items)
    the teacher doesn't ask any hard questions
    I don't have to work hard

Beliefs about the Causes of Success: "Students do well in—if …"

Interest and Effort (4 items)
    they like to work really hard they are interested in learning
Strategies and Understanding (3 items)
    they learn from their mistakes
    they try different ways of doing things
Collaboration (2 items)
    they cooperate with other students they explain their ideas to others
Superior Ability and Competitiveness (5 items)
    they try to do better than others they are smarter than the others
Extrinsic (3 items)
    the teacher likes them their work is neat
Luck (1 item)
    they are just lucky

Perceptions of the Teachers' Goals: "In—lessons my teacher …"

Mastery (5 items)
    makes sure I understand the work
    pays attention to whether I'm improving
Performance (4 items)
    says only a few students can have high marks
    likes everything to be correct the first time
Presentation (2 items)
    pays a lot of attention to neatness says we should set out our work clearly
Conformity (1 item)
    wants us to set out our work the same way

Students' Perceptions of Competence in different aspects of story writing and math: "When you—how well do you …"

Substantive competence (2 items in writing, 3 in math)
    put ideas into writing
    understand questions
Conventional competence (4 items in writing, 3 in math)
    spell words correctly
    set out work
Enjoyment (1 item)

Students' Perceptions of the Importance of Mistakes in different aspects of story writing and math
    Substantive mistakes
    Conventional mistakes

NOTES

1.   In many ways the terms within, over and across are problematic but are intended to portray the different ways in which context was used in the larger study. Variability is considered as a form of change, but few analyses statistically compared student motivation across contexts. Examination of differences in subject area contexts was made through analyses of student motivation within each context and the differences this examination highlighted.

2.   Four views of the data were examined in the research, but only two are reported here.

3.   In Australia the school year begins in February and ends in December.

4.   The analysis was conducted separately for the two subject area contexts, allowing the comparison of different patterns of change. Also, gender differences in change were explored as one approach to the investigation of interindividual differences in motivational change. These aspects are reported and discussed elsewhere (MacCallum, 1997a, 1997b) and are not the focus of this chapter.

5.   Full details of the results are available from the author.

6.   For a full discussion of subject area and gender differences see MacCallum (1997a, 1997b).

7.   Students' perceptions of the differences between primary and secondary schools and their perceptions of different subject areas were also analyzed in this way but are not reported here. A fuller account can be found in MacCallum (2001b).

8.   Another student in the interview group, Mia, had positive perceptions of the AEP class. Several teachers said that there were many students in the regular classes who were more capable than some of the AEP students and so they were receiving more challenging work too.

REFERENCES

Alsaker, F.D., & Olweus, D. (1992). Stability of global self-evaluations in early adolescence: A cohort longitudinal study. *Journal of Research on Adolescence, 2,* 123–145.

Ames, C. (1990). Motivation: What teachers need to know. *Teachers College Record, 91,* 407–421.

Ames, C. (1992). Classrooms: Goals, structures, and student motivation. *Journal of Educational Psychology, 84,* 261–271.

Ames, C., & Archer, J. (1988). Achievement goals in the classroom: Students' learning strategies and motivational processes. *Journal of Educational Psychology, 80,* 260–267.

Asendorpf, J., & Weinert, F. (1990). Stability patterns and patterns of stability in personality development. In D. Magnusson & L. Bergman, (Eds.), *Data quality in longitudinal research* (pp. 181–197). Cambridge: Cambridge University Press.

Atkinson, J.W. (1964). *An introduction to motivation.* Princeton, NJ: Van Nostrand.

Baltes, P.B., & Nesselroade, J.R. (1979). History and rationale of longitudinal research. In J.R. Nesselroade & P.B. Baltes (Eds.), *Longitudinal research in the study of behavior and development.* New York: Academic Press.

Berliner, D. (1989). Furthering our understanding of motivation and environments. In R.E. Amers & C. Ames (Eds.), *Research on motivation in education: Vol. 3: Goals and cognitions* (pp. 317–342). New York: Academic Press.

Block, J., & Robbins, R.W. (1993). A longitudinal study of consistency and change in self-esteem from early adolescence to early adulthood. *Child Development, 64,* 909–923.

Blumenfeld, P.C. (1992). Classroom learning and motivation: Clarifying and expanding goal theory. *Journal of Educational Psychology, 84,* 272–281.

Brophy, J.E. (1983). Fostering student learning and motivation in the elementary school classroom. In S.G. Paris, G.M. Olsen, & H.W. Stevenson (Eds.), *Learning and motivation in the classroom.* Hillsdale, NJ: Lawrence Erlbaum Associates.

Butler, R. (1992). What young people want to know when: Effects of mastery and ability goals on interest in different kinds of social comparisons. *Journal of Personality and Social Psychology, 62,* 934–943.

Caspi, A., & Elder, G.H. (1988). Childhood precursors of the life course: Early personality and life disorganization. In E.M. Hetherington, R.M. Lerner, & M. Perlmutter (Eds.), *Child development in life-span perspective* (pp. 115–142). Hillsdale, NJ: Lawrence Erlbaum Associates.

Covington, M.V. (1992). *Making the grade: A self-worth perspective on motivation and school reform.* New York: Cambridge University Press.

Deci, E.L., & Ryan. R.M. (1985). *Intrinsic motivation and self-determination in human behaviour.* New York: Plenum.

Deci, E.L., Vallerand, R.J., Pelletier, L.G., & Ryan, R.M. (1991). Motivation and education: The self-determination perspective. *Educational Psychologist, 26,* 325–346.

Dowson, M., & McInerney, D.M. (1997, March). *Psychological parameters of students' social and academic goals: A qualitative investigation.* Paper presented at the annual meeting of the American Educational Research Association, Chicago, IL.

Duda, J.L., & Nicholls, J.G. (1992). Dimensions of achievement motivation in schoolwork and sport. *Journal of Educational Psychology, 84,* 290–299.

Dweck, C.S. (1985). Intrinsic motivation, perceived control, and self-evaluation maintenance: An achievement goal analysis. In C. Ames & R. Ames (Eds.), *Research on motivation in education. Vol. 2. The classroom milieu* (pp. 289–305). New York: Academic Press.

Dweck, C.S. (1986). Motivational processes affecting learning. *American Psychologist, 41,* 1040–1048.

Dweck, C.S., & Bempechat, J. (1983). Children's theories of intelligence: Consequences for learning. In S.G. Paris, G.M. Olsen, & H.W. Stevenson (Eds.), *Learning and motivation in the classroom* (pp. 239–256). Hillsdale, NJ: Lawrence Erlbaum Associates.

Eccles, J.S. (1991, March). *Motivation: New directions in school-based research.* Paper presented at the 1991 annual meeting of the American Educational Research Association, Chicago, IL.

Eccles, J.S., & Blumenfeld, P. (1985). Classroom experiences and student gender: Are there differences and do they matter? In L. Wilkinson & C. Marrett (Eds.), *Classroom influences in classroom interactions* (pp. 79–114). Hillsdale, NJ: Erlbaum.

Eccles, J.S., Wigfield, A., Flanagan, C., Miller, C., Reuman, D., & Yee, D (1989). Self-concepts, domain values, and self-esteem: Relations and changes at early adolescence. *Journal of Personality and Social Psychology, 57,* 283–310.

Eccles, J.S., Wigfield, A., Harold, R.D., & Blumenfeld, P. (1993). Age and gender differences in children's self-and task perceptions during elementary school. *Child Development, 64,* 830–847.

Eccles, J.S., Wigfield, A., Midgley, C., Reuman, D., Mac Iver, D., & Feldlaufer, H. (1993). Negative effects of transitional middle school on students' motivation. *The Elementary School Journal, 93,* 553–574.

Eccles, J.S., Wigfield, A., & Schiefele, U. (1998). Motivation to succeed. In N. Eisenberg (Ed.), *Handbook of child psychology, Vol. 3: Social, emotional and personality development* (5th edition, pp. 1017–1095). New York: John Wiley.

Epstein, J.L., & McPartland, J.M. (1976). The concept and measurement of school life. *American Educational Research Journal, 13,* 15–30.

Feldlaufer, H., Midgley, C., & Eccles, J.S. (1988). Student, teacher, and observer perceptions of the classroom environment before and after the transition to junior high school. *Journal of Early Adolescence, 8,* 133–156.

Gottfried, A.E. (1985). Academic intrinsic motivation in elementary and junior high school students. *Journal of Educational Psychology, 77,* 631–645.

Graham, S., & Golan, S. (1991). Motivational influences on cognition: Task involvement, ego involvement, and depth of information processing. *Journal of Educational Psychology, 83,* 187–194.

Harter, S. (1981). A new self-report scale of intrinsic versus extrinsic orientation in the classroom: Motivational and informational components. *Developmental Psychology, 17,* 300–312.

Harter, S. (1992). The relationship between perceived competence, affect, and motivational orientation within the classroom: processes and patterns of change. In A.K. Boggiano & T.S. Pittman (Eds.), *Achievement and motivation: A social-developmental perspective* (pp. 77–114). NewYork: Cambridge University Press.

Harter, S., Whitesell, N.R., & Kowalski, P. (1992). Individual differences in the effects of educational transitions on young adolescent's perceptions of competence and motivational orientation. *American Educational Research Journal, 29,* 777–807.

Jackson, B.K., & Harter, S. (1991*). Children for whom intrinsic/extrinsic motivational orientation is, and is not, a trait.* Paper presented at the 1991 biennial meeting of the Society for Research in Child Development, Seattle, Washington.

Kagan, J. (1980). Perspectives on continuity. In O.G. Brim & J. Kagan (Eds.), *Constancy and change in human development* (pp. 26–74). Cambridge MA: Harvard University Press,

Lerner, R.M. (1986). *Concepts and theories of human development* (2nd ed.). New York: McGraw-Hill.

MacCallum, J.A. (1997a, March). A longitudinal study of student motivation in mathematics and English: Context and gender issues. Paper presented at the annual meeting of the American Educational Research Association, Chicago.

MacCallum, J.A. (1997b). *Motivational change in transition contexts.* Unpublished doctoral dissertation, Murdoch University, Australia.

MacCallum, J.A. (2000). *Motivational change: A review.* Manuscript submitted for review.

MacCallum, J.A. (2001a). A model of motivational change in transition contexts. In A. Eflides, J. Kuhl, & D. Sorrentino (Eds.), *Trends and prospects in motivation research* (pp. 121–143). Amsterdam: Kluwer Academic.

MacCallum, J.A. (2001b). The contexts of individual motivational change. In D.M. McInerney & S. Van Etten (Eds.), *Research on sociocultural influences on motivation and learning* (Vol. 1, pp. 61–97). Greenwich, CT: Information Age.

Meece, J.L. (1994). The role of motivation in self-regulated learning. In D.H. Schunk & B.J. Zimmerman (Eds.), *Self-regulation of learning and performance: Issues and educational applications* (pp. 25–44). Hillsdale, NJ: Lawrence Erlbaum.

Meece, J.L., & Miller, S.D. (2000). A longitudinal analysis of elementary school students' achievement goals in literacy activities. *Contemporary Educational Psychology,* doi:10.1006/ceps.2000.1071

Nesselroade, J.R. (1991). Interindividual differences and intraindividual change. In L.M. Collins & J.L. Hom, (Eds.), *Best methods for the analysis of change* (pp. 92–105). Washington, DC: American Psychological Association.

Nicholls, J.G. (1989). *The competitive ethos and democratic schools.* Cambridge, MA: Harvard University Press.

Nicholls, J.G., Cheung, P.C., Lauer, J., & Patashnick, M. (1989). Individual differences in academic motivation: Perceived ability, goals, beliefs, and values. *Learning and Individual Differences, 1,* 63–84.

Nicholls, J.G., Cobb, P., Wood, T., Yackel, E., & Patashnick, M. (1990). Assessing students' theories of success in mathematics: Individual and classroom differences. *Journal for Research in Mathematics Education, 21,* 109–122.

Nicholls, J.G., & Thorkildsen, T.A. (1987). *Achievement goals and beliefs: Individual and classroom differences.* Paper presented at the meeting of the Society for Experimental Psychology, Charlottesville, Virginia.

Nicholls, J.G., & Thorkildsen, T.A. (1989). Intellectual conventions versus matters of substance: Elementary school students as curriculum theorists. *American Educational Research Journal, 26,* 533–544.

Nolen, S.B. (1988). Reasons for studying: Motivational orientations and study strategies. *Cognition and Instruction, 5,* 269–187.

Nolen, S.B., & Haladyna, T.M. (1990). A construct validation of measures of students' study strategy beliefs and perceptions of teacher goals. *Educational and Psychological Measurement, 50,* 191–202.

Nottelmann, E.D. (1987). Competence and self-esteem during transition from childhood to adolescence. *Developmental Psychology, 23,* 441–450,

Pintrich, P.R. (1991). Editor's comment. *Educational Psychologist, 26,* 199–205.

Rogers, C., Galloway, D., Armstrong, D., Jackson, C., Leo, E. (1994). Changes in motivational style over the transition from primary school to secondary school: Subject and dispositional effects. *Educational and Child Psychology, 1*, 26–38.

Rogoff, B. (1982). Integrating context and cognitive development. In M.E. Lamb & A.L. Brown (Eds.), *Advances in developmental psychology* (Vol. 2., pp. 125–170). Hillsdale, NJ: Lawrence Erlbaum.

Schunk, D.H. (1991). Self-efficacy and academic motivation. *Educational Psychologist, 26*, 207–231.

Simmons, R.G., & Blyth, D.A. (1987). *Moving into adolescents: The impact of pubertal change and school context.* New York: Aldine de Gruyter.

Skinner, E.A., & Belmont, M.J. (1993). Motivation in the classroom: Reciprocal effects of teacher behaviour and student engagement across the school year. *Journal of Educational Psychology, 85*, 571–581.

Thorkildsen, T.A. (1988). Theories of education among academically able adolescents. *Contemporary Educational Psychology, 13*, 323–330.

Thorkildsen, T.A., & Nicholls, J.G. (1991). Students' critiques as motivation. *Educational Psychologist, 26*, 347–368.

Urdan, T.C., & Maehr, M.L. (1995). Beyond a two-goal theory of motivation and achievement: A case for social goals. *Review of Educational Research, 65*, 213–143.

Valsiner, J. (1987). *Culture and the development of children's action: A cultural historical theory of developmental psychology.* Chichester: John Wiley & Sons.

Valsiner, J. (1990, April). *The development of children's action.* Invited address presented at the biennial conference of the Australian Developmental Association, Perth, Western Australia.

Weiner, B. (1986). *An attributional theory of motivation and emotion.* New York: Springer-Verlag.

Weinstein, R. (1989). Perceptions of classroom processes and students motivation: Children's views of self-fulfilling prophecies. In R. Ames & C. Ames (Eds.), *Research on motivation in education, Vol. 3: Goals and cognitions* (pp. 299–315). New York: Academic Press.

Wentzel, K. (1998). Social relationships and motivation in middle school: The role of parents, teachers and peers. *Journal of Educational Psychology, 90*, 202–209.

Wigfield, A., & Eccles, J. S. (1992). The development of achievement task values: A theoretical analysis. *Developmental Review, 12*, 265–310.

Wohlwill, J.H. (1973). *The study of behavioural development.* New York: Academic Press.

Wohlwill, J.H. (1980). Cognitive development in childhood. In O.G. Brim & J. Kagan (Eds.), *Constancy and change in human development* (pp. 359–444). Cambridge MA: Harvard University Press.

CHAPTER 11

IMPLICIT THEORIES AND RESPONSES TO ACHIEVEMENT SETBACKS

Wai-man Ip and Chi-yue Chiu

ABSTRACT

For a long time, intelligence, self-confidence, and self-esteem are believed to be the most important contributors to major achievement outcomes, including performance outcomes, as well as motivational, affective and behavioral responses to achievement setbacks. In this chapter, we review evidence that challenges these assumptions. Despite psychologists' and educators' faith in the psychological benefits of intelligence, self-esteem, and self-confidence, attempts to enhance intelligence and positive self-evaluation do not always lead to the intended positive outcomes. We also propose a meaning system approach to self-regulated learning, which emphasizes the role of students' beliefs in intelligence and in the ability-effort-performance relationships as mediators of students' responses to academic challenges. We propose that adaptive, mastery-oriented responses are likely to occur when students sub-scribe to a dynamic, growth-focused meaning system, which is characterized by the beliefs that (a) intelligence is malleable, (b) effort will lead to gains in intellectual abilities, and (c) performance reflects the amount of extra effort that is required to attain one's achievement goals. In contrast, maladaptive, helpless responses are likely to occur when students adopt a static, evaluation-focused meaning system, which is constituted by the beliefs that (a) intelligence is fixed, (b) only students with limited intelligence need to work hard to compensate for their inaptitude, and (c) performance reflects one's fixed intelligence. We believe that the proposed meaning system framework has important implications for facilitating self-regulated learning in schools.

INTRODUCTION

Achievement setbacks are almost inevitable in a person's learning history. When students set reasonably challenging achievement goals for themselves, they have the opportunities to polish up their skills and develop deep understanding of the learning materials. Success in attaining challenging goals gives rise to a sense of accomplishment, which lays the foundation of positive self-evaluation and involvement in learning. However, students who take on challenging tasks are also likely to encounter learning obstacles and setbacks. Some students try to overcome learning obstacles in a mastery-oriented manner, while others respond helplessly to achievement setbacks. How students react to academic challenges should have important implications for whether students are able to attain their long-term achievement goals, and for their psychological adjustment. Therefore, it is important to understand what psychological factors contribute to mastery-oriented versus helpless responses to academic challenges.

For a long time, intelligence, self-confidence, and self-esteem are believed to be the most important contributors to major achievement outcomes, including performance outcomes, as well as motivational, affective and behavioral responses to achievement setbacks (see Hong, Chiu, & Dweck, 1995). For example, it is often assumed that intelligent and self-confident learners will have good grades, embrace challenging learning tasks, and be persistent in the face of setbacks. In contrast, learners with relatively low levels of intelligence and self-confidence will have poor grades, avoid challenges, and give up prematurely when they encounter obstacles in learning.

In this chapter, we review evidence that challenges these assumptions. Despite psychologists' and educators' faith in the psychological benefits of intelligence, self-esteem, and self-confidence, attempts to enhance intelligence and positive self-evaluation do not always lead to the intended positive outcomes. Next, we will propose a meaning system approach to self-regulated learning, which emphasizes the role of students' beliefs in intelligence and in the ability-effort-performance relationships as mediators of students' responses to academic challenges. We propose that adaptive, mastery-oriented responses are likely to occur when students subscribe to a dynamic, growth-focused meaning system, which is characterized by the beliefs that (a) intelligence is malleable, (b) effort will lead to gains in intellectual abilities, and (c) performance reflects the amount of extra effort that is required to attain one's achievement goals. In contrast, maladaptive, helpless responses are likely to occur when students adopt a static, evaluation-focused meaning system, which is constituted by the beliefs that (a) intelligence is fixed, (b) only students with limited intelligence need to work hard to compensate for their inaptitude, and (c) performance reflects one's fixed intelligence. We believe that the proposed meaning system framework has important implications for facilitating self-regulated learning in schools.

INTELLIGENCE AND ACHIEVEMENT

James Flynn (1984, 1987) discovered that, in many developed countries, there has been an average gain of about three IQ points among their citizens every ten years since 1940. In the Netherlands, IQ scores of 19-year-olds have increased by more than 8 points between 1972 and 1982. Individuals with an IQ score of 140 or above are often considered to be gifted people. In 1952, only 1 out of 126 Dutch young people had an IQ score of 140 or above. In 1982, for every 11 Dutch young people, 1 had an IQ score of 140 or above.

It is still unclear why there have been such massive gains in IQ scores in these countries. Some possible explanations are improvement in nutrition and enrichment in the environment in which people grew up. However, such impressive gains in intelligence scores have not been accompanied by similar gains in school achievement. Flynn (1984) noted that in North America, when average IQ scores have gone up, the Scholastic Aptitude Test (SAT) scores have gone down. The link between IQ scores and school achievement is not as strong as most people would expect. In a recent review of the massive literature on intelligence test scores and school achievement, Neisser et al. (1996) concluded that IQ scores explain only 25% of the variance in school performance, i.e., 75% of the variance is not accounted for by intelligence as measured by conventional intelligence tests.

SELF-ESTEEM AND PSYCHOLOGICAL ADJUSTMENT

In 1967, Stanley Coopersmith, a young psychologist in California, posited that personal judgment of worthiness and feeling good about oneself are of fundamental value in child development. Therefore, self-esteem should be a primary goal in child rearing. In the late sixties, many educators in North America accepted his view. In California, the State Government considered low self-esteem to be the cause of many kinds of developmental and social problems, including academic failure, teenage pregnancy, drug abuse, and dependence on welfare. The State Governmental also believed that fostering self-esteem is the cure for all these evils. Therefore, all schools in California were encouraged to adopt promotion of self-esteem as a teaching goal (Seligman, Reivich, Jaycox, & Gillham, 1995). Signs such as "Appreciate my own worth" and "Get used to loving yourself" were seen everywhere in school. The practice of streaming students according to their abilities was abandoned so as not to hurt the self-esteem of students with low abilities. In addition, levels of teaching were adjusted downward so as to protect slow learners' self-esteem.

Those who believe that such educational reforms would produce a generation of self-confident, self-motivated learners would be disappointed. In a 1981 survey, 95.5% of Californians who were born between 1917 and 1936 had never suffered from depression (Robins et al., 1984). The self-esteem movement had not started when this age cohort attended school. However, for those who were born between 1957 and 1963, the self-esteem movement was very much alive when they attended school. Among them, 5.4% had suffered from depression. Note that these younger people were between 18 and 24 years old when the survey was conducted. Another report (Klerman et al., 1985) revealed in the twentieth century, the prevalence rates of depression had been increasing in successive age cohorts.

In a review of a considerable amount of research evidence on aggression, Baumeister, Smart, and Boden (1996) concluded that aggressors usually have favorable views of themselves. Particularly, people with high and unstable self-esteem tend to be hostile. Baumeister and his colleagues (Baumeister & Campbell, 1999; Baumeister et al., 1996) argued that individuals who have inflated, unstable favorable views of themselves are relatively likely to use violence when they feel that their self-esteem is being threatened, attacked, or undermined by others.

This evidence seems to contradict the well-documented positive association between self-esteem and achievement. However, we cannot infer the direction of causality from a correlation. When a positive correlation is found between self-esteem and achievement, it is possible that self-esteem causes achievement, but it is equally possible that self-esteem is an outcome of achievement. The evidence to date is more consistent with the latter interpretation than with the former one. Baumeister (1993) reported that individuals do not have higher achievement when their self-esteem is bolstered. However, they have higher self-esteem when they achieve their valued goals.

The evidence for the beneficial effects of confidence in one's abilities on responses to academic challenges is also weak. In a recent review of the evidence on the role of self-confidence in achievement motivation, Hong et al. (1995) concluded that self-confidence only predicts achievement when the learning environment remains stable and contains little frustrating experiences. However, when the achievement environment becomes more challenging (e.g., when students transit from grade school to high school, or from high school to college), self-confidence does not predict achievement.

In the face of academic challenges, students may react in a mastery-oriented manner. They attribute their setbacks to lack of effort, show a high level of persistence, and prefer staying on with the challenging task than shifting to a relatively easy task. Alternatively students may react in a helpless manner. They blame some fixed aspects of the self (e.g., low intelligence) for their setbacks, give up prematurely, and avoid similarly challenging tasks in the future. Consistent with Hong et al.'s (1995) conclusion, among Hong Kong students, levels of self-confidence do not predict whether they would react in a mastery-oriented or a helpless fashion when they encounter achievement setbacks (Cheng, 2000).

Taken together, research does not support the assumption that self-esteem or self-confidence has positive effects on people's emotional adjustment or achievement.

THE MEANING SYSTEM APPROACH

The meaning system approach posits that students' assumptions about intelligence and its relationship with effort and performance provide a framework for them to interpret the meaning of achievement outcomes. How students interpret their achievement outcomes affects how they would react to such outcomes.

Implicit Theories of Intelligence

One important assumption students make about intelligence is whether intelligence is a fixed level of ability or a developing capacity for learning. Research to date has provided consistent support for the role of students' implicit theories of intelligence in determining responses to academic challenges (see Hong et al., 1995). Psychologists have termed students' lay assumptions about implicit theories of intelligence, because these assumptions are seldom openly discussed, although they provide a conceptual guide for students to make sense of their experiences in the same way a scientific theory guides scientists' understanding of their discoveries.

The belief that intelligence is a fixed trait is termed an entity theory, and the belief that intelligence is a malleable capacity is termed an incremental theory. Compared to entity theorists, incremental theorists are more likely to attribute achievement setbacks to insufficient effort (Hong, Chiu,

Dweck, Lin, & Wan, 1999). Thus, they are also more likely than entity theorists to take remedial actions to improve their abilities and to overcome learning obstacles.

For example, in one study in Hong Kong, Hong et al. (1999) measured 168 university freshmen's implicit theory of intelligence and asked the participants how much they would want to take a remedial English course in the university. The students were reminded that English was the medium of instruction in the university and that proficiency in English was important for them to succeed in university learning. When students' proficiency in English (as measured by their grade in a public examination before the participants entered university) was high, implicit theory of intelligence did not predict the motivation to take the remedial language course. As expected, the motivation to take the remedial course was low in general. However, when the students' proficiency in English was low, incremental theorists were more motivated than entity theorists to take the remedial course.

Similar findings were obtained among grade school students in Hong Kong. Cheng (2000) measured 183 students' implicit theories of intelligence and their self-confidence. Then, she had these students work on a challenging problem-solving task. As expected, the students did poorly on the task. Students who believed in an entity theory of intelligence, compared to those who held an incremental theory, were more likely to attribute this setback to low innate abilities and less likely to attribute it to insufficient effort. In addition, they were less motivated to participate in a remedial course to improve their problem-solving abilities. They were also less persistent: When given a choice, they were more likely than incremental theorists to choose an easy task that had little educational value (versus a challenging task that has higher educational value). They were also less motivated to practice their problem-solving skills after they had received the negative feedback. As mentioned, students' self-confidence did not predict their responses to achievement setbacks.

If students' implicit theory of intelligence can affect their responses to achievement setbacks, would teachers' implicit theory of intelligence be related to teachers' responses to students' learning obstacles? To answer this question, Hong (in press, Study 2) had 78 grade school teachers and 50 high school teachers read the case of a high school student whose school performance had dropped from being average in grade 7 to below average in grade 8. There was no indication that this student had any family problems or problems with drugs. The participants were asked to account for this student's poor performance in grade 8, and to decide what they would do to help this student.

The teachers' implicit theories of intelligence predicted their reactions to this hypothetical case. Compared to teachers who held an incremental theory, those who subscribed to an entity theory were less likely to attribute the student's change in performance to insufficient effort and more likely to advise the student to engage in surface learning (e.g., rote learning) to cope with the academic tasks (as opposed to encouraging the student to master the learning materials).

If implicit theories of intelligence could affect both teachers' and students' reactions to students' achievement setbacks, can these theories be changed? In another study (Hong et al., 1999, Study 3), to establish the causal role of implicit theories of intelligence in students' responses to failures, the researchers manipulated the participants' beliefs about intelligence. The participants (Hong Kong college students) were asked to read a science article that reviewed scientific "evidence" that supported either a fixed or malleable view of intelligence. Next, they worked on a nonverbal problem-solving task and received either positive or negative feedback on the task. The major dependent measure was when given a chance to take a remedial tutorial to improve their skills in solving this kind of problem before they proceeded to the next block of similar items, whether the participants would take the tutorial. When the participants received positive feedback, there was no difference in the likelihood of taking the remedial tutorial between those who were led to believe in an entity theory and those who were led to believe in an incremental theory. However, when the participants received negative feedback, 70% of the participants in the incremental condition took the tutorial, compared to only 13.3% of the participants in the entity condition. This experiment demonstrated that it is possible to alter students' implicit theories of intelligence. When students' theories of intelligence change, so do their reactions to achievement setbacks.

In sum, students' implicit theories of intelligence predict whether or not they would respond in a mastery-oriented (vs. helpless) manner to achievement setback. Among students, an incremental theory of intelligence is associated with the tendencies to attribute setbacks to insufficient effort and to take remedial actions to overcome the learning obstacles. In contrast, an entity view of intelligence is associated with the tendencies to blame one's unalterable abilities for one's failure, and to neglect opportunities to improve one's competence through remedial work. Among teachers, an incremental theory of intelligence is associated with the tendency to understand students' learning difficulties in terms of students' involvement in learning. On the other hand, an entity theory of intelligence is associated with the tendency to encourage slow learners to adopt passive learning strategies to cope with challenging academic tasks. If teachers can help students develop a malleable view of intelligence, the students may respond to academic challenge with a mastery-orientation.

Beliefs About the Relationship between Ability and Effort

Some people believe that effort and ability have a compensatory relationship; they believe that only people with low abilities need to compensate for their low abilities with greater effort. This belief may lead to the inference that if a person needs to work hard to accomplish his or her achievement goals, this person is not intelligent. Other people may believe in a positive relationship between ability and effort: If one works harder and learns more, one becomes more intelligent. Thus, if a person works hard to accomplish his or her achievement goals, this person will develop higher abilities. When students subscribe to the compensatory inference rules, they may not want to study hard because that may be seen as a sign of inaptitude. Because they are willing to spend minimal effort in their study, their long-term achievement will be severely affected.

To test this idea, in one study, Hong (in press) assessed 175 Hong Kong grade 7 students' beliefs about the relationship of effort and ability. Belief in the compensatory relationship was assessed by the extent of agreement or disagreement to statements such as "If you need to work really hard to solve some problems, this means that you are not very good at that subject," and "If you are really good at a certain subject, you don't need to work hard to get good results in examination." Belief in the positive relationship was assessed by the extent of agreement or disagreement to statements such as "If you are really good at some subjects, working hard would help you to have a thorough understanding of the subjects," and "You must work hard to solve problems in order to utilize your ability on the subjects" (Hong, in press). In this study, the belief in the compensatory rule was negatively associated with the students' school performance as measured by their final examination results.

In another study, Hong (in press) used the same measure to assess Hong Kong college students' beliefs in the relationship between effort and ability. She also assessed the extent to which these students studied with deep motivation (studying for deep understanding and personal satisfaction) or surface motivation (studying for instrumental reasons). Again, a belief in the compensatory rule was related to lower deep motivation in learning.

In sum, a compensatory rule seems to set up an interpretive framework in which effort is seen as a sign of inaptitude. To avoid unfavorable self-perceptions, students who subscribe to the compensatory rule may avoid involvement in the learning process. They are therefore less motivated to engage in deep learning and have poorer academic performance, compared to those who do not subscribe to the compensatory rule.

ABILITY-FOCUSED VERSUS EFFORT-FOCUSED FEEDBACK

The above analysis suggests that rather than focusing on the feeling good aspect of self-evaluation, to promote mastery-oriented responses to academic challenges, educators should focus on helping students develop a malleable view of intelligence, i.e., the belief that one can become a more intelligent person by working harder to improve oneself.

An important implication of this conclusion is that teachers should try to provide feedback to help students develop the belief that performance (and ability) is the result of hard work. The faith in the benefits of the feeling good aspects of self-esteem would lead teachers to believe that they should provide positive feedback or praise to students to bolster their self-esteem. In addition, teacher should avoid using negative feedback to hurt students' self-evaluation. Within the meaning system approach, students can benefit from both praise and criticism as long as the feedback focuses students on the positive relationship between effort and performance. By the same argument, both praise and criticism could lead to helpless responses to academic challenges when the feedback leads students to believe that performance reflects students' fixed intelligence. Recent research evidence on the motivational consequences of praise and criticism has provided clear support for the meaning system approach.

Ability versus Effort Praise

In a series of well-controlled experiments, Mueller and Dweck (1998) invited fifth graders to work on a set of nonverbal deductive tasks of moderate difficulty. All participants received some kind of positive feedback after they had worked on the first set of problems. The participants in the control group were told that they had many correct answers and got a high score. In the ability-focused group, in addition to the concrete feedback, participants were told that they were very smart on these problems. In the effort-focused group, participants were given the concrete feedback and were praised for their effort. At this stage, the experimenter gave the participants a choice between two kinds of problems to work on next: (a) easy problems that would show that the participants were smart, and (b) challenging problems that could help the participants to learn more. Consistent with the prediction of the meaning system approach, participants in the effort-focused group were most willing to choose the challenging problems, and participants in the ability-focused group were most unwilling to do so. Participants in the control group fell in between.

Regardless of the participants' choice, they were given the same set of extremely difficult problems to work on and they all encountered setbacks.

At this point, compared to the other two groups, participants in the effort-focused group were most likely to attribute the setback to insufficient effort and they were most persistent. In fact, when later given another set of problems that was similar in difficulty to the first problem set, their performance improved relative to their performance on the first problem set. Participants in the ability-focused group responded to the setback in a helpless manner. They were most likely to blame their ability for the setback and were least persistent. Later, when they were given another set of problems that were similar in difficulty to the first problem set, their performance declined relative to their performance on the first problem set. Again, the responses of the control group fell in between on all the measures described above.

The findings demonstrated that as long as the feedback emphasizes the link between performance and ability, it would create a tendency to display helpless responses to achievement setbacks. Even though ability praise may make students feel better about themselves, it does not foster mastery-oriented responses. On the contrary, a focus on the link between effort and performance would lead to more adaptive responses to academic challenges.

Ability versus Effort Criticisms

Analogous effects of ability versus effort criticisms have also been reported. Chan and Li (2000) replicated the Mueller and Dweck experiment with a slight modification. They had Hong Kong seventh graders worked on a very difficult nonverbal deductive task. As expected, the participants got many wrong answers. In the control condition, the participants received concrete feedback on their performance. Participants in the remaining three groups were given concrete feedback together and were criticized for (a) not working hard enough, (b) having low nonverbal deductive ability, or (c) having low intelligence. When given a choice between an easy task that would make them look smart, and a challenging task that could help them learn more, 82% of the participants in the effort criticism group chose the challenging task. The percentages in the specific ability criticism group and the intelligence criticism group were 32% and 24%, respectively. When given another task of moderate difficulty to work on, students in the effort criticism group showed an improvement over a baseline measure taken before the experiment. On the contrary, the performance of the participants in both the specific ability criticism group and the intelligence criticism group was poorer than their baseline performance. Later, in a free activity session, participants in the effort criticism group, compared to the two ability criticism groups, spent more time on learning how to solve similar deductive problems, and less time on reading an irrelevant article.

In short, according to the self-esteem approach, teachers should avoid criticizing students in order not to hurt their self-esteem, the evidence suggests that appropriate use of criticism could create beneficial effects. When criticisms focus students' attention on the link between effort and performance, students may respond to achievement setbacks in a mastery-oriented manner. However, when criticisms focus students' attention on the link between ability and performance, students may react helplessly in the face of setbacks. Taken together, to promote a mastery-orientation, it does not matter whether teachers' feedback is positive or negative. What is more important is whether the feedback focuses on effort or ability.

CONCLUSION

In the present chapter, we have posited that how students react to achievement challenges is important for their long-term achievement. Students who respond to achievement challenges in a mastery-oriented manner seek to understand their learning problems in terms of their current level of involvement in the learning process and will take self-corrective remedial actions to improve themselves. Such self-regulated learning attitude and practices are instrumental to attainment of long-term achievement goals. In contrast, students who respond to achievement challenges helplessly will blame their own abilities for the setbacks, and they are not particularly motivated to seek self-improvement through greater effort. As a result, their long-term achievement will be limited.

Under the influence of the self-esteem movement, many educators believe that the best way to promote mastery-oriented responses to achievement setbacks is to bolster students' self-esteem. However, the research evidence does not support this belief. Instead, what seems to matter most is not whether or not students feel good about themselves. Regardless of the students' levels of self-esteem and self-confidence, as long as they believe that intelligence is a developing capacity, they will think that they can improve themselves by working harder and developing better strategies. In the face of achievement setbacks, they will therefore try to overcome the learning obstacles by focusing on effort. In contrast, regardless of the students' levels of self-esteem and self-confidence, as long as they subscribe to the view that intelligence is a fixed trait, they will infer low intelligence from poor performance, and give up on the learning tasks prematurely.

In sum, to help students grow from achievement setbacks, teachers should pay attention not just to how positively students think of themselves, but also to what kind of lay theoretical framework they have developed to make sense of their achievement experiences.

REFERENCES

Baumeister, R.F. (1993). *Self-esteem: The puzzle of low self-regard.* New York: Plenum.

Baumeister, R.F., & Campbell, W.K. (1999). The intrinsic appeal of evil : Sadism, sensational thrills, and threatened egoism. *Personality and Social Psychology Review, 3,* 210–221.

Baumeister, R.F., Smart, L., & Boden, J.M. (1996). Relation of threatened egotism to violence and aggression: The dark side of self-esteem. *Psychological Review, 103,* 5–33.

Chan, Y., & Li, Y.M. (2000). *Criticism can make a difference: The role of critical feedback on children's motivation and performance.* Unpublished undergraduate thesis, University of Hong Kong.

Cheng, R.W.Y. (2000). *Implicit theories and motivational patterns.* Unpublished undergraduate thesis, University of Hong Kong.

Flynn, J.R. (1984). The mean IQ of Americans: Massive gains from 1932 to 1978. *Psychological Bulletin, 95,* 29–51.

Flynn, J.R. (1987). Massive IQ gains in 14 nations: What IQ tests really measure. *Psychological Bulletin, 101,* 171–191.

Hong, Y. (in press). Chinese students' and teachers' inferences of effort and ability. In F. Salili, C. Chiu, & Y. Hong (Eds.), *Student motivation: The culture and context of learning.* New York: Plenum.

Hong, Y., Chiu, C., & Dweck, C.S. (1995). Implicit theories of intelligence: Reconsidering the role of confidence in achievement motivation. In M. Kernis (Ed.), *Efficacy, agency, and self-esteem* (pp. 197–216). New York: Plenum.

Hong, Y., Chiu, C., Dweck, C.S., Lin, D.M.S., & Wan, W. (1999). Implicit theories, attributions and coping: A meaning system approach. *Journal of Personality and Social Psychology, 77,* 588–599.

Klerman, G., Lavori, P., Rice, J., Reich, T., Endilott, J., Andreasen, N., Keller, M., & Hirschfeld, R. (1985). Birth cohort trends in rates of major depressive disorder among relatives of patients with affective disorder. *Archives of General Psychiatry, 42,* 689–693.

Mueller, C.M., & Dweck, C.S. (1998). Praise for intelligence can undermine children's motivation and performance. *Journal of Personality and Social Psychology, 75,* 33–52.

Neisser, U., Boodoo, G., Bouchard, T.J.J., Boykin, A.W., Brody, N., Ceci, S.J., Halpern, D.F., Leohlin, J.C., Perloff, R., Sternberg, R.J., & Urbina, S. (1996). Intelligence: Knowns and unknowns. *American Psychologist, 51,* 77–101.

Robins, L., Helzer, J., Weissman, M., Orvaschel, H., Gruenberg, E., Burke, J., & Reger, D. (1984). Lifetime prevalence of specific psychiatric disorders in three sites. *Archives of General Psychiatry, 41,* 949–958.

Seligman, M.E.P., Reivich, M.A., Jaycox, L., & Gillham, J. (1995). *The optimistic child: A revolutionary program that safeguards children against depression and builds lifelong resilience.* Boston: Houghton Mifflin.

CHAPTER 12

RELATIONSHIP BETWEEN ACADEMIC PERFORMANCE AND USE OF SELF-REGULATED LEARNING STRATEGIES AMONG FORM IV STUDENTS IN ZIMBABWE

Alex R. Matambo

ABSTRACT

The aim of the study was to find out if there was any relationship between academic performance and use of self-regulated learning strategies. Fourteen categories of self-regulated learning strategies were identified from 148 students' responses to a modified Self Regulated Learning Interview Schedule (SRLIS). Three measures: total strategy use, total strategy frequency, and total strategy consistency were used to measure students reported use of self-regulated learning strategies. The scores of these three measures were related to students' performance in midyear examinations in English and Mathematics. The results showed that all measures of use of strategies were significantly and positively related to performance. There were no significant sex differences in the use of individual strategies. Other results are discussed in the paper.

INTRODUCTION

A growing body of research evidence has lent support to the positive effects of self-regulation on human functioning, especially in academic achievement (e.g., Bandura, 1982, 1986; Schunk, 1984; Zimmerman, 1983). Also, studies of expert performance and first class problem-solving models showed that self-regulation strategies play a significant role in competent performance (Glasser & Bassock, 1989). Glasser and Bassock (1989) concluded that use of self-regulatory strategies varies with individuals and those with performance difficulties have poorly developed self-regulatory skills.

Zimmerman and Martinez-Pons (1986, 1988, 1990) conducted studies on the relationship between students' use of self-regulated learning strategies and their academic performance. Zimmerman and Martinez-Pons (1986) have developed a structured interview schedule—Self-Regulated Learning Interview Schedule (SRLIS)—for measuring self-regulated learning. These researchers identified 14 categories of strategies; 13 of which were found to be positively related to achievement. They also showed that self-regulated learning measures predicted standardized achievement test scores better than either the student's gender or socioeconomic status.

In 1988, Zimmerman and Martinez-Pons investigated the construct validity of the SRLIS (Zimmerman & Martinez-Pons, 1986). They examined the relationship between students' reports of using strategies and teachers' observations of students' self-regulated learning performance in classroom situations. Teachers' ratings were also correlated with standardized measures of students' achievement. Factor analysis of the teachers' ratings along with students' scores on a standardized achievement test of Mathematics and English revealed a single self-regulated learning factor that accounted for nearly 80% of the explained variance. Students' reports of using strategies during the interview correlated .70 with the obtained teachers' rating factor.

In their more recent study, Zimmerman and Martinez-Pons (1990) considered eight different learning contexts to compare academically gifted and regular school students on their use of the fourteen strategies. They also estimated the students' verbal and mathematical efficacy. The results of this study were that: gifted students displayed significantly higher verbal efficacy, mathematical efficacy and strategy use than regular students. On the three measures of self-regulated learning, 11th grade students performed better than 8th graders, who in turn performed better than the 5th graders. Students' perceptions of both verbal and mathematical efficacy were related to their use of strategies. Analyses of sex differences in the use of strategies revealed that girls are greater users of strategies but less self-efficacious than boys.

Except for a study on learning strategies by Matambo (1982), at the time of writing, no major study on strategies had been carried out in Zimbabwe. The present study examined academic strategies as predictors of school performance in Zimbabwe. The same 14 categories of strategies identified by Zimmerman and Martinez-Pons in the United States were used to investigate the relationship between performance of some Zimbabwean "O" Level students and their use of the strategies.

METHOD

Participants

Eighty-one male and sixty-seven female form four students from Chaplin High School (a Gweru urban, former Group A school) were randomly selected from a school population of about 300. The students who participated belonged to four classes. Of the males, 28 were boarders and 53 day-scholars, while 44 females were day scholars and 23 boarders. The participants ranged from 15.5 to 20 years, with a modal age of 17 years.

Measures

The following instruments were used:

1. Modified Self-regulated Learning Interview Schedule (SRLIS); and
2. Midyear Mathematics and English tests.

In the present study, Zimmerman and Martinez-Pons' (1990) Self-regulated Learning Interview Schedule (SRLIS) was modified slightly to suit the Zimbabwean circumstances.

In the 1986, 1988, and 1990 studies, Zimmerman and Martinez-Pons found the SRLIS to be a reliable measure of the fourteen categories of strategies. Zimmerman and Martinez-Pons (1988) reported that, while students' reports of using strategies correlated .70 with teachers' ratings; these students' reports of strategy use were negatively related to students' verbal expressiveness and achievement factors. Thus, self-regulated learning construct has both convergent and discriminative validity.

Since the SRLIS was originally designed for American students, minor changes were made to make the instrument more culture-appropriate for Zimbabwean "O" Level students. In addition to the changes on the wording of items one and five; an extra item was added, thus bringing the total number of items in the Modified SRLIS to 9. Further, instead of interviewing students individually, in the present study students read the questions themselves.

These slight changes in the Modified SRLIS were made after 3 secondary school teachers, 3 Educational Psychologists and 2 Education Officers were consulted independently. Also, 8 current "O" level students from different schools in Gweru were also randomly interviewed.

To assess the utility of group administering as opposed to interviewing students individually and to check the comprehensibility of the items to the current Zimbabwean "O" Level students, a pilot study was done. The pilot study was conducted at Thornhill High School, another Gweru Urban and former Group A school. Nine boys and seven girls participated. The pilot study revealed that the Modified SRLIS reliably taps the 14 categories of strategies from Zimbabwean "O" level students' responses.

Procedures

Each participant was given a paper folder with questionnaires enclosed. The students were asked to take out the enclosed questionnaires and read number one question quietly. After about one minute the researcher read the question aloud and asked the subjects to answer parts one and two of question one only. Participants were given 5 minutes to answer the question and were further instructed to number their methods or answers using letters a, b, c, d, e and so on. Answers were to be written in point form.

After the participants had finished answering question one, they were instructed to indicate with the appropriate letter below how often they used each of the methods they had written down: A = Seldom; B = Occasionally; C = Frequently; D = Most of the time. The key was written on the chalk board throughout the experiment for the students.

Finally, the participants were asked to answer the remaining questions 2 to 9 and to answer the "How often?" part immediately after writing down a method or a way of studying/learning. Three weeks after administering the modified SRLIS, the researcher collected the students' midyear mathematics and English marks.

Scoring and Inter-Rater Reliability

All responses were scored by the researcher. Measures of total strategy use, total strategy frequency and total strategy consistency were constructed. Individual category strategy frequency measure and consistency measure were also included in the analyses.

To assess reliability, a colleague (a psychologist) independently coded 20% of the response sheets. A Pearson product moment correlation was performed on the ratings made by two scorers (.78). The correlation was high, indicating high agreement between the two judges.

DESCRIPTIVE DATA

Strategy Use

The number of strategies mentioned by students ranged from 5 to 14, with .7% of the students reporting the use of 5 strategies and 1.4% reporting 14 strategies. The modal number of strategies was 11, with 52.70% of the students reporting use of 11 or more strategies. Those strategies, which could not be suitably classified into any of the 14 categories, were grouped under the "other" category. The mean number of times strategies belonging to this category were mentioned was 2.03 with a standard deviation of 1.34.

Strategy Frequency

Strategy frequency scores ranged from zero to the total number of times the strategy was mentioned in response to each of the items. Even though there were 9 items, the maximum number of times a strategy could be mentioned was 8 because any strategy mentioned in response to the 9th question was counted only when the same strategy was not mentioned in response to any of the earlier questions.

Most of the categories of strategies had frequency of more than one except reviewing tests ($M = 0.03$), rehearsing and memorizing ($M = 0.61$), and self-consequating ($M = 0.74$). Two strategies had means above 2.00: organizing and transforming ($M = 2.18$) and seeking peer assistance ($M = 2.61$).

Strategy Consistency

Strategy consistency measures ranged from the number of times a strategy was mentioned and rated as "seldom" to each time the strategy was mentioned and rated as "most of the time." This gave a range of scores of 1 to 4. Hence the greatest possible value of strategy consistency was 32.

The means for strategy consistency measures ranged from a minimum of 1.02 for reviewing texts to 7.46 for seeking peer assistance. These low mean scores reflect that, besides reporting the use of few strategies, most students also reported that they seldom used the strategies they had reported.

Using the SPSS+ program (Norusis, 1988), the non-self-regulated response ("other" category), the consistency measure and the fourteen category of strategy consistency variables were submitted to a principal component analysis, followed by an oblique oblimin factor rotation and varimax rotation. Both oblique and orthogonal rotations were used because of the controversy in the literature as to which procedure is better than the other (e.g., Cattell, 1952; Nummally, 1978).

The principal component analysis extracted six factors, which accounted for 56.2% of the total variance. The communalities of variables ranged from .40 to .73. The varimax and the oblique oblimin rotations came up with similar factor matrices. The only difference was that, the four variables that loaded highly on factor three of the oblique rotation factor matrix loaded highly on factor four of the varimax rotation factor matrix.

CORRELATIONAL ANALYSES

All measures of use of strategies were significantly and positively related to performance. These results are compatible with reports in the literature, which stated that learning strategies are highly associated with academic achievement. However, in the present study the correlations between strategy measures and performance were in general moderate. When analyses were done with individual categories, most relationships were weak.

The correlational nature of the study leaves open several alternative interpretations of these findings. One plausible explanation is that the modified SRLIS tapped students' knowledge of, not their use of strategies. The argument seems to hold when one considers that on average each participant mentioned more than ten strategies out of a total of fourteen strategies.

An analysis of some of the strategies classified under the category of goal setting and planning revealed that many of the strategies mentioned by the participants are desirable and could lead to positive learning outcomes when used appropriately, Most of the responses were suggestive of the fact that the participants involved knew about good study habits but might not engage in such desirable behaviors.

Consistent with earlier studies on self-regulated learning strategies (e.g., Zimmerman & Martinez-Pons, 1986); the non-self-regulated response (the other category) had negative relationships with all the performance measures.

Although females reported slightly greater numbers of strategies than did males, supporting Zimmerman and Martinez-Pons' (1990) findings, males attained a slightly greater strategy frequency mean and slightly greater strategy consistency mean than did females.

Analysis of sex differences in use of individual strategies revealed that for most categories of strategies, there were no significant differences. However, contrary to Zimmerman and Martinez-Pons' (1990) findings, males used significantly more self-evaluation and information seeking strategies. Again, unlike Zimmerman and Martinez-Pons' findings, females surpassed males in the use of the non-self-regulated ("other") strategies. Nevertheless, the difference was not statistically significant.

On the school status differences, day schoolchildren used the strategy of seeking adult assistance significantly more frequently than did boarders. One apparent reason for this difference is that, day schoolchildren generally have more interactions with adults (excluding teachers) than do boarders. Another interesting outcome is that day schoolchildren used more environmental structuring strategies than boarders. Although the difference was not significant here, the direction of the differences supported the social cognitive theorists' contention that less structured environment demands more self-regulation than more structured environments (e.g., Zimmerman, 1986). Compared to the day schoolchildren's circumstances, the boarders' environment is generally more structured and more conducive to academic learning. However, the non-significant difference might result from the fact that the two comparison groups came from the same school.

Analyses of three separate stepwise multiple regression of the three performance measures on total strategy use, total strategy frequency and total strategy consistency measures revealed that total strategy consistency was the only significant predictor for all performance measures.

These results agreed with Zimmerman and Martinez-Pons' (1986) findings that, strategy consistency measures were the most effective in differentiating higher academic achievers from lower achievers.

In keeping with Zimmerman and Martinez-Pons' (1988) findings, the results of the present study showed that the modified SRLIS was not seriously affected by individual differences in verbal facility. This argument holds when we consider the fact that total strategy consistency, which produced the only significant regression correlation was based on a nonverbal rating scale (Zimmerman & Martinez-Pons, 1986). Unlike strategy use and strategy frequency measures, which depend on verbal fluency, for strategy consistency measure, the student's task was to simply choose an appropriate word or phrase from a given list.

The other predictive models analyzed in the present study depicted that, among the fourteen categories of strategies, reviewing texts was the single most important predictor for the three measures of performance. Other predictors selected were: self-consequating, keeping records and monitoring, rehearsing and memorizing, environmental structuring, seeking information, and organizing and transforming.

Two possible reasons for the category of reviewing texts' being the best predictor of the "O" level students' mid-year results are:

1. When textbooks are available, they are the most accessible sources of information for students.
2. Teachers, usually, construct test items using textbooks as their main sources.

Factor analysis procedures resulted in a six-factor solution. From these results it can be concluded that categories of self-regulated learning strategies are generally related but factorially distinct from each other. Hence each factor makes an important contribution to Zimmerman and Martinez-Pons (1986) self-regulated learning strategy model. Further support for this conclusion is rendered by the fact that the seven important predictors listed above loaded highly on separate factors, with self-consequating and reviewing texts loading highly on the same factor. Thus, although the correlational nature of the study and the type of instrument (self-report) placed limitations to the interpretation of the results, the present study has added support to the self-regulation/performance function.

In summary, the findings of this study suggest that at least at the form four level, no student is totally devoid of the ability to self-regulate his or her academic learning process. Since the least number of strategies reported by each student was five, with more than 50% of the students reporting more than 10 strategies out of a total of 14 strategies, it seems that the type of combination of, and the rate of using strategies determine the quality of any given student's academic self-regulation. Further, the effectiveness of strategies also seems to depend on the type of academic task and the prevailing circumstances.

For instance, the best two predictors for English were different from the best two predictors for Mathematics. Thus, it is possible that if History or Science test scores were collected and analyzed, different strategies could have emerged as the best predictors. This observation is in line with research evidence, which had revealed that different tasks demand different strategies.

CONCLUSION

Since students seem to be very much aware of various self-regulated learning strategies, they therefore require information as to when and where, as well as how, to use self-regulated learning strategies. To this end, future studies should investigate the relation between individual differences in choice and use of self-regulated learning strategies and academic performance. Also, the research question should be expanded to include personal factors such as the student's attitude, ability and personality. One way of achieving this is to use observation, ratings (by teachers and peers) and interviews in addition to the self-report instrument used here.

Further, the relationship between the use of self-regulated learning strategies and other academic subjects should also be examined. For instance, in the modified SRLIS, item number 4 asked for strategies which students use when completing homework assignments such as science reports or English grammar exercises. Here it is possible that some students mentioned learning strategies which are applicable to science reports but not to English grammar exercises. Thus it is suggested that in future, individual items should be more subject or situation specific.

All in all, the results of the present study are encouraging and they could be used as a base for more vigorous research, which in turn may lead to the development of a diagnostic test to be used for counseling students in academic difficulty.

REFERENCES

Bandura, A. (1982). Self-efficacy mechanism in human agency. *American Psychologist, 37,* 122–147.

Bandura, A. (1986). *Social foundations of thought and action: A social cognitive theory.* Englewood Cliff, NJ. Prentice-Hall.

Cattell, R.B. (1952). *Factor analysis.* New York: Harper and Row.

Lutz, G.M. (1983). *Understanding social statistics.* New York: Macmillan.

Matambo, A.R. (1982). *An investigation of learning strategies and levels of performance in some secondary schools, Teachers' Colleges and University of Zimbabwe.* Unpublished doctoral dissertation, University of London, Institute of London.

Nourusis, M.J. (1988). *SPSSIPC + or The IBMPCIA71AT.* Chicago: SPSS Inc.

Nummally, T. (1978). *Psychometric theory.* New York: McGraw-Hill.

Runyon, R.P., & Haber, A. (1980). Fundamentals of behavioral statistics (4th ed.) Reading, MA: Addison-Wesley.

Shunck, D.H. (1984). Self-efficacy perspective on achievement behaviour. *Educational Psychologist, 19,* 848–857.

Shavelson, R.J. (1981). *Statistical reasoning for the behavioral sciences.* Boston: Allyn and Bacon.

Siegel, S. (1956). *Nonparametric statistics for the behavioral sciences.* New York: McGraw-Hill.

Wright, (1976). *Understanding statistics: An informal introduction to the behavioral sciences.* New York: Harcourt.

Zimmerman, B.J. (1983). Social learning theory: A contextualist account of cognitive functioning. In C.J. Brainerd (Ed.), *Recent advances in cognitive developmental theory* (pp. 1–49). New York: Springer.

Zimmerman, B.J., & Martinez-Pons, M. (1986). Development of a structured over-view for assessing student use of self-regulated learning strategies. *American Educational Research Journal, 23,* 614–628.

Zimmerman, B.J., & Martinez-Pons, M. (1988). Construct validation of a strategy model of student self-regulated learning. *Journal of Educational Psychology, 80,* 284–290.

Zimmerman, B.J., & Martinez-Pons, M. (1990). Student differences in self regu-lated learning: Relating grade, sex and giftedness to self-efficacy and strategy use. *Journal of Educational psychology, 82,* 51–59.

CHAPTER 13

AN INVESTIGATIVE RESEARCH IN TEACHING AND LEARNING

David Yau-fai Ho, Si-qing Peng, and Shui-fun Fiona Chan

ABSTRACT

The authors report a distillate of observations on Confucian-heritage education, following the methodology of investigative research that integrates ethnographic research and investigative reporting. The composite picture is that students as well as their parents have to endure a great deal of pain to secure the promised rewards of education—earning a better living and gaining upward social mobility. The pain comes from preoccupation with examinations and excessive amounts of homework. Keeping silent and assuming a passive role by students impede effective learning. Chinese students commonly manifest fear, docility, silence, negativism, resentment, and outward compliance (but inward defiance) in front of their teachers; disrespect, noncompliance, and passive-aggression behind their backs. In recent decades, traditional educational values are being eroded. Students have become more openly defiant and disrespectful of teachers. In sum, the pains of education appear to outweigh the rewards. Confucian-heritage education prepares students poorly for higher education and eventually for life. The evidence shows a weakness in the mastery of approaches to learning and metacognitive abilities among university students in Hong Kong. Underlying the resistance to educational reforms are authoritarian values, a manifestation of which is the ubiquitous ranking of students, teachers, and schools.

INTRODUCTION

In this chapter, we aim to accomplish two objectives. The first is to provide a demonstration of investigative research in teaching and learning, guided by a relational analytic framework. The second is to report some data based on this research, which may help to resolve what we have termed the paradox of Confucian-heritage education (Ho, Peng, & Chan, this volume—to be read as a companion chapter). Briefly stated, the paradox refers to the apparent contradiction between the alleged superior educational achievement of schoolchildren and the many ills of educational systems in Confucian-heritage cultures. More importantly, the data speaks to a central issue in education: What is academic success and how can it be meaningfully assessed?

Readers of the relevant literature are confronted with a schism: Supporters and critics of Confucian-heritage education appear to have been engaged in disparate social constructions of reality. One construction is largely based on massive quantitative data obtained by international researchers (see Ho, Peng, & Chan, this volume, for a summary). The other grows mainly out of the critics, especially insiders, of Confucian-heritage cultures who have an in-depth knowledge of the workings of their educational institutions.

The critics are at a disadvantage, however. Unlike their opponents, they lack massive quantitative data in support of their position. There is a tendency to dismiss their criticisms, on the grounds that they are largely based on "anecdotal evidence" or "qualitative data." A bias in favor of the quantitative over the qualitative may be discerned. But the quantitative-qualitative dichotomy is specious (Ho, Chan, & Chau, 2000). For both are needed to describe the same social reality—only because the human intellect is too limited to comprehend, much less to represent, the whole all at once. Qualitative data may be quantified or described in terms of logical-mathematical relations.

What is desirable is quality data that reflect closely and accurately social realities. With this in mind, we provide some of our own empirical data derived from replicated observations in diverse contexts that cannot be dismissed as merely anecdotal. We attach great importance to relational contexts in our investigative research. As we shall see, the behavior of Chinese students may be radically different in the presence or absence of authority figures and, more generally, in different interpersonal relationships.

METHOD AND ANALYTIC FRAMEWORK

The method we have used is *investigative research* (Ho, Chan, & Chau, 2000), which allows the investigator to observe closely and directly the phenomenon of interest. Although it does not preclude other techniques for gathering data, investigative research tends to rely on disciplined, naturalistic, and in-depth observations over a time span in diverse contexts. It is particularly suitable for uncovering, understanding, and reporting social phenomena that may be hidden from or not easily accessible to observers. Because appearance is often misleading or deceptive, investigative researchers have good reasons to delve into open secrets, insiders' views, rumors, remarks made off the cuff, and activities behind the scenes; to treat official pronouncements with skepticism, and to tap informal networks of communication as an alternative source of information (Ho, Chan, & Chau, 2000). Being close to the phenomenon under investigation helps to ensure that the information obtained is trustworthy and accurate in reflecting realities.

Methodological relationalism provides the analytic framework for guiding our investigative research (Ho, Peng, & Chan, this volume). It acknowledges the importance of relational contexts within which teaching and learning take place. Accordingly, the analysis of relational contexts precedes those of individuals and situations. Methodological relationalism employs two basic units of analysis: (a) *persons-in-relation* (focusing on persons, e.g., teachers and students, interacting within a learning context), and (b) *student-in-relations* or *teacher-in-relations* (focusing on a student or a teacher in different learning contexts). Our strategy is to analyze roles and relationships as a vantage for understanding individual students.

Although investigative research differs from formal surveys, the basic notions of research design and measurement are no less relevant to it. Placing the emphasis on depth means that investigative researchers typically cannot afford to have large sample sizes. And reliance on naturalistic observations makes it impractical to follow formal sampling procedures. However, having a sampling frame in mind helps the investigator to identify representative cases and areas where more information is needed.

We used diverse sources of data, including observations, mostly unobtrusive, of everyday experiences pertaining to teaching and learning; and unsolicited or spontaneous utterances by, and conversations with, teachers, students, parents, educators, psychologists, and colleagues. The observations were made inside and outside the classroom, in families (e.g., during a family gathering) as well as at public settings (e.g., in the street, waiting rooms, and eateries). Our role as researchers overlapped with those of students, teachers, and parents. At times, we acted as participant observers; at other times, we were detached observers.

In a sense, our minds have become the repository of vast amounts of data. A part of the data is recorded in the form of a personal journal. The challenge was to retrieve, organize, and report them—not an easy task even when it is computer assisted. We are aware, of course, that the problems of selecting and interpreting the data are intractable. We have attempted to follow the rigorous standards of investigative research described by Ho, Chan, and Chau (2000). Ultimately, however, this report is our interpretive account of social realities, filtered through our world views, particularly educational values. But, as we shall see, realities are often disturbing, even embarrassing—a price to be paid for honesty.

The present report represents a distillate of the results of our investigative research, organized under four major headings: (a) a personal journey; (b) the pains and rewards of education; (c) teacher-student interactions; and (d) approaches to learning and metacognitive abilities. Theoretical linkages among these areas are given in the companion chapter (Ho, Peng, & Chan, this volume), and will not be repeated here. In reading the following account, the reader should assume some responsibility for avoiding unwarranted generalizations. Virtually all assertions should be read as qualified by such phrases as *tend to, by and large, in some* (or *many*) *cases, in some learning contexts,* or *in the context of some interpersonal relationships.* The quantifiers *some, not all,* or *many* apply to class names such as *parents, teachers,* and *students.*

A PERSONAL JOURNEY: OBSERVATIONS IN THE EAST AND IN THE WEST

The first author has been conducting investigative research for more than 30 years, when opportunities have arisen to search for answers to intriguing educational questions, in the East and in the West. To those who are bent on quantification, we might add that his direct observations as a teacher in the classroom alone adds up, by a conservative estimate, to some 5,000 hours. These observations were made in diverse geographical locations: Canada, Continental United States, Hawaii, the Philippines, Taiwan, Hong Kong, and Mainland China. Because of his training as a clinical psychologist, the first author also made extensive use of clinical observations and case studies. We present three vignettes that are representative and illustrative of the first author's experiences as a student and teacher. (The I in these vignettes refers to the first author.)

Vignette 1: University Life in Canada

At the age of 16, I went overseas to study in Canada. I found myself awfully unprepared academically, even though I had graduated from a so-called famous school in Hong Kong. But that was not the main reason why my grades were bad: Unlike other Chinese students, I was not a "good" student. To me, attending university was like a child entering a playroom full of intriguing toys for the first time. Finally, I thought to myself, I was out of the intellectual dark ages of my secondary-school days. Homework was no longer doing repetitive exercises; composition was no longer drudgery to be suffered; and learning was no longer unrelated to life.

Mingling with Canadian students in extracurricular and social activities was an eye-opening experience. They worked together; they practiced democracy; and they knew how to have fun. In sharp contrast, I found that my fellow Chinese students, all of whom were from Hong Kong, did not know how to work together. Most of them were reluctant to assume leadership positions, and treated those who did as targets of animosity. During meetings, they bickered endlessly among themselves, with nothing much accomplished in the end. They were not quite "a pile of loose sand," as Dr. Sun, the founder of the Chinese Republic, used to say—but an assembly of warring cliques. Defying stereotypes (particularly of cross-cultural psychologists), the Canadians were behaving like "collectivists," and the Chinese like "individualists."

Although my major was physics, I could not resist the temptation to explore other subjects. So I roamed the library, made a diagnostic assessment of professors on the inspiring-boring dimension, and sat for courses in which I was not registered. During my first year, I audited a course called Personality Dynamics. That was my very first exposure to psychology. There were no lectures, only discussions. No syllabus, no lecture notes, and no formal examination. Textbook learning was not emphasized. To a Chinese student, this was strange indeed! The students did not appear knowledgeable, even to one as ignorant as I was. Yet the remarkable thing was that most of them seemed genuinely interested in the subject matter and participated actively in discussions. They struggled to apply psychological principles to better understand their own life experiences. They expressed their opinions freely, often arguing among themselves and even with the professor. At first, I was hesitant to speak. One day, I marshaled enough courage to open my mouth. No one laughed at me. The professor, in particular, encouraged me to speak up more. Since then, I have found it difficult to keep my mouth shut.

I was not sure what I had learned, probably not much that could be measured in a traditional examination. Nonetheless, I began to ponder about questions I had never before encountered. The seeds for a lifelong quest had been sown. Five years later, after obtaining a degree in physics, I decided to enter graduate school to study psychology—to the dismay of my parents and the bewilderment of other Chinese students. And that is why I am a psychologist today. Had I been deprived of the opportunities in North America, I might have survived the suffocation of, but not eliminated the Hong Kong educational system.

Vignette 2: Teaching in a University in Taiwan

After receiving my Ph.D. degree in 1968, I went to teach in a leading university in Taiwan as a visiting professor. Setting foot on Chinese soil for the first time after having lived in North America for 12 years, I was extremely excited about teaching psychology to Chinese students. I thought that I could help to bring an important segment of Western learning that has been relatively neglected in Chinese societies. During classes, I found myself compelled to lecture—to do all the talking. Nothing I did succeeded in getting the students to participate in the learning process, to ask questions or engage themselves in discussions. To challenge my ideas was unthinkable. I experimented with dividing the class into discussion groups. I used every trick I knew about group dynamics to encourage participation, but nothing worked. At the end of the course, one student gave a lengthy written dissertation in which he explained in great detail the reasons why the discussion groups did not work. I said to him, "If you have such good ideas, why didn't you express them in the discussion group?" He did not or could not answer this question.

I befriended some of the students, and became less of an authority figure. Outside of the classroom, they were freer to express themselves and engage in discussions. Some were intellectually curious and took scholarship seriously, with well thought out ideas about human behavior and society.

Vignette 3. Teaching in a University in Mainland China

In 1981, I was invited to teach at a major university in Mainland China as a visiting professor. The university's mission was to provide leadership in education, specifically the training of teachers. On my first day of teaching, the whole class stood up in unison to salute my entrance. Totally unprepared for such an occasion, I was petrified instantaneously. Again, the students seemed as determined as any I have encountered not to participate actively in the learning process. Some informed me quietly that it was considered impolite to ask questions in class. In many ways, the university reminded me of a *sishu* (private school) in past centuries.

The controlled atmosphere was not confined to the classroom. Typically during an academic or professional forum, the chairperson, who was most likely male, would begin by setting the tone and defining the perimeters of the ensuing discussion. The vice-chairperson, if there was one, would be the next to speak. After that, others would take turns to speak, according to an order of authority or status. Participants who occupied a low status spoke little or kept silent. Toward the end, the chairperson would summarize the main points and conclusions, if any, of the discussion. Clearly the right to voice an opinion correlated closely with authority ranking.

My identity was that of a "foreign expert." Like other foreign experts, I was housed in a hotel miles away from the university. A car brought me from the hotel to the university to deliver my lectures. As soon as the class was over, I would be brought back to the hotel. After a while, I "rebelled" against such an arrangement. I requested permission to stay behind after classes to meet with the students informally. There the situation changed. The students became more alive. Some were impressive: motivated, knowledgeable, and analytical. I learned that they had great misgivings about boring lectures, the lack of library and other facilities, and restrictions on access to materials that were considered to be "spiritual pollution" from the West. One student told me in private that interacting too closely with a foreign expert was politically hazardous.

At the end of my visit, I submitted a lengthy statement, containing personal observations and proposals, to ranking officers of the university. Here is an excerpt, indicating that the institutional context simply did not encourage or allow, let alone promote independent learning.

> I find that lecturing is still the prevalent mode of teaching. Students are highly reluctant to ask questions in class, and do not seem to engage in discussion readily ... There are severe limitations to the lecturing method, as almost everyone I have talked with seems to agree ... I find that both students and teachers are very unhappy about the lack of accessibility to reading materials in the library and other resource centers. There are too many restrictions and too many forbidden territories! The library seems to function more like a place for storing books ... The difficulty lies not so much in the lack of materials as in the lack of circulation.

I did not expect to receive a reply, and in fact did not. Instead, I was invited to a banquet, during which no one mentioned any of the issues I raised.

Conclusion

The similarity in teaching and learning styles between Taiwan and the Mainland is striking, and in sharp contrast to those in North America. My observations in Taiwan and Mainland China have been replicated innumerable times with Hong Kong students as well as Chinese students studying in North America—just as my experiences with the Canadian students have been replicated with American students. These observations lead to a conclusion: North American students are by far more active learners than their Chinese counterparts; they are much more willing to participate in discussions and much less hesitant to challenge their teachers. Two words, passivity and silence, capture the essence of my observations about Chinese students.

THE PAINS AND REWARDS OF EDUCATION

We all have our personal journeys, in which we become more alert to the pains and rewards of education in Confucian-heritage societies. This is now the focus of our investigative reporting. The pains and rewards are those of not only students but also teachers and parents. We include, in addition to direct observations, comments, mostly spontaneous or unsolicited, made by parents, teachers, and students. To preserve their anonymity, we omit their names and those of the specific institutions mentioned; however, we give relevant information on their roles, the context, and the year in which the comments were made (in parentheses). The comments have been edited, with their gist being preserved.

The Career of Asian Students

The career of the Asian student is a hard one. The pressure to succeed academically is immense, beginning from the tender years of early childhood. Learning is hardship, not enjoyment. Traditionally, playing and studying is viewed as mutually exclusive. Parents believe that play is antagonistic to learning, because it "prevents students from concentrating on studying." (A popular saying in the West expresses a similar view: "Work while you work, and play while you play.") Education is regarded as a means to an end, not as an end in itself. Securing academic qualifications enables one to make a better living, and to gain upward social mobility. In other words, the rewards come later—or never at all, if one does not succeed.

To ensure success, it is vital to start early by getting the child admitted into a prestigious kindergarten or even nursery school. In some extreme cases, mothers practice antenatal training in the hope of producing super-babies that will sail through the educational system. In Hong Kong, the child's earliest experience with formal education may well be an entrance examination, including an interview, into a kindergarten or nursery school. The earlier rigorous academic training begins, the better, parents commonly believe. A kindergarten principal (2000) explains: "In many nursery schools in Hong Kong, children at the age of 3 to 4 years are forced to write a lot of Chinese characters—in utter disregard for maturational readiness. Many parents think that this will prepare their children well for getting into the so-called famous schools later on. This takes the joy out of learning."

Academic ranking. In Confucian-heritage societies, ranking is ubiquitous. Students, teachers, professors, and educational institutions are all ranked. Social ranking is determined according to not only a person's performance or status within an institution, but also the status of the institution with which he or she is affiliated. Institutional affiliation may assume overriding importance in defining *shenfen* (social identity), and in affecting attitudes and behavior. In social encounters, knowing a person's ranking functions to locate his or her place in the hierarchy of statuses, an important piece of information for "proper" interactions.

In Hong Kong, schools are categorized into five bands. (The Education Commission of the Hong Kong Special Administrative Region, 2000, has recommended that the number of bands be reduced from five to three.) Within schools, classes at the same grade may be ranked, and generally students are ranked within classes. Students, teachers, and administrators in the lowest band schools see themselves as "oranges at the bottom of the basket." Students in the "notorious" low-band schools or low-ranking classes therefore generally have terrible self-esteem. As do students admitted into tertiary institutions perceived to be at or near the bottom. In one such institution, innumerable students we talked with said that they felt ashamed and depressed, especially during the first year after admission. On the other hand, students admitted to ranking institutions are prone to have an attitude problem, namely, arrogance. They find it difficult to admit that they may have learning problems, and so they tend to blame their teachers. An American professor, teaching in a ranking university (circa 1985), summed it up: "The students are bright. But their [defensive and self-aggrandizing] personality is such that they can't learn." Likewise, a university teacher in a top-ranking institution in Beijing (1998) said: "The students at this university today are very arrogant, although they may be actually quite ignorant." We call this the *famous-school syndrome.*

Thus, for both the top and the bottom, there are serious adverse consequences for learning as well as mental health. The Hong Kong educational system functions like a huge machine, sorting students into institutions ranked hierarchically and warping their development in the process. A clinical psychologist (circa 1980) put it this way: "You couldn't design a more efficient system for producing generations of intellectually stifled, emotionally crippled, psychologically illiterate, politically apathetic, and socially cynical citizens—and thus ensuring the continued employment of mental health professionals." These education-induced pathologies are not unique to Hong Kong. In the Mainland, students' rankings are still announced in class and delivered to parents. New policies prohibit such practice, but most teachers will probably continue doing it. It is not difficult to imagine what happens to the self-esteem of students, numbering in the millions.

Examinations and homework. Students are preoccupied with passing examinations. They concentrate their studies on materials prescribed in the syllabus. Some students approach their teachers prior to examinations in the hope of getting "tips" on what questions might be set in examinations. We should add that schoolteachers, no less syllabus bound in their mentality, cover only or mainly materials prescribed in the syllabus.

In order to do well in examinations, one has to be diligent. This means that one must do lots of homework. Parents commonly believe that the amount of homework given to students is an indication of the school's academic standing. Trying to get children to do their homework looms largely in Chinese family life. In large measure, it is a parental obsession and a focal strife in parent-child relations—enough in itself to keep educational and clinical psychologists busy. We can hear parents saying to their children: "You will become a beggar if you do not study hard." A common parental habit is asking the child, many times daily: "Have you done your homework yet?" Not surprisingly, the frequency of such verbalization is negatively correlated with its effectiveness. In families as well as public settings, a common topic of conversation is the frustration of not being able to overcome the child's refusal or reluctance to do homework. Some parents (usually the better educated), however, complain about the excessive amount of homework their children have to do.

> I have little time to play with my daughter [who is attending primary school]. She has so much homework to do. (A psychiatrist in Hong Kong, 1974)

> My daughter, in Form 4, a good student, has to stay up until midnight every night to memorize the English prepositions. A "D" is a good grade. (A professor in Hong Kong, 1991)

Children, of course, suffer no less. The mutual torture between parents and children over homework sometimes reaches tragic proportions. Xu Li, a 17-year-old student, struggled to meet his mother's demand that he places within the top 10 of his class. He managed the 18th place; his mother refused to let him play football with his friends and threatened to break his legs. In a moment of rage, the quiet and well-behaved youngster bashed her head with a hammer. Of course, it would be a mistake to read too much into a single case. However, Xu Li's case has touched a raw nerve, prompting all of China to talk about education. There are signs that educators are beginning to take action for reforms. Beijing's Ministry of Education has announced that students in Grade 1 will get no homework in the second semester of the academic year 1999–2000. Grades will not be made public. Class rankings will no longer be based solely on examination results. (But note that class rankings will continue to be practiced.)

Educational and career goals.   How do students make decisions on their choice of academic concentration? Hardly a process of self-discovery: Left out of consideration are the ideas of human development and individuality. Personal interests, aspirations, or aptitude play little or no part in their decision making. Rather, decision making is externally directed. The determinants are parental and peer-group pressure, examination marks, availability of places in target institutions into which entrance is sought, and job market conditions. In Hong Kong, students are sorted into two streams, arts and science, at the beginning of senior secondary school (Form 4)— long before they have the maturity to make any informed decision. (It is encouraging that the Education Commission of the HKSAR, 2000, has recommended the premature streaming be abolished.) No wonder we find that many university students have no idea why they have ended up where they are. A student in her final year of study (1990) said: "I don't know why I am in psychology." Many are unhappy: "My parents want me to study medicine, but I am more interested in psychology." And many have a narrow, instrumental conception of career goals: "I chose business studies because that will get me a good job."

In Mainland China, the negation of personal aspirations is rooted in the ideology of collectivism. Individuals are obligated to place collective interests and needs above their own, and to follow the "centralized allocation" of job assignments by state bureaucracies after graduation. Considerations for personal career plans were attacked as "careerism" (Oksenberg, 1969, p. 213). In talking with cadres in educational institutions during his visit to Mainland China in 1971, the first author found that even the idea of individual differences in aptitude was negated. By 1981, while teaching in a Mainland university, he discerned an ascendancy of individualism among students. As one student put it: "To think of the state's needs is rather "abstract." We have to consider our own future." The system of central allocation has been loosened considerably in the last two decades, giving more room for personal choice. Young people are now given freedom to choose their career goals. However, in actuality there are many hurdles that may not be easily overcome. For instance, difficulties in relocation in effect restrict one's alternatives.

We may reflect on the struggle for autonomy in making two of life's vital choices, for one's marital partner and one's career, in Chinese societies. The May Fourth Movement early in the twentieth century saw a rebellion of the youth against parental domination, in which a central victory was won for the right to choose one's marital partner on the basis of free love. The struggle, for the right to choose one's own educational and career goals, has yet to be fully won.

Preparation for higher education and beyond.   A common complaint among professors is that the schools have failed to prepare students for higher education, and freshmen generally find it difficult to adjust to the independent style of university learning. But that is to be expected: To play the academic game, the strategy is to study hard in order to gain entrance into a university; after admission, many students feel that they may now "relax." Professors complain that students often behave as if they were entitled to a diploma, without having to work hard to earn it. Several years ago, there was a popular saying around campuses on the Mainland: "Long live 60 marks [the minimum for passing examinations]."

Obtaining the diploma marks a milestone in the career of being a student. Presumably, it means that one has played the academic game "successfully." But many graduates we have talked with have doubts. They do not think that they are well prepared for life and work ahead of them. A university graduate with a major in economics in Taiwan (1967) explained: "I have no interest in economics. My marks at the university entrance exam were not high enough to get me into some other subject ... I just studied lecture notes and textbooks to pass exams. I really learned nothing." Going to graduate school may not mark a departure from the pattern we have described. As a graduate student in North America (1964) observed: "Chinese [male] graduate students are typically preoccupied with getting a degree, a job, a wife, in that order, and not much else. They are poorly informed outside their area of specialization. They congregate among themselves; as a result, they have hardly absorbed the essence of their host culture."

There is irony in this. Students have gone through an educational system that is highly structured, with rigidly defined paths to be followed. Yet, graduates are at a loss if they are asked to reflect on why they have "chosen" their academic concentration and career, and what they have really learned to prepare themselves for life. In terms of human development the end result may be summed up as a lack of inner direction.

Silence and Passivity

To many a teacher, one of the "pains" in education is the students' lack of responsiveness. A generalization that no one, to our knowledge, has disputed is that the majority of Chinese students play a passive role in learning. They expect their teachers to instruct, and expect themselves to be instructed—"spoon fed." They rely heavily on handouts and notes taken in lectures. The popular teachers are those who prepare detailed handouts and give lessons in an orderly (uninspiring?) manner that makes it easy for note taking. Independence and initiative are lacking. Looking for direction and structure, students expect their teachers to give them explicit directions on what to study, what materials they should read and when to read them, and what tasks or assignments they should complete and how to do them. They feel uneasy about unstructured situations or freedom of choice. Looking for guidance, they ask: "What should I read?" "What topic should I choose for my assignment?" "What should we discuss today?" They are hesitant to ask questions and do not participate actively in class. In discussion groups, typically students take a long time to warm up. They look at one another, with nothing much to say. We call this the phenomenon of silence and passivity. Because it is one of the most pervasive and intractable obstacles to effective learning among Chinese students, we decided to investigate this phenomenon in greater depth.

Political control. To begin with, the generalization has to be qualified, particularly with respect to Mainland China. The first author had an unusual opportunity to visit the mainland as a member of a group of overseas Chinese scholars. The time was 1971, just after the "ping-pong diplomacy" and before Nixon's visit to China. The visit lasted nearly a month. It was, in every sense, a guided tour. Nonetheless, everyone in the group was impressed with the eloquence of students at various levels of education everywhere we went. Of course, the students uniformly spoke according to the party line. But their assertive expressiveness in front of authority figures (teachers and professors) was not something the first author had witnessed before, or has witnessed ever since the visit, among Chinese students. It remains an anomaly to this day. To account for this anomaly would go beyond the scope of this chapter. It does show, however, that the phenomenon of silence and passivity is subject to change according to not only cultural, but also political forces.

Political control over university students has loosened considerably, compared with the time, in 1981, when the first author taught in a mainland university. According to our informants from the mainland, in many universities nowadays students in classes taught by foreign teachers can be very active. More generally, the teacher's quality and style is a main determinant of the level of participation. Still, even in ranking institutions, such as Peking University and the People's University, the majority of students are passive and keep their silence.

Explanation. To account for the phenomenon of passivity and silence, first we note that the pressure to keep silent has ancient roots, culturally reinforced for centuries. In Confucianism, exercising caution in speaking is a virtue; spontaneity is recklessness (Ho, Peng, & Chan, this volume). Opening one's mouth exposes one to various dangers, such as invoking the anger and retribution of authority figures, appearing immodest, or ridicule by one's peers. In educational settings, the most parsimonious explanation is that passivity and silence result directly from role definitions: The teachers impart knowledge, and the student listens (Ho, Peng, & Chan, this volume).

Generally Chinese teachers put great emphasis on maintaining order in the classroom. They usually set aside some limited time for students to ask questions during class. Many consider asking questions outside this "question time," impolite or disruptive. Also, questions have to be raised in a respectful, submissive manner—asking for "correct" answers or guidance. Asking "difficult" questions is threatening to teachers, given that they are supposed to be knowledgeable and have the answers. Asking challenging questions is worse. On their part, students hesitate to ask questions, because they are afraid of appearing unprepared or ignorant in front of the teacher and classmates, running the risk of challenging the teacher's authority, or being seen as showing off (a serious social blunder where modesty, not assertion, is a virtue).

But why the great reluctance to speak during discussion periods, when they are expected to participate? Here are some of the answers most frequently given by students.

"I don't know if what I want to say is correct"

"I am afraid of how other students may react to what I say."

"I don't want to use up class time."

"By the time I want to speak up, the class has already moved to a different topic."

These answers do not, however, tell the whole story. Talking with students in-depth and in private reveals that many factors may be operating to inhibit discussion: (a) the very presence of the teacher, seen as an authority figure; (b) passive resistance to the teacher; (c) lack of interest; (d) lack of experience with spontaneity and freedom of expression in the students' educational history; (e) conformity to the norm of silence and fear of ostracism by classmates; and (f) feeling intimidated when the size of the group is too large, say exceeding ten students.

An experiment.   A simple experiment shows that the level of student participation changes when the relational context is altered. In a Hong Kong tertiary institution where he was teaching, the first author found, as expected, a near-zero level of spontaneous participation in discussion groups. Giving encouragement and other inducements had little effect. He then divided a discussion group into two subgroups, each with a size of about nine students, and moved back and forth between the subgroups in the same classroom. Almost immediately the level of spontaneous participation increased dramatically. In subsequent discussion sessions, participation level decreased, just as dramatically, whenever the group was not so divided. Subsequent replications with more than 10 other groups over a two-year period led to the same result. Having a smaller group size obviously helped to reduce inhibition, the students admitted. But the critical factor was that the teacher, seen as an authority figure, was "absent" from each subgroup approximately half of the time.

The experiment demonstrates that passivity and silence are not incurable. It also highlights the overriding importance of authority relations within which teaching and learning take place. In a section below, we focus our report on the overriding importance of authority in teacher-student interactions.

Departure from tradition. In recent decades, keen observers have remarked that Confucian educational values, such as respect for learning, authority, and order, are becoming increasingly irrelevant. This raises the question of whether the notion of Confucian-heritage education is still applicable. Students have become more openly defiant and disrespectful of teachers. Impertinence and aggressiveness are becoming more direct. In Japan, a new term has appeared in the lexicon: *gakkyu hokai* (classroom collapse). Many teachers complain that they find it difficult, even unable, to control classes which have degenerated into anarchy, with children running around, playing, fighting, or sleeping. In Hong Kong, listening to teachers and students reveals a high level of mutual antagonism; each side has a low opinion of the other. This can be verified as easily as listening to comments teachers and students make about each other in elevators within university campuses. The remark most frequently made by students is: "The lecture was boring. I have no idea what [the professor] was talking about." Seldom heard are statements indicative of accepting personal responsibility for having difficulty in following lectures. Teachers, in turn, regularly complain that present day students have no manners and are "hard to teach."

My colleagues and I have noticed that, in the last few years, students have become unpleasant. That takes the joy out of teaching. (An American professor teaching in Hong Kong, 1990)

Teaching has become a revolting vocation. (A professor in Hong Kong, 1990)

My colleagues complain that many students have bad manners, such as dribbling into the classroom late, by as much as half an hour, without apology. Some students have the annoying habit of talking among themselves during class, in disregard for the professor and other students present. In some classes, some students may be seen dozing off, reading newspapers, or answering their mobile phone. In one of my own classes, a male and a female student embraced each other "amorously," without the slightest embarrassment, even after I warned them not to do so. I have not seen this kind of behavior before. The student culture is changing, and many professors are shaking their heads. The same male student acted like a smart aleck during discussion sessions. None of the other students present showed the slightest disapproval of his behavior; some even regarded him as a "hero." Apparently, some students take a perverse delight in publicly embarrassing their teachers. (A professor in Hong Kong, 1998)

The students see themselves as consumers. Teachers are paid to cater to their needs. (A university teacher in Hong Kong, 2000)

A university graduate applied for a position in our publishing house. During the recruitment interview, the interviewer asked him, "Which course did you like the most when you studied in the university?" "I don't know," the graduate replied. "Why?" "Because I hardly went to class." (Head of a publishing house in Beijing, 2000, professing surprise at the applicant's behavior)

These comments reflect troubles running deep in contemporary Chinese educational institutions—and more generally in the wider society. They warrant urgent attention by researchers.

TEACHER-STUDENT INTERACTIONS

A common stereotype is that Chinese students are obedient and respectful of their teachers. However, observations outside of the classroom, and especially during the absence of teachers or other authority figures, reveal that this stereotype is misleading. Let us tune in to hear what the students say among themselves under these circumstances.

Hong Kong

Most students we have talked with each have their own tales of horror to tell. As the following sample of comments illustrates, the school environment in Hong Kong is commonly perceived to be competitive, harsh, and punitive; teachers are stingy in giving praise; many humiliate their students publicly.

My son failed his math exam. Only two students in the whole class passed. The teacher humiliated the students ... When I talked with the teacher, he said that my son was good at neither studying nor anything else. (Mother of a secondary school student, 1986; the student is now an engineer.)

The school principal made the boy stand in the hallway, wearing a placard on which was written: "I received a zero-egg [a zero mark]." He is now utterly resentful of all authority figures. (A clinical psychologist, to whom the boy was referred for psychotherapy, circa 1987)

In Primary 1, my teacher used a wooden ruler to hit my hand every time I wrote, because I didn't hold the pencil "correctly." I didn't agree with her. So I kept holding the pencil my way when she was not looking. (A university teacher in Hong Kong, 1998)

Not surprisingly, students tend to be fearful and resentful of authority figures. Among the most salient ways of coping is passive aggressiveness. Too
many students have learned to be fearful, suspicious, and resentful of
teachers through this oppressive school system; and they bring this attitude
with them into university life.

> The students have a basic problem of passive aggressiveness. That's the con-
> clusion I have reached. (A visiting professor from Japan in Hong Kong, circa
> 1970)

> The students come into my office like scared rabbits or mice seeing a cat, for-
> mal, stiff, and uneasy. They come in small groups whenever possible. That
> way they feel more secure. (A professor in Hong Kong, circa 1975)

> Students are naturally antagonistic toward teachers. It's nothing personal … I
> find it hard to call you by your first name. It's a real problem I have to struggle
> with. (A graduate student in Hong Kong, speaking with his teacher, circa 1980)

> The more he gets annoyed, the more they do it. The students are perfectly
> capable of playing in tune. He has a lot to learn yet. (A British professor in
> Hong Kong, commenting on his colleague in the department of music who
> had not been in Hong Kong for long and got very upset with students who
> didn't play in tune, circa 1985)

> The students laugh at the wrong moments, like when you make a mistake. (A
> Chinese-American visiting professor in Hong Kong, circa 1985)

Mainland China

We owe the following vignettes to informants from Mainland China.
The vignettes were shown to several graduate students, also from Mainland
China; all these students agreed that they captured the essence of some
common aspects of secondary school life on the mainland. We have translate them from Chinese for presentation here.

Vignette 1. Shaming in public. This vignette illustrates public shaming
commonly used by teachers as a technique for moral education. A student
stole an apple from a plantation to eat. He was discovered by the horticul-
turists, who reported the incident to his teacher. In front of the entire class,
the teacher criticized the student and asked his classmates to join in the
criticism. One student protested: "He stole the apple mainly for fun. It was
not that serious. He cannot be counted as a thief." The teacher became
angry and said: "When one is young, one steals a pin; having grown up one
steals gold. Today he steals an apple; after he has grown up, he will rob a
bank." The classmates dared to say no more. After class, a student whis-
pered to his good friend: "My father and the teacher were classmates. My

father said that both of them were very naughty when they were schoolchildren. Together they went to steal not only apples, but also water melons." His friend replied: "Then our teacher must have stolen gold by now."

Vignette 2. Imaginary numbers.   A teacher tried to explain the concept of imaginary numbers to a class of secondary school students. After trying three times, the students still did not understand. The teacher was flustered, and the students laughed. He became angry, and hitting the table, said that the students were stupid. He explained no further; instead, he demanded the students to copy five times from the instruction notes a page about imaginary numbers. Then he rushed out of the classroom in a state of agitation. No sooner had he left, the students voiced their opinions.

> If we can understand by copying five times, what do we need him to teach?

> I think that the teacher himself doesn't understand. That's why he didn't explain clearly.

> Right. "Illustrious pupils come from famed teachers.' Of course, the stupid ones are the product of stupid teachers.

> I estimate that our teacher copied this page only three times. That's why he hasn't understood it. Wait till he has copied it two more times. Perhaps he will then explain it clearly.

Vignette 3. Dozing off during class.   A student dozed off during class. The teacher was very angry and hit him with a stick. The student felt he had been wrongly treated and cried. The teacher said: "Hitting is affection; scolding is love. Without control and instruction, students will become bad. I hit you because I love and care about you. Do you understand?" Still crying, the student said: "I know." After class, a classmate said quietly to the student: "The teacher showed so much loving care toward you. From now on you may show the same loving care toward his beloved son."

Apparently, some teachers have not yet learned from Chairman Mao (1964/1974), who said:

> There are teachers who ramble on and on when they lecture; they should let their students doze off ... Rather than keeping your eyes open and listening to boring lectures, it is better to get some refreshing sleep. You don't have to listen to nonsense. (p. 205)

An interpretation.   These vignettes are a gold mine for psychological insights. We see authoritarian moralism on the part of teachers: the emphasis on proper conduct and obedience, the demand for respect from students, the assertion of authority, and the use of public shaming as a technique of discipline. The Confucian ideal of loving and caring for one's students continues to exert its influence on contemporary teachers; and so does the injunction: "Teaching without strictness is the negligence of the teacher." On the part of students, the pattern of ventilating anger in the form of passive, and sometimes displaced, aggression may be discerned. However, their independence of thought, eloquence, and even sense of humor survives their teachers.

Comparing students' behaviors during and after class, and more generally in the context of different interpersonal relationships (e.g., peer vs. teacher-student), should be instructive to researchers. It should occasion pause to those who think of Chinese students as obedient and respectful of their teachers. In the great 18th century novel, *Dream of the Red Chamber*, a passage described the rambunctiousness of pupils attending a *sishu*. Reading this passage should alert us to the possibility that the "docile, obedient, and well-behaved Chinese student" may have already been a myth centuries ago.

We might reflect further on the incident of the student's theft. Moral judgments are dependent on the interpersonal context in which an action is performed. Traditionally, stealing food for one's parents, especially if they were hungry, would have been lauded as an act of filial piety (as in one of the Twenty-Four Stories of Filial Piety). We might also compare it with the story about George Washington cutting down a cherry tree with an ax when he was a boy, and his father's handling of the incident. Washington was not humiliated but was led to admit courageously his wrongdoing. He did not become resentful toward his father.

A perusal of the mainland press suggests that teacher brutality may be more common than what has been acknowledged, especially in rural areas. In one notorious case (though by no means representative), a fourth-grade teacher boxed a student's ears and kicked him to the ground, because he failed to hand in his homework on time. What followed was a chilling reminiscence of Nazi officers in concentration camps during World War II. According to media accounts, the teacher ordered other students in the class (numbering 50) to give the boy 10 lashes each with a stick, adding that those hitting hard would be commended and those hitting lightly would be given 10 lashes themselves. Most students participated in the beating, which lasted more than 40 minutes. One newspaper showed a photograph of the kids smiling, saying: "We have beaten our classmate according to command." The boy, 9 years of age, was given 280 whacks in all. He could not refrain from urinating and defecating. Eventually he was taken to a hospital, his backside pummeled to a swollen, purple pulp. The national attention this case received signals that the phenomenon of teacher brutality is no longer ignored.

Concern over teachers' treatment of students and teacher-student relationships has been voiced among educators. Chen (1995) reported that 43.8% of students seeking counseling in Beijing suffered from school phobia, of which 90% resulted from teachers' improper punishment. Huang

(1998) quoted one student as saying: "If you ask me whom I hate the most, the answer is 'teacher'! If you ask me whom I dislike the most, the answer is 'teacher'! If you ask me whom I look down on the most, the answer is 'teacher'!" (p. 315).

Unresolved Problems with Authority

Based on the data gathered, we characterize the typical teacher-student relationship as follows.

1. Status disparity creates a gulf, seemingly unbridgeable, between teachers and students. Role definition, rather than personality, predominates in determining how the student perceives the teacher—primarily as a teacher and only secondarily as a person.
2. Teacher-student relationships tend to be marked by affective distance. The greater the disparity in status, the greater the affective distance. Students generally feel closer to teaching assistants than to professors.
3. The flow of information between teachers and students is impeded, or even blocked, in proportion to affective distance. Communication is typically unidirectional, from the teacher to the student. This makes it difficult for the student to make known his or her concerns and problems to the teacher. In turn, the teacher is ill informed about the real condition of the student. Problems may not be identified and reported early enough for remedial actions to be taken effectively. Often, untreated problems surface only when they are already too advanced for solutions.
4. Students tend to perceive the exercise of authority by teachers as something over which they have little or no control—often arbitrary, absolutists, even oppressive. Resignation, passivity, and anger may result.
5. Potential conflicts are kept dormant and unresolved, masked by the facade of harmony. Repressed anger on the part of students has to be held in check by psychological or institutional control mechanisms.

Given such teacher-student relationships, unresolved problems with authority can cause serious problems. Observations of Chinese students reveal some common patterns: fear of teachers often generalized to other authority figures; maintaining respect, at least superficially, in front of teachers; criticizing teachers, calling them names, or playing tricks on them behind their back; keeping affective distance from teachers; and adopting silence, negativism, or passive resistance, even passive aggression, to deal with teachers' demands. Passive resistance and passive aggression are expressed in acts of commission (e.g., doing things that the teacher does not want students to do) as well as omission (e.g., not following directions, "forgetting" to keep appointments and giving no apology afterwards, and failing to submit assignments on time and to give due notification).

Some teachers have attempted to be more democratic and bridge the gulf between themselves and their students. But problems remain. As political scientists know, to practice democracy in a society without a democratic tradition is hazardous. Likewise, to practice democratic-permissive teaching is fraught with dangerous contradictions. One runs the risk of creating an environment not in keeping with one's educational setting in particular and with society in general. The dilemma is that the student may flourish in this "unreal" environment, but cannot survive elsewhere. To be democratic and permissive is not enough! The teacher has to help students to make distinctions, so that they will be better equipped to cope in different situations.

Another problem relates to the inability of many students to cope with the democratic-permissive situation itself—which is, to them, highly unfamiliar, in view of their educational history. Hostility toward authority figures is likely to find more direct expression when tolerance is increased and the threat of retaliation is reduced. Thus, ironically, the democratic-permissive teacher has to be prepared to face more, not less, hostility from students, until they have gained sufficient maturity to know how to divert their aggression to constructive channels.

Unresolved problems with authority have consequences beyond teaching and learning. Chinese students are poorly socialized at home and in school for democratic functioning. Recall, in this connection, the contrast between Canadian and Chinese students described above (Vignette 1: University Life in Canada). Our investigative research reveals that we must confront these unresolved problems with authority if democracy is to take root in Chinese societies. Redefining the teacher-student relationship is fundamental to this process.

APPROACHES TO LEARNING AND
METACOGNITIVE ABILITIES

The following account is focused on the mastery of approaches to learning and metacognitive abilities at the tertiary level of education. It should be informative on how well the schools have prepared students for higher education, as well as how tertiary students are equipped for life after graduation. We need to stress that the account pertains to Hong Kong, because at present we lack data on other Chinese societies. Nevertheless, among academics as well as employers in Hong Kong, a commonly held opinion is that Hong Kong university students compare poorly with their counterparts in Singapore, Taiwan, or Mainland China. As the following comments testify, teachers regard students as poorly motivated, immature, and uninformed.

> The students are just interested in getting a job, not in studying. They give you a blank look when you ask them a question. You have no idea if they know the answer. The probability is that they don't. You get no reinforcement ... Students in Taiwan are academically more serious. (A professor in Hong Kong, 1990)

> The students expect the most for the least amount of effort. I doubt if they spend more than a few hours per week on each course. They don't read much. About a third of the students in the course on psychotherapies were indifferent and hardly said anything at all during the entire semester. (A Chinese-Canadian tutor in Hong Kong, 1991)

> The students here say quite openly that they don't study. They don't think that it's important. (A graduate student from Singapore studying in Hong Kong, 1991)

> Perhaps 10% are interested in studying. Little or no intellectual discussion takes place outside of the classroom. They don't have manners ... The English standard is perhaps lower than junior secondary level. Very passive ... Their general knowledge is poorer than Canadian students. (A tutor in Hong Kong, having returned from Canada, 1991)

> The students here like to blame their teachers, but do not accept responsibility for learning. They are rather immature and less independent in comparison with university students in Beijing. (A graduate student from Beijing studying in Hong Kong, 1991)

> The students expect to get something for nothing [obtaining a degree without having to work for it]. (A professor in Hong Kong, 1998)

Employers we have talked with complain that fresh graduates in Hong Kong are "inept, poorly trained, and expect much more [in remuneration] than they are worth." Some put it bluntly: "Most of them are unemployable." The main complaints by employers that have been made to the University Grants Committee, the body responsible for allocating public funds to tertiary institutions in Hong Kong, "relate to a lack of social skills, and a lack of communication skills" (Higher Education in Hong Kong, 1996, p. 155). The University Grants Committee itself "has been sufficiently unhappy with the language skills of recent graduates" (p. 64); it states that: "In the 1980s, a perception began to take hold that there was a decline in the ability of tertiary students to communicate effectively either in Chinese or in English" (p. 70).

This is all the more disturbing in view of the fact that tertiary education in Hong Kong is among the most expensive anywhere in the world. The unit cost for publicly funded tertiary institutions for the academic year 1995–96 was projected to be HK$201,842 or US$25,877 per student per year (Higher Education in Hong Kong, 1996, Table 36.1, p. 137; unit cost = nonspecific institutional annual expenditure divided by the full-time-equivalent number of students). It is also paradoxical that Hong Kong's universities are well regarded internationally. According to a ranking by Asiaweek (Bacani, 1997, May 23, pp. 34–37, 42–43), 3 Hong Kong universities were among the top 10 institutions in Asia and Australia.

Reading and General Knowledge

Lack of reading accounts for the students' poor general knowledge. During interviews, most applicants seeking university entrance frankly admit, without the slightest embarrassment, that they do not read newspapers or magazines (especially those in English) on a regular basis. The reason given is that they have no time left for outside reading, after studying for the Advanced Level, the entrance examination. But reading does not seem to improve after admission. Students are generally reluctant to spend money on required textbooks, let alone recommended texts, even though they do not lack the means at all. Based on their sales record, university bookstores regularly order only a fraction of the textbooks specified by professors. In recent decades, comics have become their favorite reading material (a phenomenon that may be observed in the Mainland also), and cartoons are among their preferred TV programs. In some cases, the degree of ignorance and lack of willingness to do anything about it reaches an extreme.

Some students in my course on psychotherapies did not know what neurology meant. (A professor in Hong Kong, 1991)

During discussion, one of the students asked: "Is Chairman Mao the same person as Mao Tse-tung?" (A professor in Hong Kong, 1999; this is just a more extreme case of the students' general ignorance of Mainland China and contemporary Chinese history.)

One student came into my office for help on an assignment. I referred her to some introductory texts. She looked surprised and asked: "But do I really have to read books?" (A professor in Hong Kong, 1999)

Reading Examination Scripts: A Seasonal Depression

Officially, only a handful of tertiary students in Hong Kong ever fail their examinations. This is not to say that there is grade inflation, as it is practiced in the United States. Very few obtain a First Class Honour; most obtain a Second Class Honour. But we are not concerned with published results here. Rather, we report on a different reality, one that reflects common views of insiders expressed in private. For many conscientious teachers of humanities, social sciences, and business studies, the month of June is a time of seasonal depression, induced by the experience of marking examination scripts.

In 1970, at a time when tertiary education in Hong Kong was still "elitist," a visiting professor of sociology wrote to his colleagues to express his concerns about the students' "poor English, poor thinking, or poor thinking because of poor English," after his ordeal of reading examination scripts. An excerpt is reproduced here.

> It was a strenuous, painful and often depressing experience. The quality of the answers as a whole was poor … [In an answer on a theorist's definition of institutions], the original definition is totally garbled, as if the student had tried to memorize it like a machine (without understanding its meaning at all) and failed … [In another case], it does not seem that [the student] tried to memorize something and then failed in reproduction, because I cannot find in my lecture notes anything that could be garbled up [the way it was by him] … the student did not understand what I said. Accordingly, this student shows … [a] "lack of thinking through" (durchdenken) rather than the failure in expression due to poor English … The students had to think, or try to think, to produce an answer to [a question on the definition of social psychology, because no definition was ever given in my lectures and there was nothing for the students to "memorize"]. Many must have done so in English and some, fortunately not many, failed disastrously, becoming almost incoherent.

In giving an oral feedback to the teaching staff, an external examiner stated: "There is a weakness in the construction of arguments. Facts are presented. But one does not feel that an argument is presented, even among the better examination scripts. There is a lack in using evidence and citations in support of views presented." His concerns have long been widely shared by those who have had the experience of teaching the humanities or social sciences in Hong Kong. Even graduate students have great difficulties. An external examiner's report stated: "The impression is gained that students tend to regurgitate lecture notes. There is not as much evidence of independent thought as might be desirable in a postgraduate course." His impressions are shared by internal examiners.

Metacognitive Abilities

Some time ago, we formulated a set of criteria for grading assignments in psychology and related subjects. The criteria for superior performance, which requires the mastery of metacognitive abilities, were:

> Superior writing skills; accurate, clear, and concise expression of ideas; consistent adherence to a commonly accepted style; comprehensive coverage of the relevant literature; in-depth discussion of issues; insight into the significance of the topic under discussion in a broader theoretical context; good logical organization and integration; critical, reflective, and/or original thought; coherent development of arguments supported by evidence or rational analysis; insight into relations between academic learning and everyday life experiences; applying knowledge acquired to solve problems (where relevant); giving illustrative examples.

To obtain an A-grade for a major assignment, at least half of the criteria should be met. Some tutors commented that, if the criteria were strictly applied, no undergraduate student would get an A-grade. Our own experiences are in agreement with their assessments; furthermore, few graduate students would either.

The evidence from oral discourse points to the same assessment. In small-group discussions, few undergraduate students demonstrate the mastery of metacognitive abilities. Rather, symptoms of compartmentalization are evident. Too often, little or no trace can be found that they have integrated (a) pieces of information into a coherent body of knowledge; (b) academic and experiential learning; and (c) knowledge gained from courses they have taken, especially those in different academic disciplines. Most students do not know how to formulate probing questions. When they do speak, their verbalizations tend to be short, not exceeding a few sentences. They have great difficulty in sustaining an interchange focused on a topic under discussion. As a professor (1980) remarked: "The students have a talent in turning intellectually exciting questions into boredom." And they seldom engage in intellectual discussions outside the classroom. Graduate students fare better; still, many perform poorly. Students in clinical or educational psychology, who have met relatively stringent entrance requirements, find it difficult to interrelate theory and practice, formulate diagnostic and treatment plans, or to integrate what they have learned into a coherent framework.

Thesis Supervision

University teachers' experiences in supervising students working on their theses, both undergraduate and graduate, speak most directly on the students' mastery of metacognitive skills and learning strategies. Such mastery, or the lack of it, is a telling indicator of what the end products of the Hong Kong educational system are like. One point we should first make clear: Despite their difficulties, a minority of students do manage in the end to produce a thesis of respectable quality. However, the somber experiences of supervisors in psychology we recount below compel us to ask: What have most students learned? This is a question that professors typically dread to ask.

Comments from supervisors. The following off-the-cuff comments reflect the common experience of supervisors.

> They don't even begin to know where to begin. (A Chinese-American professor in Hong Kong, referring to graduate students doing their theses, circa 1985)

> The students have no idea how to do research. They don't want to make the effort, just the least amount of work. (A professor in Hong Kong, in a conversation with her colleagues, 1991; another professor present expressed the same opinion.)

> It's like "pulling a cow up the tree." It makes a travesty of research. (A professor in Hong Kong, 1998)

A written report.   A teacher became very concerned about what the students were doing and wrote a report about her experiences to her colleagues. An abridged excerpt is reproduced here.

> The students seem to have a lot of misconceptions about thesis writing … Most students came in with very little preparation … Some were not clear on what they would like to find out from their study … In one consultation session, a student suddenly asked me how many variables one should have in a thesis. She worried that her study did not have enough variables. Another student had great difficulty understanding that it makes no sense to compute correlations with only a single variable. Students doing a qualitative study approached me for advice on what statistics might be used so that the word significant could appear in their thesis.

Vignette.   The essence of some of our own encounters with undergraduate supervisees may be captured in the following vignette.

Supervisor: "What's the research question? That is, what is the question on which you could provide an answer through your research?" The supervisee looks perplexed, as if she were thinking to herself: "But shouldn't professors instruct their students on what they should do?" Appealing to authority, the supervisor says: "Albert Einstein says that the formulation of a problem is often far more essential than its solution."

Supervisee: "I would like to study Chinese personality."

Supervisor: "That's a grand aim. Are you committed for 6 years, rather than 6 months? Would you please narrow the scope of your thesis and be more specific?"

A few supervisory sessions afterwards, the supervisee asks: "What are the instruments or tests I should use?"

Supervisor: "That's like putting the carriage in front of the horse. Instrument-driven research is no good. Without their tests, some psychologists wouldn't know what to do. How about developing a theoretical rationale first?"

A few more sessions afterwards, the supervisee looks frustrated, complaining: "So many theories, all saying different things. Which theory should I choose?"

Supervisor: "Do they really say different things? The whole point of doing research is to constrain theorizing, to see which theory can better account for empirical facts." The supervisee looks more frustrated, as if the supervisor has provided no guidance.

Summary

The evidence suggests that neither undergraduate nor graduate students in Hong Kong compare favorably with their counterparts in North America or other Chinese societies. Many teachers and employers perceive them as poorly motivated, immature, and uninformed. Students' reading is very narrow and thus their general knowledge is poor. In particular, students in the humanities, social sciences, and business studies perform poorly in examinations, in terms of integration of ideas and not merely regurgitation. They lack the mastery of metacognitive abilities.

CONCLUSION

A composite picture of teaching and learning emerges from our investigative research. Educational systems function like huge machines, sorting students according to examination marks into institutions ranked hierarchically and warping their development in the process. Symptomatic of the syllabus-bound mentality, teachers teach and students study only or primarily prescribed materials. The careers of Chinese students are hard ones. Under immense pressure to succeed academically and preoccupied with examinations, they have to study diligently and do lots of homework. Education is viewed as a means to an end, not an end in itself. Learning is hardship to be suffered, not enjoyment. Humiliations by teachers may have to be endured. Decisions on one's educational and career goals are dictated largely by external factors, leaving little or no room for personal interests and aspirations to be considered. If and when one "succeeds" academically, the end result may be a lack of inner direction and preparation for life and work. If one does not, it means elimination from the educational sorting machine, and the expected rewards of securing a good job and higher social status vanish.

Adopting a passive role and keeping silent constitute a major impediment to effective learning. The majority of Chinese students expect to be given direction by teachers. They do not participate actively and tend to keep silent in discussions. Teacher-students interactions are marked by affective distance and unidirectional communication from the teacher to the student. Students are generally fearful, even resentful, of teachers. But the idea of the docile, obedient, and respectful Chinese student is a myth. Many learn to be passive aggressive in dealing with teachers and other authority figures. These unresolved problems with authority are serious, with adverse consequences for learning—and for democracy.

Given what we have described, it is not surprising to find students poorly prepared for higher education. The evidence converges on the conclusion that, at least in Hong Kong, students lack the mastery of approaches to learning and metacognitive abilities for learning in tertiary institutions. Comments by teachers as well as employers about the quality of graduates are predominantly negative.

In recent decades, a departure from the traditional pattern may be discerned. Confucian educational values, such as respect for learning, authority, and order, are becoming increasingly irrelevant. Students have become more openly defiant and disrespectful of teachers. Impertinence and aggressiveness are becoming more direct. Teachers, in turn, regularly complain that present day students have no manners and are "hard to teach." These symptoms forebode a crisis in contemporary Chinese educational institutions.

In sum, the pains of education appear to outweigh the rewards. Some readers may feel that our account is biased toward the negative. To this, we respond by saying that we report only what we have indeed seen and heard sufficiently to indicate a discernible trend. The poverty of positive comments made by various people should be gauged against cultural norms. Unlike the American one, the Chinese norm is biased against giving compliments, except as expressions of politeness. Parents tend not to praise their children, nor teachers their students—especially in the presence of others, because they do not want to appear immodest. As a clinical psychologist observes: "The United States is a nation of flatterers; there I would discount the 'positive reinforcements' people give to one another. In Hong Kong, you should be satisfied if people don't curse you."

We wish to emphasize that nothing we have stated should be construed to imply anything inherent in parents, teachers, or students. Many teachers are devoted and caring in the best of the Confucian tradition. We marvel at how some students have managed to survive the educational system they have gone through, bearing testimony to the resilience of the human spirit. Intellectual curiosity and creativity, it appears, are difficult to extinguish. We regard research framed in terms of the inherent characteristics of individual learners (e.g., predisposition toward rote memorization) as simplistic. We reject the simplistic view that learning follows from inherent characteristics. Rather, we view learning and social relations as interactive. As we have explained, the conceptual framework guiding our investigative research does not focus on the individual, but on the individual-in-relations. It also provides a strategy for effecting changes: to alter the relational contexts within which teaching and learning take place. As our experiment (section on the phenomenon of passivity and silence) demonstrated, learning behavior may change dramatically when authority relations are altered. Redefining the teacher-student relationship is central to promoting better teaching and learning.

We have alluded to the fact that educators are beginning to action for reforms. However, we must also take note of the fact that repeated calls for reforming education in Asia have been voiced for decades. Not much seems to have been accomplished. If anything, academic pressure has intensified, and has even extended into nursery schools. The resistance to reforms is deeply entrenched. We argue that to a large extent underlying this resistance are authoritarian values, a manifestation of which is the ubiquitous ranking of persons and institutions. So, are educators, especially those in responsible positions, prepared to de-emphasize ranking according to examination marks as a start? And eventually to stop educational systems from functioning like sorting machines that warp rather than develop human potentialities?

REFERENCES

Bacani, C. (1997, May 23). Asia's search for excellence. *Asiaweek*, pp. 34–36, 42–43.

Chen Y.H. (1995, December 24). On "school phobia." *Beijing Youth Daily*, p. 8. (In Chinese. Reprinted in D. P. Yang, Ed., Jiaoyu: Women you hua yao shuo [Education: We want to say something about it], pp. 25–32. Chinese Social Sciences Publishing House.)

Higher education in Hong Kong: A report by the University Grants Committee. (1996, October). Hong Kong: Government Printer.

Ho, D.Y.F., Chan, S.F.F., & Chau, A.W.L. (2000). *Investigative research as a knowledge-generation method: Disciplined, naturalistic, and in-depth observations.* Manuscript submitted for publication.

Huang, B.L. (Ed.). (1998*). Blind spot: A report on the educational crisis in China.* Beijing: China City Publishing House. (In Chinese)

Mao, T.T. (1974). Remarks at the Spring Festival (summary record). In S. Schram (Ed.), *Mao Tse-tung unrehearsed: Talks and letters*: 1956–71 (J. Chinnery & Tieyun, Trans.; pp. 197–211). Middlesex, England: Penguin. (Originally given on 1964, February 13).

Oksenberg, M. (1969). Local leaders in rural China, 1962–65: Individual attributes, bureaucratic positions, and political recruitment. In A.D. Barnett (Ed.), *Chinese communist politics in action* (pp. 155–215). Seattle: University of Washington Press.

AUTHOR INDEX

Y

Z

SUBJECT INDEX